Victorian
Melodramas

VICTORIAN MELODRAMAS

Seven English, French
and American Melodramas

Edited and introduced by
JAMES L. SMITH

Dent, London

Rowman and Littlefield, Totowa, N.J.

© Introduction, editing and selection,
J. M. Dent & Sons Ltd, 1976
All rights reserved
Made in Great Britain
at the
Aldine Press · Letchworth · Herts
for
J. M. Dent & Sons Ltd
Aldine House · Albemarle Street · London
First published 1976
First published in the United States 1976
by Rowman and Littlefield, Totowa, New Jersey

This book is set in 11 on 12 point Garamond type (156)

Dent edition
ISBN 0 460 10193 5

Rowman and Littlefield edition
ISBN 0-87471-767-1

CONTENTS

ILLUSTRATIONS

Between pages 104 *and* 105

1. *Mazeppa* at Astley's, 25 April 1831. A large poster with the type printed in red and the block in black. As the untamed steed scrambles ashore with Mazeppa, lightning flashes, a vulture hovers, and two hungry wolves snap at his flanks. A backstage view of this scene is presented in Plate 4. *British Theatre Museum.*

2. John Cartlitch as Mazeppa, King of Tartary. A 'penny plain' portrait published by T. J. Brown, probably in 1831. Cartlitch created the role at Astley's, and played it for many years; here, he prepares for battle with the Poles. In the background, an 'extensive Tartar encampment'. *British Theatre Museum.*

3. Miss Adah Menken as Mazeppa, in her sensational and brief costume. A lithograph by Concanen, Leek and Siebe, *circa* 1864. *British Theatre Museum.*

4. Backstage at *Mazeppa*; a drawing by Tenniel showing Astley's in 1851. The untamed steed is guided by a patient groom, the vulture is on wires, and the wolves are cut-out heads with hinged mouths

manipulated by two kneeling stage hands. A Polish knight and two Tartar chiefs stand by in the wings. *Punch*, 8 November 1851. *Reproduced by permission of* Punch.

5. Stock poster for *Nick of the Woods*. The terrifying Jibbenainosay, looking like a most respectable Victorian gentleman, is precipitated down the cataract in a canoe of fire. The cataract may be real water, or crumpled green and blue gauze with a steaming kettle for the spume; the flames of the canoe are probably streamers of red and orange silk agitated by a fan. In the foreground, a dead Indian with the Jibbenainosay's mark carved on his chest. Ledger cut no. 377. *British Theatre Museum*.

6–7. Designs for the two vision scenes in Charles Kean's production of *The Corsican Brothers* at the Princess's in 1852. On the the left, Lloyd's design for the château of the Dei Franchi in Corsica; the back wall is painted on gauze, and seems to disappear when a strong light is placed behind it, revealing a vision of Louis' death in the Forest of Fontainebleau. On the right, Gordon's design for the Forest scene, which dissolves in turn to show the château of the Dei Franchi. All the clocks have stopped at ten past nine, but the curious observer will note several minor inconsistencies between the acts. *British Theatre Museum*.

8. Sarah Bernhardt as Marguerite Gautier in *The Lady of the Camellias*: 'If only I could live until the spring! Oh, how changed I am!' Photograph by M. Walter Barnett. *British Theatre Muesum*.

INTRODUCTION

Most of the melodramas in this book were written to amuse Joe Whelks of the New Cut, Lambeth, and his many friends in New York, Paris, Bradford or the Edgware Road. By 1800 every industrial city in Europe and America had its legions of Joe's army, slums to house them, factories to exploit them and theatres to keep them happy. Not that Joe was often found at the Comédie-Française or Drury Lane, where you paid two shillings for a bench up in the gods while well-dressed midgets thirty yards away adopted noble postures and declaimed interminable verse by Otway or John Home. Fortunately, new theatres designed exclusively for Joe's convenience were springing up in some less fashionable quarters of the great metropolis where he lived. The Ambigu-Comique in Paris opened in 1797, the Bowery in New York in 1826; London boasted the Surrey (1810), the Coburg (1818), the Whitechapel Pavilion (1828), the Britannia in Hoxton (1841) and many more. Most of them seated upwards of three thousand people at prices everybody could afford. At the 'Brit' in 1850, for example, admission to the boxes cost a shilling, the pit sixpence, the lower gallery fourpence and the upper gallery threepence; at the first three you could come in for half-price at half-past eight. These 'minor' theatres were Joe's own kingdom. Instead of squinting round a pillar in the gods, Joe and his friends now occupied the entire auditorium. Boxes, pit and gallery alike were packed each night with costermongers, cobblers, convicts, clerks, dock labourers, stay-makers, ladies' maids, shop girls and their beaux, theatrical young gentlemen, apprentices, pickpockets, prowlers, idlers, pimps and whores, bold mothers suckling babes in arms and young mechanics in limp caps with cravats tied round their necks like eels or hanging down their chests like strings of sausages. So Dickens describes them in *Household Words* (30 March 1850) and *The Uncommercial Traveller* (25 February 1860). They surged into the theatre at six o'clock, fortified themselves at intervals with huge ham sandwiches, pigs' trotters, fried soles, chipped potatoes, cans of porter and flat stone bottles filled with beer, and then stayed on till after midnight, sometimes rapt in wonder, sometimes bursting into song, exchanging salvoes with friends across the auditorium, quarrelling and fighting, cheering, hissing, clapping, booing, stamping and stinking to the very rafters. This was the truly popular audience such theatres had to please.

But how? Certainly not with Sheridan or Shakespeare. Until the Theatre Regulation Act of 1843, the English classics were monopolized by the patent theatres in Drury Lane and Covent Garden; the minors could attempt them only in burletta-form, cut down to three acts apiece with frequent musical additions. A Surrey-side Macbeth in 1809 brought the house down with a song beginning

> Is this a dagger which I see before me?
> My brains are scatter'd in a whirlwind stormy.

But Joe still found him wordy, dull and difficult to follow. A costermonger interviewed by Henry Mayhew tells us why:

> Love and murder suits us best, sir. . . . Of *Hamlet* we can make neither end nor side; and nine out of ten of us—ay, far more than that—would like it to be confined to the ghost scenes, and the funeral, and the killing off at the last. *Macbeth* would be better liked, if it was only the witches and the fighting. The high words in a tragedy we call jaw-breakers, and say we can't tumble to that barrikin.
> (*London Labour and the London Poor* (1851), I. 15)

So *Hamlet* and *Macbeth* gave way to farce, burlesque and pantomime, which combined a minimum of dialogue with a maximum of spectacle, and allowed for clever managers to introduce a dazzling display of acrobats and tightrope-walkers, jugglers, fireworks, infant prodigies, performing dogs, hornpipes, highland flings, plaintive songs and comic choruses in which the entire audience could join. What could be better than *Harlequin and Cinderella*, or *Antony and Cleopatra Married and Settled*, or *Did You Ever Send Your Wife to Camberwell?*

But these were mindless recreations, and did not satisfy Joe's need for a theatre which faced up to the difficulties of the real world he lived in. Melodrama met that need. Country folk bred in the simple reassuring certainties of village life were suddenly thrust into the moral chaos of the mighty city, tied down twelve or fourteen hours a day to humdrum machine tasks, left to the mercies of a culture they did not understand, and kept economically dependent on the chance decisions of an inscrutable employer. Melodrama brought these moral and emotional insecurities under strict control; it dramatized Joe's problems and provided them with perfect answers; it faced his fears and fantasies and exorcised them all. In the ideal world of melodrama, life is once more simple and uncomplicated, character and motive are reduced to blackest black or whitest white, coincidence and chance are tamed, unlucky accidents are overcome, and virtue after many thrilling and precipitous reversals is guaranteed to triumph over vice and end up with a choice assortment of material rewards. This strict poetic justice means that melodrama is never down-beat or depressing; its nightmare fantasies can be enjoyed in all their palpitating horror because Joe knows that they are always bound to fail. Its violent extremes of emotional distress and physical disaster, its threats of instant death by pistol, poison, buzz-saw, rope or steel or railway track, its hostile universe of earthquake, ice-floe, avalanche and mill-race, its terrifying bandits, pirates, gypsies, tyrants, vampires, werewolves, gliding ghosts and flying Dutchmen, its prisons, gallows, chains and racks and wheels, its gloating villains, tortured heroes and defenceless heroines are all no more than a thrilling prelude to the ultimate defeat of guilt and final tableau of triumphant innocence. Sometimes this ideal world depicts with photographic accuracy every surface of the life Joe sees around him every day in factory, pub and tenement; sometimes its settings offer unashamed escape into a never-never-land of medieval castles, Mayfair opulence or oriental splendour. Always it holds up to Joe's eye a mirror which reflects life not as it is but as it ought to be: clear-cut, simple, morally benevolent and enormously exciting. Once this simple pattern is perceived, the apparently absurd conventions of the form—its cardboard characters, haphazard plots and predetermined justice, its scenic marvels and sensational effects, its rapid shift from windy rhetoric to crummy jokes or maudlin pathos, its songs, parades and miscellaneous *divertissements*—all slide smoothly into place. They are the means by which this comforting illusion can be made to live upon the stage.

The characters of melodrama are a set of walking clichés who invite snap moral judgments the moment they appear. No teasing niceties of plausibility or motivation are allowed to clog the action or obscure Joe's rigid line between the Bad Guys whom he hisses and the Good Guys whom he cheers. That well-knit young man at present swearing honourable love in halting couplets is, of course, our handsome hero, who is always brave and kind and strong and chivalrous and often quite absurdly stupid. Ever-eager to defend the innocent and the oppressed, he walks straight into every trap that fortune can devise, and consequently spends long sections of the play cast adrift on stormy seas, wandering in foreign parts, or tied up and left senseless at the bottom of a mine-shaft. To compensate for these long periods of idleness, the hero is permitted a large stock of reviving moral platitudes which emphasize his noble nature and bring a cheer from his supporters in the gallery and pit. Who could resist the fervency of

> Withered be the arm that hesitates to strike against a treacherous,
> remorseless tyrant!   (Samuel Arnold, *The Woodman's Hut*, 1814)

or

> Angela thine? That she shall never be! There are angels above who
> favour virtue, and the hour of retribution must one day arrive!
>   (Matthew Lewis, *The Castle Spectre*, 1797)

ix

This optimistic faith in heavenly justice is echoed by the beauteous heroine, a paragon of feminine perfections whom the hero worships wholly for her mind. Loving, loyal and uncomplaining, she wanders through the forest glades to gather herbs for remedies, and sits up sewing half the night to earn a crust of bread. 'I am an orphan, and obliged to work for every meal', says pretty Mary Maybud in John Haines' *My Poll and My Partner Joe* (1835); 'I am content to do so, because I think, somehow, that the bread we have earned must eat the sweeter.' If this Cinderella is suddenly transported to the gilded realms of luxury and wealth, she masters the intricacies of courtly etiquette with consummate ease, quickly tires of pleasure, pomp and equipage, and joyfully sneaks off to the local cottages with tea and sugar for the old folks, individual jellies for the sick and Christian tracts to save the wicked.

With heroine and hero thus assured of Joe's unswerving sympathy, the melodramatist is ready to begin the plots against them. These have two functions. They provide the play with its emotional excitements, and by their ultimate defeat show Joe that honour, virtue and a good straight left are enough to overcome a sea of troubles far more stormy than his own. Their *primum mobile* is, of course, the villain—a heartless libertine in shiny boots and jet-black whiskers whose whole existence is devoted to encompassing the heroine's chastity, the hero's downfall, or their combined destruction. His diabolical malignity, which makes Iago look a tyro, provides a melodrama with its motor power. He plots and counterplots, gloats, wheedles, threatens, curses, cheats, steals letters, forges cheques, hides wills, kills witnesses, wrecks trains, blows up banks and air-balloons, and generally does his bit to get the action started. He may join forces with the villainess, a luscious vamp with crimson lips, raven tresses and a paste tiara. Sometimes he subcontracts a pair of minor thugs for routine dirty work. One of them is a bloody homicide who dies cursing the creation, the other a semi-comic ninny who usually deserts to virtue. They argue heatedly in front of the traverse cloth while heavy scenery is changed behind.

This league of darkness is always just about to be entirely successful. By its diligence, the hero may be chloroformed or clobbered, coshed, abducted, lynched, exploded, executed, shot, speared, poisoned, punctured, set on fire, locked in a condemned cell or private lunatic asylum, precipitated from an iceberg, mountain peak or high stone wall, attacked by lions, cobras, dervishes, Jahrejahs, revolutionaries or redskins, asphyxiated by the Upas Tree, or dumped overboard tied in a sack and weighted down with heavy rocks. But he is indestructible. At the eleventh hour he always reappears in perfect health to thwart the villain, claim the bride and collect the jackpot. The heroine is a much better risk. All the dangers which beset the hero are liable to lie in wait for her as well, but in addition she must protect her honour from the villain's clutches, and she lacks the hero's muscle power to do so. He is the superman who does what Joe would like to do but never dares; she is the hapless innocent who sums up his inability to cope with the hostile world around him. Naturally, it is her harrowing distresses which provide the focus of the play. Helpless and unprotected, broken-hearted and alone, she staggers through the windy wood, prairie wild or city snow, pursued by human bloodhounds armed with daggers, tomahawks or warrants for her immediate arrest. She may be auctioned as an octoroon or buried in an avalanche, tied senseless to the railway track or stranded on a sea-girt rock with big waves lapping round her ankles, chained to her bed in the stateroom of a burning river-boat, drugged with chloral-impregnated whisky on the upper storey of a burning house, or locked in the ship's boiler by a jealous lady matador who then proceeds to turn on the hot water. She is usually exhausted, frequently delirious and sometimes goes quite crazy in a simple muslin dress with pale blue tucks. A host of stock supporting characters augments her woe. Doting mothers fret for her, angry fathers turn her out of doors, and avaricious bailiffs eject her from the mortgaged garret she has made her home. And then there are pathetic angel children, who cry for bread when she is penniless, ask artlessly if Grandmamma has gone to heaven yet, and always want a good-night kiss from Daddy when he's doing six months' hard labour for the villain's crime. Sometimes they fall sick and die, like Little Willie in Palmer's version of *East Lynne* (1874), whom Isobel has nursed as 'Madam Vine':

> Speak to me, Willie! (*Throws off her disguise*) This cannot be death so soon; speak to me, your broken-hearted mother. Oh! Willie! my own darling! . . . Oh, Willie, my child! dead, dead, dead! and he never knew me, never called me mother! (*Falls sobbing across the body*)

Meanwhile, round every corner of the plot the villain waits to take advantage of her misery and press his suit with promises or threats. These lead inexorably to the 'Hands Off!' scene, a classic confrontation where his triumph seems assured until the hero turns up unexpectedly to disappoint him. Here they are at the beginning of the century in *Adelmorn the Outlaw* by Matthew Lewis (1801):

> *Brenno.* Hold! you fly not! That passion burns in my veins, which if you refuse to satisfy, force shall compel.
> *Innogen.* Force!
> *Brenno.* Think on your situation—
> *Innogen.* Unhand me—
> *Brenno.* You are alone—
> *Innogen.* Monster!—
> *Brenno.* Your cries will be unheard—
> *Innogen.* Oh, Heavens!—

Brenno. Nay, this struggling—
Innogen. Help, help! Oh, Adelmorn—
Adelmorn. (*rushing from his concealment*) What shrieks—Villain, desist.

And here again, over eighty years later and still virtually unchanged, in *The Harbour Lights* by George R. Sims and Henry Pettitt (1885):

Squire. You are lost, lost beyond recall, Dora Vane. You leave this house as my affianced wife, or you shall never hold up your head before the world again. (*Clasps her in his arms and kisses her*) I love you, Dora.
Dora. Help, help! (*She breaks away and rushes to the folding doors at back, as* Squire *intercepts her and fastens them*)
Squire. Not this way—my pretty bird. (*Business worked up, she rushes to the window, draws aside the curtain, and bursts open the windows as* David *appears, who throws down the* Squire *and takes her in his arms*)
Dora. David, thank God!
David. Lie there, you hound. Come, Dora, this is no place for you.

After which the Squire retires to gnaw his lip in fury, and the funny man comes on in a bright red tie with purple spots to entertain the audience with mirthful anecdotes and groansome puns. Often he is joined by the funny woman, an impudent soubrette or superannuated spinster who cuffs his ears and dances breakdowns as she crosses busy Main Street or goes about the housework; together, they ad-lib slapstick routines and comedy duets on the front-stage. Joe never finds incongruous melodrama's sudden switchback of emotions. When he has finished sniffing for the heroine or cheering on the hero, it makes a welcome change to join in the chorus of a comic song; and it all adds up to a good threepenny-worth of entertainment. Besides, the funny man does more than change the mood. As able seaman, private soldier, servant, muffin man or shoeblack, he is the closest of the characters to Joe's own social class; he steers Joe's sympathies around the play and acts as their dramatic spokesman. Of course, he sticks up bravely for the hero when all the world is set against him, and often rushes to the rescue of defenceless innocence when his master is incarcerated in the robber stronghold or mouthing patriotic speeches beneath the tropic sun. There is a valuable contrast here of style and attitude. The hero's language walks on stilts. 'There is a gilded foliage round that pill that makes its nausea palatable', says Milner's *Masaniello* (1829), without explaining why a pill wrapped in gold leaf is more easily swallowed than, say, one coated with sugar. Often the hero rises to unconfessed blank verse or talks of himself in the third person; and like the heroine he always describes his sufferings with absurd composure. 'Pray, pray let me drag you to the spot where my husband lies weltering in his gore', requests Geraldine politely in Buckstone's *The Green Bushes* (1845).

But the funny man, like other low-life characters in melodrama, confines himself to a racy lingo based on current slang, and always presents his feelings with an admirable brevity and punch. 'We never meet but like gunpowder and fire there is an explosion', says Jerrold's *Black-ey'd Susan* (1829). Writing like this inevitably cuts the hero down to size, puncturing his high-flown lyricism with unsentimental common sense. While the hero lives on love alone, the funny man orders up hot meat and vegetables and gravy. His function, apart from being funny, is to voice Joe's latent scepticism of the heroic code within the confines of the play itself; this siphons off Joe's disbelief, and strengthens his committed sympathy for noble but impracticable virtue.

Early melodrama uses music for much more than comic songs. Obedient to the Theatre Regulation Act, the minor houses thronged the stage with medieval jesters, gypsies, peasants, huntsmen, nuns and wedding guests, who were obliged by law to burst into a little number at least five times in every act. The fleet could never sail without its complement of farewell shanties, and the Bastille never fall without a full rendition of the *Carmagnole*. In between these set *divertissements*, the orchestra provided background music aimed, like a film score, to establish character, underline emotion, screw up the tension and bang the crises home with thunderous chords. Music precedes and announces the arrival of every character in Holcroft's *The Lady of the Rock* (1805), and in his *Tale of Mystery* (1802) the first scene alone asks for '*confused music*', '*threatening music*', '*sweet and cheerful music*' and '*soft music, but expressing first pain and alarm; then the successive feelings of the scene*'. Assassins always creep about the stage to pizzicato strings, heroines bewail their woes against a surging wash of violins, and heroes battle to the blare of cornets and the throb of drums, parrying upon the beat, resting their minim rest, and striking home the fatal blow to a strong chord. So H. B. Baker recalls them in *Belgravia* (May 1883).

As the century advanced, the melodramatist relied for theatrical excitement far less on music and far more on the resources of the scene painter and stage mechanic. Eye-glutting spectacle was always popular, and enterprising managers risked huge sums on new sensations. In *The Caravan* by Frederick Reynolds (1803), the hero's dog leaps from a rock into the sea to save a child from drowning. *The Dog of Montargis* (1814), which Thomas Dibdin cribbed from Pixerécourt, is even cleverer. He digs up the body of his murdered master, raises the alarm, pursues the killer and at the showdown springs at the villain's throat; the actor wore protective bandages which hid small sachets of convincing 'blood'. Monkeys, jackals, lions, elephants and giant cobras came soon after, and in Fitzball's *Thalaba the Destroyer* (1836) ostriches made their début on the melodramatic stage. At Sadler's Wells in 1804, the boards were ripped out and relaid over a huge tank fed by the New River; here Charles Dibdin staged *The Siege of Gibraltar* (1804), which culminated in the burning of the model Spanish fleet and the rescue from real water of small children dressed as sailors. A smaller tank later built into the roof permitted the display of stunning waterfalls and giant cascades. At other theatres, the stage floor could be raised or sunk in sections, allowing snowdrifts to pile up over Alpine cottages and giant rocks to sink into a sea of green-gauze waves. Backscenes could be flown or sunk, or divide in two and do both simultaneously. The diorama, a backcloth painted on long strips of canvas wound between two vertical rollers, enabled characters to travel from Paris to Vienna in full view of the audience. Sometimes sections of the floor were replaced by laths of wood glued onto canvas loops to form caterpillar tracks; armies could march for miles on them, and horses gallop at full stretch without stirring from the spot. Fix the track to an ascending trap, and ghosts or visions can glide *sideways* as they rise up through the floor. Gas lighting, introduced in the first quarter of the century, brought with it undreamed wonders. Buildings painted on transparent gauze dissolve at once by turning up the light behind them, and reappear when it is dimmed. Fog effects are made by stretching gauze across the arch of the proscenium, towers drawn on thin wooden blocks collapse in ruins when a string is pulled, and flames are red silk streamers agitated by a fan. The results were certainly spectacular. The villain in MacFarren's *Malvina* (1826) falls into an '*extensive mountain torrent*', ships sink in flames in Fitzball's *The Red Rover* (1829), an earthquake destroys an amphitheatre in Medina's *The Last Days of Pompeii* (1834), and in Boucicault's *Pauvrette* (1858) an avalanche 'entirely buries the whole scene to the height of twelve or fifteen feet'. When poor Lina is trapped on a cliff-ledge in *The Harbour Lights*, the tide rises, the cliff sinks, a wave sweeps her out to sea, and she is rescued by a passing boat. *Masaniello* shows Vesuvius in eruption:

> *The crater of the volcano emits torrents of flame and smoke—forked lightnings rend the sky in every direction. . . . A terrific explosion ensues from the mountain, the lava impetuously flows down its side, and extends itself into the sea.—The people, awe-struck, bend in submission to the will of heaven, and the curtain slowly descends.*

But this is nothing compared to Moncrieff's *The Cataract of the Ganges* (1823), which winds up with an orgy of fire, horses and real water:

> *As the scene draws, the whole of the Trees are discovered in flames. . . . The burning trees fall on all sides, and discover the terrific Cataract of Gangotri, supposed to form the source of the Ganges. The Emperor and the Bramin's troops appear, pouring down the rocky heights around the Cataract in every direction. . . . Zamine mounts the courser of Iran, and while he keeps the foe at bay, dashes safely up the Cataract, amidst a volley of musketry from the Enemy on the heights. . . . The contest becomes general—horse and foot are engaged in all parts. . . . Iran brings forward Zamine in safety—the Rajah joins their hands—and the Curtain falls on the shouts of the Conquerors.*

It always does. These sensational effects are not just exciting spectacles; they increase the persecutions of the villain by exposing helpless heroines to all the terrors of a hostile universe, and then heighten Joe's delight by allowing virtue to emerge from the ordeal unscathed. This is the great design all melodrama bends to serve. The cavalry comes thundering across the plain to save the decimated garrison, the hero is cut down from the gallows by a last-minute reprieve, long-lost clues are conveniently pieced together from the debris of waste-paper baskets, unexpected riches tumble from the lining of a waistcoat or the innards of a taxidermist's dog, and stolen infants reared in poverty are identified by lockets, scars or gooseberry birth-marks as the long-sought heirs of vast domains. In the real world, Joe's life is ruled by accidents which lack all palpable design; in the ideal world of melo-drama they subserve a universal moral order which makes sure the villain's luck runs out before the final curtain. Some early pieces based on sentimental French originals let him get off scot-free. In *Deaf and Dumb* by Thomas Holcroft, for example, he bursts into tears when con-fronted by his wickedness, writes a full confession and is saved from public shame by the good old man. That was in 1801; most later melo-dramas refuse to countenance such weakness. Their villains are betrayed by bunglers or blackmailed by accomplices, tricked into confession by a verbal slip, snapped by a camera at the moment of their crime, arrested by exchange telegraph or Scotland Yard, accidentally self-poisoned, hurled from the Monument, shot down from the Mansion House, blown up on a paddle-boat, run over by an express train or roasted to a crisp in forest fires. There are no loose ends left dangling. In the last act of Augustus Harris's *The World* (1880), one wretch is stabbed in error for the hero, another turns Queen's Evidence, a third is crushed by a descending lift and two more are arrested at a fancy-dress ball disguised as the Sultan of Turkey and his attendant monk. All villains are made painfully aware of their final destination. Tyrants unmanned by conscience sit trembling on their usurped thrones, and wander through the Alps tortured by agonies of hideous remorse. Here is the vile Romaldi in Holcroft's *Tale of Mystery*, who leaps from rock to rock

> *pursued as it were by heaven and earth.* Whither fly? Where shield me from pursuit, and death, and ignominy? My hour is come! The fiends that tempted now tear me. (*Dreadful thunder*) The heavens shoot their fires at me! Save! Spare! Oh spare me! (*Falls on the bank*)

Carlos puts a bolder face on things in Lacy's version of *The Sea of Ice* (1853):

> Death! To me, who can pay armies and purchase kingdoms! 'Tis impossible—impossible! You triumph! . . . Oh, that I could spit

poison upon you! My curses, my dying malediction upon you!—
upon you all!

Clearly, there is no hope of pardon here. Nor does the melodramatist
allow his well-known tenderness for the weaker sex to pervert the
course of justice. Erring wives and ruined maidens regularly lose their
reason, leap from bridges, plunge into volcanoes, intercept the villain's
bullet, or die of sin, a fatal disease in all true melodrama; and tawny
villainesses always pay the full price of their crime. Nothing is allowed
to compromise the rigorous enforcement of a code which confirms Joe in
the comforting illusion that the heavens are just, crime never pays, and
the wages of sin is inevitable death. In this final victory of the hero and
the heroine, Joe can enjoy at one remove a temporary triumph over all
the persecuting tyrannies and misadventures of real life. And as he
walks back home to Lambeth, with the huzzas of virtue ringing in his
ears, he may resolve to bring the ideal world of melodrama closer to
the real world he knows. With hard work, honesty and simple faith to
guide him, perhaps tomorrow or the next day he too will reap his just
rewards.

The basic pattern of all popular melodrama remained unchanged for
upwards of a century. To keep Joe coming back for more, authors had
to find new ways of wrapping up the old, familiar, story. They gutted
history books and atlases, adapted Byron, Scott and Dickens, wove
instant fantasies around newspaper stories of national battles, new
inventions, murder trials and recent shipwrecks, and kept a plagiarizing
eye upon the billboards of their competitors in Europe and America.
Above all, they sought out new periods and settings for their plays. The
earliest were gothic, exotic or plain horsey. *Mazeppa*, the first melodrama in this book, owes something to all three. Gothic melodrama
deals in ruined abbeys, moonlit churchyards, crumbling castles, suits of
armour, blood-filled goblets, haunted chambers, sliding panels, dripping
dungeons, shrieking phantoms, nightmares, serpents, skeletons,
monsters, vampires, ghouls, blue fire, ghosty music, thunderbolts, total
darkness and tormented tyrants hiding dreadful crimes from questing
heroes. Lewis's *The Castle Spectre* led the field in 1797. Exotic melodramas simply transport this whole bag of tricks to Turkey, Tartary
or the battlefields of Ahmedabad by moonlight. These colourful enter-
tainments provided ideal material for the Royal Circus and Astley's
Royal Amphitheatre, where spectacular pantomimes like *Rinaldo
Rinaldini* (1801) and *The Blood-Red Knight* (1810) filled the stage with
Turkish tyrants, tournaments, equestrian parades, assaults, pitched
battles, gunfire, conflagrations, waterfalls and fireworks. At first these
were performed in dumbshow and eked out with explanatory placards
which proclaimed 'AURELIA ACCUSED OF INCONTINENCE AND TREASON'

or 'DEATH WHEN I PROVE FALSE'. Their orthography was sometimes shaky, and one spectator recalled that 'LEAD HER TO THE BRIDLE HALTER' announced a princess's nuptials, while orders to explode a corsair's haunt appeared as 'BLOW UP THE COURSER'S AUNT'. Snippets of song and dialogue were gradually introduced, gothic supernaturalism was engulfed by oriental splendour, and while heroes stormed cardboard battlements upon the stage, on the other side of the orchestra pit warriors in gold and silver armour rode squadrons of real horses round and round a sawdust ring. With its simple tale of romantic love and parental tyranny, its songs and choruses, Polish court, Tartar landscape and moving diorama of the Dnieper, its parades, processions, knightly tournaments, burning forest, military ballet and sensational untamed steed, *Mazeppa* shows this early melodrama at its most exotic and appealing. It opened Astley's summer season in 1831, and was promptly pirated in New York and Philadelphia.

Most early melodramas in America were foreign imports clearly labelled 'Made in England'; the rest were modelled on those jingoistic spectacles typified by Dibdin's *Siege of Gibraltar*. While Napoleon lost Trafalgar and Waterloo once again at Sadler's Wells and Astley's, on the stages of the eastern seaboard Washington marched on to victory and General Warren died for a free America in John Burk's *Bunker Hill* (1797). Whatever the setting, there were the usual sieges and manoeuvres, forts exploded, fire-ships stormed, tattered flags hoist up in triumph and mournful bugles sounding the retreat. But despite the patriotic speeches and a cast of national heroes, these melodramas were little more than carbon copies of their European rivals; it was with plays of pioneering life that native melodrama came of age. Best of them all is *Nick of the Woods*, which is set in the outback of Kentucky in 1782, and comes complete with rocky passes, forest wilds, savage panthers, log stockades, abductions, tortures, redskins, burning wigwams, a generous discharge of firearms, and the terrifying vision of the Jibbenainosay, a homicidal maniac who appears '*precipitated down the cataract in a canoe of fire*' while the injuns utter yells of terror and the paleface folks evince polite astonishment. Two innovations set this play apart from earlier Indian dramas like John Stone's *Metamora* (1829). Firstly, Metamora and his fellows are all chivalrous and noble savages, distinguished from more classic heroes only by their gaily decorated tomahawks and feathered headgear. Bird's novel, upon which *Nick* is based, looked at the aborigine with less sentimental eyes, and found instead of nature's gentleman a filthy and ferocious savage happy only when out hunting for a white man's scalp. Medina's play reflects Bird's prejudice, presents Wenonga and the Shawnees as the second sons of Satan, contrasts them with the noble pioneers of Brucetown Station, and so blazes out a trail for Tom Mix and *The Virginian*. Secondly, Bird and Medina treat the cliché leatherstocking as unglamorously as the cliché

xvii

Indian. Ralph Stackpole is no idealized backwoodsman, though he wears the buckskin trews and cooncap of the tribe, but a reckless, roaring, ring-tailed rough-neck, boaster, hoss-thief and barbarian, afraid of nothin' that walks or crawls or swims or flies; he whoops like an injun, neighs like a hoss, crows like a cock, and vows to tote the angeliferous heroine down the falls in his canoe or else be tee-to-taciously expluncti- fied. What is more, he does. Add to these excitements all the spicy thrills of a sadistic blackguard who tangles dangerously with noble innocence, and it is easy to see why *Nick of the Woods* remained the most successful American melodrama for more than half a century.

Meanwhile, liberals on both sides of the Atlantic were focusing on Joe's most pressing social problems. In village plays like Buckstone's *Luke the Labourer* (1826) and Jerrold's *Rent Day* (1832), grasping lawyers foreclose mortgages, cruel stewards squeeze horrendous rents from the downtrodden peasantry, ruined farmers are evicted and lovely village maidens almost ravished by the wicked squire in a black frock coat and sideburns. The virtuous young ploughman whose heroic speeches rail against such manifest injustice is promptly packed off to the neighbouring township, where he is arrested as a vagrant, vic- timized by mercenary factory owners, beaten up by guttersnipes, or conned by city slickers into sampling the depraved delights of prosti- tutes and booze. Titles like Taylor's *The Factory Strike; or, Want, Crime, and Retribution* (1838) and Stirling's *Mary of Manchester; or, The Spirit of the Loom* (1847) are enough to show the social message and domestic interest of English factory plays, which continued well into the second half of the century with Boucicault's *The Long Strike* (1866) and Fenn's *The Foreman of the Works* (1886). None of them is more committed than *The Factory Lad*, which uses melodrama's black and white morality to prop an uncompromising drama of industrial unrest. The villain is a sneering factory owner who sacks half a dozen honest weavers to replace them with the new steam looms. Emigration, poaching and the workhouse are canvassed and dismissed as answers to their penury. In desperate revenge they set the factory ablaze and smash the new machines, only to be hunted down and brought before Justice Bias. The factory owner is assassinated by a half-crazed poacher, and as the curtain falls the men are left awaiting trial and sentence, transportation or the noose. There is no happy ending here, no songs, no jokes, no light relief, and precious little pathos; all are sacrificed to make this savage propaganda play a grim tract for grim times. In its militant class consciousness and powerful dramatic life, *The Factory Lad* anticipates by more than half a century the problem plays of Galsworthy and Shaw. The chances are it would revive as well today.

Unlike *The Factory Lad*, most domestic melodramas in America were able to encompass social problems without surrendering the comedy and optimism of the form. The Abolition movement inspired

Boucicault's *The Octoroon* (1859) and Aiken's *Uncle Tom's Cabin* (1852), in which the wicked slavers are precipitated from a mountain top, the heroine escapes pursuit by floating over the Ohio River on a handy cake of ice, and Little Eva goes to heaven on the wings of a milk-white dove. Uncle Tom, who dies in holy innocence before his manumission is received, is of course a complete abstainer who weans his master from strong drink. Temperance melodramas concentrate exclusively upon this edifying spectacle. Some of them are nothing more than dreary sermons with a cast of crude abstractions driving home the message with the finesse of a battering-ram. In *The Trial of Baneful Alcohol*, for instance, Baron Drinkwater speaks for the prosecution, with Lusty Tippler, Pale Ale and Dismal Destitute for the defence. Beardsall's *The Trial of John Barleycorn* (? 1850) is conducted by Chief Justice Impartiality and his trusty clerk Mr T. T. Temperance. Other melodramas wrap the sermonizing up in an exciting tale of village life. The hero is usually a weak-willed dipsomaniac who drives his wife into the workhouse, beats his starving angel-child, takes off for the sinful city, pawns his shirt to purchase rum, and winds up his degradation with a protracted and spectacular display of *delirium tremens*. Sometimes he kills himself and his family, or ends up in the madhouse; more often he is rescued *in extremis* by a temperance philanthropist who administers The Pledge. 'Louisa,' cries the wretched Mordaunt in Taylor's *The Drunkard's Warning* (1856),

> Louisa, hear me while I swear ne'er again to pollute my lips with that accursed fluid that has brought this misery upon us both! Heaven hears my vow, and surrounding seraphs record the oath on high!

After which, the melodramatist is morally obliged to give the hero back his fortune, family and friends, and restore them in the last scene to that same rural paradise where the drama had begun. This is certainly what happens in *The Drunkard*, which for good measure also boasts a pathetic and much bowdlerized Ophelia, a lascivious villain called Lawyer Cribbs, and for light relief a superannuated spinster who parades down Broadway in her bloomers and is at pains to let us know age cannot wither her nor custom stale her infinite vacuity.

The other three plays in this book show some of the developments which melodrama suffered as the century advanced. Many early theatres had followed the example of Pixerécourt's *Latude* (1834) and specialized in recent crime. The Royal Victoria did so many *Sweeney Todds* that Joe affectionately christened it 'The Bleedin' Vic', and when the Surrey staged the Thurtell-Weare case as *The Gamblers* (1823) it got hold of the actual furniture the murderers had used and gave the audience an extra thrill by using it again upon the stage. In crime plays like Moncrieff's *The Scamps of London* (1843), this cult of realism was extended to embrace a riff-raff cast of railway porters, ruined roués, drunkards, cadgers, shoe-blacks, vagabonds, bill-discounters and policemen. They speak a racy Cockney slang, and play out exciting scenes of metropolitan depravity in hotel rooms and railway stations, garrets, gaudy pleasure gardens, miserable dives and brickfields close to Battersea. The technical developments of gaslight and built scenery enabled later managers to show the seamy side of urban life with still more nauseating thoroughness. When Sims' *The Lights o'London* appeared at the Princess's in 1881, *The Theatre* critic threw in his towel and cried enough:

> If anything, it is all too real, too painful, too smeared with the dirt and degradation of London life, where drunkenness, debauchery, and depravity are shown in all their naked hideousness. Amidst buying and selling, the hoarse roars of costermongers, the jingle of the piano-organ, the screams of the dissolute, fathers teach their children to cheat and lie, drabs swarm in and out of the public-house, and the hunted Harold, with his devoted wife, await the inevitable capture in an upper garret of a house which is surrounded by the police.
>
> (IV. 239–40)

London by Night, which dates from 1868, does not go as far as this. But it has all the local colour of *The Scamps of London*, upon which it is based, plus the thrilling rescue of a female suicide and a full-sized express train which dashes right across the stage '*with a roar and a whistle*'. In 1868, this great sensation was alone enough to guarantee the play's success. Later, Joe demanded something just as thrilling in each act. Hence *Pluck*, by Henry Pettitt and Augustus Harris (1882), which combines a burning house, a grand snow storm, a heroine who exits in a carriage with real horses, a bank with real glass windows broken by an angry mob, and a terrific railway accident in which a second express train crashes headlong into the wreckage of the first.

While Joe Whelks and his friends were held in thrall by these new wonders, the middle classes were lured back into the theatre with promise of more subtle fare. Buckstone at the Adelphi had begun the movement in the 1840s, and he was followed by the gentlemanly management of Charles Kean at the Princess's (1850–9), Squire Bancroft at the Prince of Wales's (1865–79), and Irving's long reign at the Lyceum (1878–1902). In these smaller and more fashionable houses, actors were no longer forced to rant and rave like lunatics. Their scripts became more conversational, their acting more restrained. Strong emotions were conveyed by well-bred reticence, and comic scenes depended less on fisticuffs than wit. The leading actor schooled his company into a fine ensemble, and assumed complete responsibility for every aspect of the show. Settings, costumes, properties and furniture were assembled with an eye upon their unified effect. In modern plays the curtain rose upon a perfect copy of the bourgeois drawing-room the audience had just vacated; in costume dramas it disclosed a *mise en scène* which was historically accurate as well as picturesque. Lighting changes, music cues and off-stage sounds received the same attention; supernumeraries were drilled like soldiers, and the stage crew went on overtime to make each scene change smooth. The melodramas of the period reflect this new sophistication. Without the most scrupulous stage management, the double vision scenes and gliding ghost of *The Corsican Brothers* could easily be muffed; so could the all-important substitution of the hero's double at the climax of the final duel in the frozen glade. But this play has more than stage illusion to commend it to the middle classes. Its novel form, in which the first two acts are supposed to take place concurrently, shows a degree of structural complexity quite foreign to the simple stories which amused Joe Whelks. Again, its subject matter treats of love and chivalry in the swishy sword-and-caper style of D'Artagnan and Monte Cristo. And to this romantic interest Boucicault has added a sure-fire snob appeal. He draws his supers from Society, and titillates the audience with daring glimpses of their naughty night life with the *demi-monde*. His villain is a gentleman, his heroine an admiral's lady, and his hero owns ancestral acres and a mansion house in Corsica. The plot turns on a duel of honour. When Kean and Wigan acted it in 1852, their muted, untheatrical delivery lent the lines an inner truth which terrified the first-night audience. A serious revival could have the same effect today, for underneath the splendid trappings of this drama is a simple tale of honour, love and vengeance which still tugs at the heart.

The other French play in this book is a four-act adaptation of *The Lady of the Camellias*. Its wordy dialogue, genteel style, 'strong' emotive situations and cast-list drawn from High Society all indicate another bourgeois drama. But Dumas *fils* is much more daring here than Boucicault had been. He dispenses with the spectacular machinery of Paris, Corsica and Fontainebleau, and sets the play in drawing-rooms and salons; while Marguerite goes off to a masked ball at the Opera, the audience stays at home and watches Varville quiz Nanine. Secondly, he does away with melodrama's black and white morality, and shades some of his characters in muted grey. No one in the *demi-monde* seems more frivolous and selfish than the dissipated Gaston Rieux, but it is he who sits up all night by Marguerite instead of dancing both his feet off at a ball. The melodramas Joe admired deal harshly with the girl who sins; in *Masaniello*, for example, poor Fenella leaps into a sea of molten lava with the minimum of fuss. The code grew weaker as the century grew old. In Landeck and Shirley's *Tommy Atkins*, which dates from 1895, an unmarried mother purifies her soul by touring through the battlefields of Europe as a Red Cross nurse, and is rewarded for her trouble with the hand of Harold Wilson, an energetic curate she has loved right from the start. Such bliss is not available to Marguerite in 1852. She spends the last two acts atoning for her scarlet past by nobly giving up the man she loves and forcing him to hate her. And then she dies, but not till Dumas has invested her supreme self-sacrifice with fifteen minutes of the most exquisite pathos. 'Sleep in peace, Marguerite!' says dear Nichette, who has fallen on her knees beside the body. 'Much will be forgiven you, because you greatly loved!' And Dumas' mastery of tears has made sure that the biblical allusion sums up our judgment too.

By 1900, melodrama was almost invalided from the stage. Sir Henry Irving played to thinning houses at the Lyceum, forfeited the lease, and spent his last years on the road. The middle classes were deserting to the murder mystery and the witty social comedies of Wilde; Ibsen and Shaw provided for the intellectuals, and Joe Whelks took himself off to the Music Hall, the Grand Guignol, or the thrilling hippodramas of the Buffalo Bill Roadshow. The friendly theatres of the East End and the Bowery struggled through the Great War on a repertoire of blood and thunder, and then sold out to seedy strip shows, boxing bouts, and blue revue. By their side sprang up new pleasure domes called Odeons, and suddenly the melodrama was reborn anew. Joe found the clichés of the stage new-minted marvels on the silent screen. Ships were sunk and trains exploded with a realism far beyond the theatre's power, and instantaneous cross-cutting did away with all those pauses while the stage crew cleared the mess. Famous actors came before the cameras in all their greatest scenes; James O'Neill was seen as Monte Cristo in the Gorbals, and the Marguerite of Sarah Bernhardt was billed nightly at the Trocadero, Golders Green. Soon, the cinema developed its own perfect melodrama in the western, where the good guys and the bad guys are instantly identified, injuns on the warpath add the necessary thrills, music heightens every scene of tenderness or tension, and the cavalry always come galloping across the prairie in the nick of time. Television, too, has spawned new melodramas in the shape of science-fiction fantasies, or thrillers where the incorruptible police force wages ceaseless war against the Soho underworld, Chicago gangsters, dope rings in Marakesh, or lethal vamps with slightly parted lips. Some of these series have been on the air for years; clearly, they fill a real need. At certain times, we all need to slump into a sofa, turn the box on, and escape into an ideal world of superheroes, thrilling conflicts and pre-determined victory. Joe Whelks would not judge us harshly. Must we judge him?

1974   James L. Smith

FOR

ROLAND MACLEOD

sine quo non

Mazeppa

A ROMANTIC DRAMA IN THREE ACTS BY H. M. MILNER

First performed at the Royal Amphitheatre, London, 4 April 1831

CAST

Poles

PREMISLAS, COUNT PALATINE	Mr S. Foster
THE CASTELLAN OF LAURINSKI	Mr Hart
RUDZOLOFF, Chamberlain of his household	Mr Lawrence
DROLINSKO, a servant	Mr Herring
OFFICER	Mr J. Smith
SENTINEL	Mr Taylor
OLINSKA, daughter to The Castellan	Mrs Pope
AGATHA, her nurse	Mrs Bradley
ZEMILA, a servant	Mrs Yates

Knights, officers, guards, heralds, soldiers, pages, grooms, ladies, domestics, priest, envoy, &c.

Tartars

ABDER KHAN, King of Tartary	Mr Gomersal
MAZEPPA, his son, known in Poland as CASSIMIR	Mr Cartlitch
THAMAR ⎫ conspiring chieftains	⎧Mr S. Smith
ZEMBA ⎬	⎨Mr Taylor
KOSCAR ⎫ shepherds	⎧Mr West
KADAC ⎬	⎨Mr Fillingham
ELDERS OF THE PEOPLE	Mr Gough, Mr Montgomery and Mr Yates
ONEIZA, a shepherdess	Mrs J. Ducrow
SHEPHERDESS	Mrs Dawson

Chieftains, warriors, priests, guards, shepherds, shepherdesses, &c.

The First and Third Acts are set at the Castle of Laurinski in Poland. The Second Act is set in Tartary.

Period: 1672

HENRY M. MILNER

Life unknown. Flourished mightily between 1820 and 1840 as hack melodramatist for the minor houses. Adapted many plays for the Coburg, including *Frankenstein* (1823) from Mary Shelley, *The Lovers of Verona* (1826) from Shakespeare, *The Hut of the Red Mountains* (1827) from Ducange, and *The Fair Maid of Perth* (1828) from Scott. At Astley's, followed *Mazeppa* (1831) with *Chevy Chase* (1832), an equestrian burletta. Last known work: *Dick Turpin's Ride to York* (1841).

MAZEPPA

The story goes that when Ivan Stepanovich Mazepa-Koledinsky (?1644–1709) was a young man at the court of Casimir of Poland, his intrigue with a married lady was discovered by her husband; outraged, he tied the naked Ivan to the back of a wild stallion and sent him forth to wander on the steppe. Rescued at the point of death by Cossacks from the Dnieper, Ivan recovered to become their leader and most influential hetman. Byron retold the tale in a poem called *Mazeppa* (1819), which several hippodramatists adapted for the stage. Milner's version was presented at the Coburg (3 November 1823), and Cuvelier and Chandezon's at the Cirque Olympique, Paris (11 January 1825); John Howard Payne's translation could not find a London theatre. When Milner became house dramatist at Astley's, he dug out his old play and rewrote it under Ducrow's supervision. Decked out with splendid scenery, exotic costumes, and a cavalcade of horses, the new version opened Astley's summer season on Easter Monday, 1831, and met an instantaneous success. The iron-lunged John Cartlitch played Mazeppa, with Gomersal, a famous Napoleon, as Abder Khan. But it was the headlong dash of the untamed steed which drew the most applause. Next day *The Morning Chronicle* reported:

> There was something almost terrific in his first start with the victim lashed to his back; and the way in which he bounded up the different platforms . . . gave no faint idea of the speed with which the real

steed might have dashed along precipices and mountains. Next to this, the best effect produced was where he is seen with his burthen immersed in the Dnieper, with the wolves in his train, and the birds hovering over head, in search of their prey.

For nearly fifty years *Mazeppa*-fever raged through every hippodrama house in England and America. Astley's revived the show for season after season. In 1833, there were two rival productions in New York and two more in Philadelphia. St Louis succumbed in August 1838, and San Francisco in December 1851. Sanger's tent circus toured the play through Scotland in 1854. Cartlitch alone played the young hero more than 1,500 times, and wept aloud when, in view of his advancing years, he was demoted to the Tartar Khan. But history's most famous Mazeppa was the actress Adah Isaacs Menken, who made her début in the role at the Green Street Theatre, Albany, on 7 June 1861, and in the next five years went on to conquer New York, San Francisco, London and Paris. Baltimore showered her with flowers and diamonds; Virginia City gave her a bar of bullion. Swinburne, Dickens and the elder Dumas acknowledged her fascination. She fought the combat scenes, according to *The Times* (7 October 1864), 'with wonderful vigour and spirit', and—greatly daring—rode the Tartar horse wearing pale pink fleshlings and tight-fitting trunks of white linen. As her New York manager advertised,

> Miss Adah dresses the part very prettily, and displays a leg—or rather, two legs—in silk fleshlings of such delicate proportions that they would have made St Anthony lift his eyes from his prayer-book. To see Miss Adah in the matured beauty of her womanhood, costumed as she is costumed, is alone worth the price of admission.
>
> (Bernard Falk, *The Naked Lady* (1934), p. 155)

There is no record of her acting ability.

The text of Milner's revised *Mazeppa* survives in two versions: one in Dicks' Standard Plays, the other in Cumberland's Minor Theatre, which is reprinted line for line in Lacy. The present edition is based on Cumberland, which is far the earliest. One or two effective touches are introduced from Dicks, together with a few cuts sanctioned by the later acting text.

ACT I

Scene 1. The court-yard of the castle of Laurinski, bounded by the buildings of the castle, its moat and adjacent lake. It is approached by a series of drawbridges over the moat and branches of the lake. In the background, the distant country. Castle gates L, two large windows L, the nearest of which has a practicable balcony. The moon seen to set. Lights are observable in the castle windows, which are gradually extinguished as the morning advances.

A Sentinel *discovered, pacing the drawbridge which leads across from* R *to* L. *Enter* Cassimir *cautiously, and crossing to the window* L.

Cassimir. (calling softly) Olinska.

Sentinel. (halting on the drawbridge) Ha! Who goes there? No answer? (Cassimir *conceals himself behind a buttress*) By the uncertain glimpses of the moon, I can distinguish no one. All is silent. It could have been but the wind sighing amongst these ancient battlements, whistling along them as it does through my ribs, which—by the time they keep me on the watch—I suppose they think as tough and as weather-proof as the walls themselves. I shall take the liberty of making free with the porter's fire in the hall, for a few moments.

(Music. Exit into the portal)

Cassimir. (advancing from the buttress) Olinska, dear Olinska! Ere yet the envious daylight robs my soul of this sweet privilege, of drinking from thine eyes deep draughts of the bright liquid fire which, as from twin stars of love, streams through my enraptured heart, appear, dear life! Raise me to that throne of glory monarchs might envy me, Olinska's love!

Music. Olinska *appears in the balcony.*

Olinska. Cassimir! Thou here? Hence, hence! Wert thou discovered, think how fearfully my father's wrath would fall on the clandestine suitor to his child.

Cassimir. What can Cassimir dread, ennobled and emboldened by thy love?

Olinska. It cannot be a noble or a worthy love, that thus beneath the mask of night must steal to lay its homage on the shrine.

Cassimir. Dost thou reproach my rash presumption?

5

Olinska. No; but my own unworthy cowardice. Cassimir, I will no more of this, no longer stoop to tremblingly conceal affections in which my soul should glory. No. At my father's feet I will avow it all, will plead thy gallant services—thy exalted deeds, charge him, as he values my happiness or peace, to grant Olinska's hand where her fond heart is pledged, and gain a son who'll be an honour to his name.

Cassimir. To thee and to thy love I do commit me!

Olinska. But see, the dawn advances. The moon has sunk behind yon hoary hills, the glimmering lights are one by one expiring, and the hum of busy menials speaks approaching day. Away, my love, away!

Cassimir. May all propitious powers smile down upon the pleadings of thy virtuous love, waft thy soft breathings deep to thy father's heart and win him to our cause! Then should thy doting Cassimir in the broad blaze of day boast of his bliss and be all Poland's envy.

The drum of the guard is heard. Cassimir *climbs a buttress and passionately kisses* Olinska's *hand, then effects his escape. Sound approaches. Re-enter* Sentinel *on the drawbridge.* Olinska, *after watching* Cassimir, *retires from the balcony. Enter a* Patrol *who crosses the drawbridge and relieves the guard.* Domestics *enter and go into the castle, followed by* Rudzoloff *and* Drolinsko.

Drolinsko. Come! bustle, bustle, you lazy-pated varlets! Why, it's day, broad day! And is not today to be a remarkable day, a glorious day, a day of festivity? Is there not to be a grand tournament? Are not all the neighbouring knights, ladies, esquires and gentry invited? Is not an envoy from the Count Palatine Premislas expected? And an't I expected to take a leading part in all the games?

Rudzoloff. But what an odd freak of our Lord Castellan to choose such a day as this for the attempt to subdue the unbreakable, fiery, wild Tartarian horse, so long the terror of all our grooms and the executioner of so many rough-riders! He'll kill all the men, and frighten the women into fits.

Music. Domestics *return from the castle, cross stage and exeunt.* Cassimir *follows them on and remains listening at the back.*

See, there goes Cassimir, the idol of all the women, and the envy of all the men.

Drolinsko. Not of all the men, godfather; for my part, I think his brother, the wild horse, the more amiable barbarian of the two. Let my lady beware, or she may find, too late, that she has caught a Tartar.

(*Chord*)

Cassimir. (*rushing forward, and giving* Drolinsko *a violent slap on the shoulder*) What says the slave?

Drolinsko. (*aside*) By all that's terrible, the Tartar has caught me.

Cassimir. No muttering, sirrah; you spoke of me.

Drolinsko. Did I? Well, then, I'm sure you must have been delighted to hear the complimentary things I said of you. You can't think how prodigiously we shall all regret—I speak of myself in particular—that your duty must presently take you from us.

Cassimir. What means the slave?

Rudzoloff. Why, as you know that my Lady Olinska is going to be married to the Count Palatine Premislas, one of the richest and most powerful noblemen in Poland——

Cassimir. How said you? Married—married to another?

Rudzoloff. Another? What other? Why, she was never married before, was she?

Drolinsko. A despatch late last night, conveyed to the Castellan's chamber after he had retired! Ay, ay, it's we folks of consequence in the establishment that come at the earliest intelligence. Bless your heart, the envoy is expected today, to make the formal proposal to my lady.

Cassimir. (*aside*) Against this blow, support me, heaven! She never will—she never shall be his!

Drolinsko. Shan't she, though? There, I think, you'll find yourself mistaken, young fellow. Not that you need to put yourself into such a taking about it, for I dare say, as you are her favourite page, she will prevail on the Palatine to make you one of his esquires.

Cassimir. (*seizing* Drolinsko *by the throat*) Wretch, how dare you thus insult me? But no, reptile, thou art not worth my anger.   (*Rushes out*)

Drolinsko. I thank you for appreciating me so justly. Godfather, mark my words, that man will never come to any good. Oh, that the Castellan would clap him on the back of his brother devil the Tartarian horse, and send them off to Tartary—or Tartarus!

Rudzoloff. Tush, fool! The Lady Olinska approaches. Out of the way, numskull; away, to speed the preparations for the festival.

Music. Rudzoloff *drives* Drolinsko *out, who has hardly recovered from the effects of his shaking. Enter* Olinska *with* Agatha.

Agatha. Why, how is it my pretty bird has left her nest so early this morning? And, oh! those downcast eyes and colourless cheeks assure me she must have passed a sleepless night.

Olinska. Oh, I am deeply to be pitied!

Agatha. Pitied! You, you to be pitied! When there's nothing talked of through all the castle but your approaching nuptials with a young nobleman so rich and so——

Olinska. Those nuptials never can take place. My heart, my soul, each energy of my existence—all, all is Cassimir's.

Agatha. Cassimir's! Heavens! A friendless youth, an orphan boy, a foundling Tartar!

7

Olinska. The idol of my fond affections! This very morning, yielding to the prayer of Cassimir, I went to make an avowal to my father; but judge of my astonishment, my agony, when he announced to me that he had solemnly engaged my hand to the Count Palatine, who in the recent war had rescued him in battle. You know my cruel situation; judge, condemn me, if you can, but you must at least pity the unhappy Olinska. (*A noise of hurried footsteps is heard without*)

Agatha. Some one approaches.

Olinska. Ah, 'tis he—'tis Cassimir! Great heaven, how agitated!

Re-enter Cassimir *suddenly.*

Cassimir. (*with suppressed anger*) Noble lady—— (Agatha *retires, watching*)

Olinska. Speak without reserve, Cassimir; my second mother here knows all.

Cassimir. Before her, then, pronounce my fate.

Olinska. Your fate!

Cassimir. Yes. On you, and on this moment, depend the destinies of my life.

Olinska. What mean you?

Cassimir. We must fly. The deserts of Tartary, where I first drew breath —from which we are only separated by a river—offer us an assured retreat. Then seek with me, in my own country, that happiness which is denied us here!

Olinska. How, with barbarians? With the enemies of Poland? Never!

Cassimir. Then let this hated rival tremble.

Olinska. Listen to me, Cassimir——

Cassimir. I care not for life. I am ready to sacrifice it. But I will not perish alone!

Agatha. (*advancing*) Your father comes. Cassimir, away!

Music. *They separate. Enter the* Castellan *with his suite, including* Rudzoloff, *from the castle gate. He seems surprised at observing the embarrassment his presence occasions, and testifies his astonishment on beholding* Cassimir.

Castellan. (*aside*) Cassimir! (*Aloud*) What do you here, Cassimir?

Cassimir. (*confused*) My Lord Castellan——

Agatha. (*fearing he may betray himself, hastens between him and the* Castellan) My lord, Cassimir was just come to—to—to—to request my influence with the Lady Olinska, to obtain for him the situation of first esquire with her intended husband.

The Castellan, *with a scrutinizing glance, surveys the lovers, who remain abashed and confused.*

Rudzoloff. This young man's intrusion on my lady's privacy——

Castellan. It would be your duty to punish, but I am willing to excuse. I call to mind his uniform good conduct, his courage and fidelity,

8

which deserve reward. I name him officer of men-at-arms, whom I
am sending to Warsaw to be incorporated in the royal guard. He will
depart tomorrow at daybreak.

Cassimir. My lord, permit me——

Castellan. Rudzoloff, I rely on you to see my wishes fulfilled. Away now,
and prepare for your appearance at the approaching fête.

Rudzoloff. Enough, my lord.

Exit Cassimir, *with gestures of submission to the* Castellan *and darting
glances of piercing scrutiny on* Olinska—Rudzoloff *following.*

Castellan. I find by the Count Palatine's despatch that this proposed
marriage is likewise sanctioned by the sovereign himself.

Olinska. (*aside*) Support me, oh, support me!

Castellan. The Count Premislas wished to come even on the instant and
present to thee his homage, but an ancient custom does not permit a
Palatine of Poland to offer his vows in person, till after a solemn
ceremony. The countess's coronet must be presented to the intended,
and she return her ring in exchange. From that moment, she is his
affianced bride. The envoy of the count this day will come on the
important mission.

Olinska. How, my father? This very day!

Castellan. Even so. Prepare for his reception, my daughter; obedience
should be easy, when honours and fortune are its reward.

Music. Enter an Officer, *on platform.*

Officer. My lord, a splendid cavalcade of knights and warriors even now
is discerned from the battlements, approaching the castle. By the
bearings on the banners, we perceive it is an envoy from Count
Premislas.

Castellan. Let him be conducted hither, with all the honour due to his
noble master. Bid my pages and officers of my household attend me
here. Olinska, be mindful of your duty.

Music. Olinska *bends in submission. The* Officer *retires. Enter* Rudzoloff,
pages including Cassimir, *ladies, and guards from the castle, at the gates, and
form round the* Castellan, Olinska, *and* Agatha, *who advance near the front.
Enter a Guard of Honour from the castle, crossing the back drawbridge.*

Chorus.   Songs of gratulations raise,
           Hymns of triumph, songs of love;
        In the sweet Olinska's praise
           A warrior's ardent passion prove.
        Hark! The drum approaches near,
        Sound triumphant to the ear.
        Songs of love and sweet Olinska—
        And shout—sweet Olinska—Olinska!

9

THE GRAND PROCESSION

moves on, consisting of soldiers, knights, officers, ladies, and attendants, who form on the L side and across the back. A small ornamental car is drawn on, under the canopy of which is a cushion with a countess's coronet. The Envoy *advances, the* Castellan *leads forward his daughter, and with her takes a position* R. *Two ladies place a cushion* C, *on which* Olinska *kneels. The* Envoy *brings forward the coronet, and presents it to* Olinska. *It is received by her attendants and placed on her head.* Cassimir *anxiously beholds the ceremony; he passes round the back, and takes a situation behind* Agatha; *on* Olinska's *receiving the coronet, he expresses rage and despair. The* Castellan *now reminds her to present her ring. With trembling agitation she draws it from her finger and approaches the canopy,* Cassimir *watching with a degree of intentness wrought up to agony. As she drops the ring on the cushion,* Count Premislas *bursts from the drapery of the car, seizes the ring, and advances to the front.*

Olinska. (starting) What do I see?
Castellan. The Count Premislas!
Premislas. 'Tis even so!
Cassimir. (aside) Down, rebel nature, down!
Premislas. Pardon me, beautiful Olinska, for not awaiting the sentence which was to decide my fate. Had my homage been rejected, I should have quitted the castle without intruding upon your presence; but on seeing you accept the diadem, I hastened to receive, myself, this precious pledge of happiness. *(Showing the ring)*

Music. He takes the hand of Olinska *and kisses it.* Cassimir *makes a movement as if, in his jealous fury, he would spring upon his happy rival, but is restrained by a sudden thought of more effectual vengeance.*

Cassimir. (aside and earnestly to Olinska) This very night—vengeance—death! *(Exit)*
Castellan. Deign to accompany me, count. Everything is prepared to receive you with the honours due to him who, becoming my son, will presently have a right to command, where now he is a guest. Never could your arrival have been better timed. This day I had prepared a solemn tourney, in which the pages of my household and friendly knights will contend in those manly sports which form the warrior's earliest lesson. To this festivity your presence will add a tenfold brilliance. Forward, and prepare the arena.
Premislas. Count, with the utmost joy I shall attend you. *(To* Olinska) Lady, may I be honoured with your hand?

Music. He offers his hand to Olinska, *who with diffident reluctance yields hers. The procession moves on towards the castle, and the scene closes.*

Scene 2. *A gothic apartment in the castle.*

Music. Enter Zemila.

Zemila. Well, so my Lady Olinska is going to be married. I wish I was
going to be married, for then I should no longer be a maid; no,
indeed, I'd be a mistress, as my husband would be pretty quickly
convinced. There's that lout Drolinsko has been casting sheep's eyes at
me for months past; but the dolt scarcely knows his own mind, I fancy.
There's but one reason I can conceive for having anything to say to
such a numskull: if I married him, he'd save me the trouble of making
a fool of him, for he's ready made to my hand. Give me a dashing,
spirited fellow, I say, who would run away with you in spite of
fathers, uncles, cousins—ay, for the matter of that, in spite of
yourself.   (*Song for* Zemila *introduced*)

Enter Drolinsko.

Drolinsko. (*meeting* Zemila) Ah, pretty Mistress Zemila! What may you
be seeking in such a bustle?
Zemila. No such trash as you; so mind your own business and let me
pass.
Drolinsko. Well now, for my part, I don't know what a likely young
woman, such as you, can meet more suited to her wants and inclina-
tions than a tidy husband.
Zemila. A husband! (*Laughing*) Ha, ha, ha, ha, ha! As if, were I inclined
for a husband, I should for a moment dream of such a thing as you!
Drolinsko. Such a thing as me! What the devil do you mean by that?
Why, what's the matter with me? I'm all right and tight, snug and
comfortable, as any young woman could desire.
Zemila. No, Drolinsko; you want one very material article to make a
man of you.
Drolinsko. No, you don't say so!
Zemila. Not that it's so essential to a husband.
Drolinsko. Well, I'm glad to hear that, at any rate.
Zemila. (*touching his head*) You want it here, my poor fellow: empty as a
scooped-out cocoanut shell!
Drolinsko. Want it there, do I? Now it strikes me very forcibly that if I
were your husband, you would furnish me with something more
than I should want—there.   (*Pointing to his forehead*)
Zemila. Now, if you were anything like such a person as the Tartar,
Cassimir——
Drolinsko. The Tartar Cassimir! Only to hear the women talk! He's a sort
of a wild beast, and all the women are weaving nets and meshes to catch

11

him; and if they can't tame him, he's a wild devil indeed. But I've stopped Mr Cassimir's pranks for a while.

Zemila. You stop him, Drolinsko? (*Laughing*) Ha, ha, ha! That's an excellent joke.

Drolinsko. I don't think he'll find it so. The slave had the presumption to intrude on the Lady Olinska's privacy, whilst taking a walk on the terrace of the castle, and even to touch her hand.

Zemila. Like a spirited young fellow, as he is.

Drolinsko. There I caught him—so did her father.

Zemila. (*sneering*) Well?

Drolinsko. The father did not seem inclined to say much. But I gave Mr Tartar pretty plainly to understand that if ever he attempted the like liberty again, he would incur a pretty considerable portion of my displeasure.

Zemila. (*derisively*) Your displeasure! Poor, poor Drolinsko.

Drolinsko. I'd a good mind to give him a bit of a shaking, then.

Zemila. You give Cassimir a shaking! Why, you'd shake in your shoes if he did but raise a finger.

Drolinsko. I say, Zemila, how provokingly beautiful you do look, to be sure. Do you know, I should so like to——

Zemila. Well, then, why don't you take courage and try?

Drolinsko. Egad, that's a pretty fair invitation, and here I go.

(*He attempts to kiss her; she slaps his face*)

Zemila. Smack for smack, my fine fellow, all over the world is fair play, you know.

Drolinsko. That's what you call giving a modest young man proper encouragement, I suppose.

Zemila. Recollect, Drolinsko, that till a recruit has learned to stand fire, he's never fit for the field of action.

Enter Rudzoloff.

Rudzoloff. Come, come, none of your billing and cooing here; all should be bustle and activity. The tournament is about to take place, the Lady Olinska is to crown the conqueror, and the presence of Count Premislas inclines my lord to wish the entertainment more brilliant even than he had intended.

Drolinsko. Lovely Mistress Zemila, were it your task to crown the conqueror, I feel that I should overthrow all before me.

Zemila. Then it must be with a crown of thistle and dandelion, ornamented with a pair of ass's ears. (*A trumpet heard without*)

Rudzoloff. Hark! That's the first signal. Hasten to take your place.

Drolinsko. My soul's in arms, and eager for——

Zemila. The encounter?

Drolinsko. No; for the sumptuous banquet that is to take place afterwards.

Trio

Zemila.
Oh! 'midst the clash of war's alarms,
    Delightful hurry scurry!
Where 'midst of trophies, plumes, and arms,
    The men each other worry.
How high each damsel's bosom beats,
    How beam her sparklers bright,
To think, with all their gallant feats,
    For her the heroes fight.

Drolinsko.
No doubt, for those who get the best,
    'Tis very pretty fun,
But ah! the thought that fills my breast
    Is care of number one.
What silly sport for fighting elves,
    Into each other pitching!
They'd better pitch into themselves
    The comforts of the kitchen.

Rudzoloff.
Oh, the thought of martial glory
    Warms the breast and fires the heart!
Though my war-worn locks are hoary,
    I could play a soldier's part.
Still the falchion could I wield,
    Still enjoy the trumpet's clang,
Still my heart to beauty yield,
    And each haughty rival bang.

ALL TOGETHER

Zemila.
Ever still must martial glory
    Tend a woman's heart to win;
Still they love a warrior's story,
    Though they dread the battle's din.

Drolinsko.
It's very well to talk of glory;
    Something better I would win.
With a jovial feast before me,
    I but wish a good tuck in.

Rudzoloff.
Still my heart beats high for glory,
    Fresher laurels yet I'd win;
As I tell each martial story,
    Fight the battle o'er again.
        (*Exeunt*)

13

Scene 3. *The Grand Arena, prepared for the tournament, surrounded on three sides by an elevated gallery. An arched entrance under the gallery. Near the front a canopied couch.*

Music. The galleries are filled with spectators. The limits of the arena are maintained by heralds and mounted men at arms. In the centre are drawn up the pages and knights, proposed combatants; Cassimir *is amongst them. The couch is occupied by the* Castellan, Olinska, *and* Count Premislas, *surrounded by their attendants.*

Castellan. My friends, display before us your address and courage. These noble sports are the image of war; learn from them to defend your prince and country. My daughter will crown the conqueror. Let the signal be given for the games to begin.

Music. The Castellan *sits.* Rudzoloff *makes a signal, on which a trumpet sounds and the respective champions take their stations. First, a small sword combat between two of the pages. Then a tilt of mounted and armed knights with spear and battle-axe, of whom* Cassimir *is one. Then a sword combat on horseback between* Cassimir *and his opponent. In both of these* Cassimir *is successful. Then a broadsword combat of four, in which* Cassimir *is also the victor. The conquerors advance towards the* Castellan.

Castellan. Cassimir, it is with pleasure I behold you the victor. I have before remarked your courage and address. I have distinguished you from the crowd of my pages; merit always thus my favour, and new rewards will be the result. The evening's shadows, now gathering o'er the valley, remind us to conclude our sports and taste the banquet's joys. Now let the trumpet speak the contest o'er, and in the joyous goblet's cheering draught let each drink happiness to my daughter and her noble spouse.

The victors are crowned by Olinska *with laurel;* Cassimir *receives also a scarf. They then approach a small table which has been prepared; each takes a goblet of wine, and as they are in the act of drinking, the scene closes.*

Scene 4. *A gallery of the castle, conducting to the sleeping rooms. An entrance from the armoury* L.

Music. Enter Count Premislas, *preceded and followed by his pages and gentlemen of his household, some of whom bear flambeaux. Three pages bring on table and chair. One takes his hat, another his mantle, which he lays over the back of a chair; a third places his sword on a small table.*

Premislas. You may now retire; I dispense with all further service for the evening. (*Pages &c. retire; the* Count *sits on a chair*) I shall presently be united to Olinska, called by my sovereign to one of the first offices of the state. Love and fortune unite to crown my wishes. Still the extraordinary emotion of Olinska haunts me—her disturbed looks, her eyes moistened with tears. What would be her hand without her heart? Perhaps some knight more blessed than I——. (*Rises and advances*) But no, Olinska has been brought up in retirement; her heart will be thoroughly her husband's.

Music. Enter Cassimir, *disguised in a black helmet with black plumes, the visor closed, and a long black mantle. He stands before* Premislas, *as he is turning towards his chamber.*

Premislas. (*seizing his sword*) Who art thou?
Cassimir. Thine enemy.
Premislas. How entered you this castle?
Cassimir. What matters that to thee?
Premislas. What is thy will?
Cassimir. Thy death.
Premislas. Would'st thou be my murderer?
Cassimir. No. I would meet thee in equal encounter of man to man.
Premislas. (*haughtily*) Thy name?
Cassimir. Thou shalt know that when thou art conquered.
Premislas. This arrogance——
Cassimir. Befits a jealous and offended man.
Premislas. What can you be?
Cassimir. Your rival.
Premislas. (*with anxiety*) Beloved?
Cassimir. Till yesterday I believed so.
Premislas. (*exultingly*) But today thou findest that the beautiful Olinska accords to me the preference.
Cassimir. Not to thee, but to thy honours and thy titles.
Premislas. Dar'st thou insult me?
Cassimir. I have told thee but the truth. My sword shall do the rest.
Premislas. Rash intruder! Think'st thou a Palatine will deign to measure swords with an unknown, doubtless unworthy of that honour?
Cassimir. My sword shall teach thee whether I be worthy.
Premislas. Hence, or my servants shall chastise thy boldness.
(*Proceeds to ring a bell*)
Cassimir. (*presenting two pistols*) One word, one gesture, and I stretch thee at my feet.
Premislas. Coward! Were our arms but equal——
Cassimir. (*laying aside his pistols and drawing a sword*) They are so. Behold, my bosom is unarmed. (*Throws open the mantle*) I wear this helmet for concealment, not protection. Aim at my heart; it has no defence but courage and this good sword.

Music. Pressed by the attack of Cassimir, Premislas *places himself on his defence, and a combat ensues. Unable to resist the vigour of* Cassimir's *onset,* Premislas *is wounded, and falls.*

Premislas. I yield.
Cassimir. (*resuming his mantle*) I am revenged.

Music. A tumult is heard without. A crowd of the Count's *attendants and other of the* Castellan's *household rush on, headed by* Drolinsko.

Drolinsko. I tell you, the unknown who stole the armour is in that gallery. See—behold him—there, there he is.

Those of the Count's *household, perceiving him fainting in the chair, rush to his assistance. The others are about to rush on* Cassimir, *who stands near the entrance to the armoury, but are kept in check by his presenting his pistols. He rushes off by the passage leading to the armoury, and they follow him. Enter the* Castellan, Rudzoloff, *and other attendants.*

Rudzoloff. Great heaven! The Palatine assassinated!   (*Goes to him*)
Premislas. (*partially reviving*) A rival—vengeance!
Castellan. You shall obtain it; and whoever the murderer may prove, it shall be terrible.

Music. Two discharges of pistols heard without. Enter Drolinsko, *running backwards.*

Drolinsko. We've got him! He's taken! He's taken!

The three pages bring in Cassimir, *still concealed by the visor and mantle. He shakes them off and quietly takes his station, the servants behind him.*

Premislas. (*pointing to* Cassimir) That is the assassin.
Castellan. Remove the mantle that conceals the wretch.

Music. As the servants are about to do so, Cassimir *casts off both the mantle and the helmet.*

All. Cassimir!
Castellan. My suspicions were, then, true.
Knights. Let him die!   (*All draw and rush upon him*)
Castellan. Hold! Reserve him for the punishment inflicted on rebel slaves. Lead in the Count; let every aid be lavished to restore him. (*Approaching the* Count *and grasping his hand. The* Count's *followers support him off*) Tremble, ungrateful miscreant, at the punishment reserved for outraged hospitality. Lead the vile Tartar hence. (*Grooms rush on with cords; they bind him*) Strip him of that garb he has degraded. (*They proceed to remove his dress*) Let not the arms of my house be sullied by adorning a traitor who raises his assassin arm

against my friend, under the very roof that gives him shelter. Lead out the fiery untamed steed—prepare strong hempen lashings round the villain's loins—let every beacon-fire on the mountain's top be lighted, and torches, like a blazing forest, cast their glare across the night. (*Exit page*) This moment let my vengeance be accomplished, that I may see him borne beyond my domain.   (*Exit* Rudzoloff) Away!

Music. Exit the Castellan, *followed by his principal officers.* Cassimir *is dragged out by the servants.*

Scene 5.   *Part of the gardens of the* Castellan.

Music. Enter Rudzoloff *and* Zemila, *meeting. Enter* Drolinsko, *running, and his clothes in great disorder.*

Zemila. Well, Drolinsko, what dismal fate has happened to you now?

Drolinsko. Dismal fate, indeed! The dismal fate has not happened to me, but it might have done; I am perpetually led into predicaments by my unquenchable courage.

Zemila. Or your unquenchable thirst? Which, Drolinsko?

Drolinsko. There, his lordship has ordered them to bring out the wild Tartar horse, and strap Cassimir to his back. Lord love you, there stood the poor wretches about him; not one of them had courage to approach him. But my eagerness for difficult adventures inspired me; I approached the infuriated monster and seized him by the mane, when he turned round and savagely tore——

Rudzoloff. Tore! My poor dear fellow, are you seriously hurt? What did he tear?

Drolinsko. Why, he tore what I won't venture to mention.
                    (*Turns round and discovers his small-clothes* [1] *torn*)

Music. Enter two Grooms, *who cross from* L *to* R. *One of them appears wounded.*

Rudzoloff. (*to the other*) Hasten to my lord; entreat him to forego his purpose, ere half his household is destroyed.   (*Exeunt* Grooms)

Drolinsko. Why, truly, it seems as if the wild horse would make the castle an hospital. His countryman, Mr Cassimir, began that game; but, thank heaven, we are likely to get rid of them both now. I've often said the best thing our Lord Castellan could do, would be to bind them back to back and send them off to their own country together. Egad! If we don't run we shall miss the sight, and the opportunity of wishing our Tartar friends goodbye for ever.
                        (*Music. Exeunt running*)

---

[1] *small-clothes* breeches

Scene 6. *The outer terrace of the castle, overlooking a tract of desolate country composed of precipitous mountain ridges abounding with cataracts. The rocky pathway crosses a stupendous waterfall by a slight rustic bridge, and is finally lost in a chain of lofty eminences stretching into the distance.*

Music. Enter the Castellan, Rudzoloff, Drolinsko, *and several of his suite, male and female.*

Castellan. Is my will obeyed, and the wild horse secured?
Rudzoloff. All is as my lord commanded.
Castellan. Bring forth the miscreant.

Music. Olinska *rushes in, followed by all the females of her household, and approaches the* Castellan. *At the same time* Cassimir *is dragged on by several of the household.*

Olinska. (*throwing herself at her father's feet*) Oh, my father! Pardon for him who saved your daughter's life!
Castellan. Unworthy girl! All power on earth were ineffectual to assuage my vengeance.

Music. Enter Count Premislas, *followed by his officers.* Olinska *and the females instantly surround him, kneeling at his feet as if entreating his interference.*

Premislas. (*approaching the* Castellan) Hold, my lord. From vengeance such as this, even my indignant bosom shrinks with horror.
Castellan. You plead in vain. Bring forth the untamed steed.

Music. The horse is brought forward by three or four grooms, who with difficulty restrain him. He is led to the centre. Cassimir *indignantly bursts from those who hold him, and, advancing to the front, surveys the horse. The spectators, in alarm, run to the corners, front.*

Now bind the traitor on his back. Let scorching suns and piercing blasts, devouring hunger and parching thirst, with frequent bruises and ceaseless motion, rend the vile Tartar piecemeal.

Music. Cassimir *is now bound to the horse's back.*

Olinska. Yet, dearest father, in mercy hear me!
Cassimir. (*on the horse*) Plead not for me, Olinska. Perish as I may, it is sufficient glory that I die for thee.
Castellan. Now launch the traitor forth, and let the story of his fate strike terror throughout Poland!

Music. The horse is released, and immediately rushes off with Cassimir. *He presently re-appears on the first range of hills from L to R, all the spectators rushing to the L, and as he crosses again from R to L, they take the opposite side. When he has reached the third range of hills, they commence pursuing him up the hills, and as he progresses, they follow. When he has disappeared in the extensive distance, the whole range of hills is covered by the servants, females, guards, and attendants, shouting, waving their arms and torches, forming an animated tableau.* Olinska, *who has fainted, is supported by* Agatha *and* Premislas *in the front, whilst the* Castellan *expresses exultation, completing the picture, lighted by the glare of torches and red beacon-flares, on which the drop falls.*

ACT II

Scene 1.   *Moving panorama of the course of the Dnieper River, running from L to R. On the flat is seen its bank, with a tract of wild country. A tremendous storm of thunder and lightning, hail and rain.*

Music. Mazeppa *discovered on the wild horse, stopping a few moments, apparently from exhaustion.*

Mazeppa. Exhausted nature for a moment stays his furious course. Eternal heaven, where will these horrors end? Oh, would I were released from suffering, if but in the endless calm of death. Ah! Again he urges on his wild career.

The wild horse gallops off with Mazeppa, *R. Music. The storm abates, the sun rises, and the panorama begins to move. The horse, still bearing* Mazeppa *fastened to his back, is seen wading up the stream from R to L.*

Ah, how refreshing is the cool stream to my racked, fevered limbs. Ah! Could my parched lips but catch its moisture, it would soothe the burning thirst that preys upon me. But here, like Tantalus, I feel the limpid luxury wash past my mouth, whilst my arid throat is denied the sweet relief. (*Music. A group of wolves is seen on the opposite bank, as if watching and pursuing the horse and* Mazeppa) Though nigh exhausted by the strong exertion, yon group of ravening wolves scare the affrighted beast from off the bank. Already have their gnashing teeth been buried in my flesh; and I could almost wish again to feel their horrid grip, if perchance it might free me from the cruel thongs that eat into my flesh and squeeze my swollen veins almost to bursting. Surely the power of the maddened brute must be well-nigh exhausted! Though my dim sight imperfectly distinguishes, it seems as if the current was so strong as to impede his course. These waters, then, shall be my welcome grave. And see! (*Music. An enormous vulture is seen hovering above him*) Yon horrid bird of prey, now hovering over its destined victim, forewarns me that my torments soon shall end. It brings me, too, the sacred consolation that I have reached my native Tartary, to which its form and plumage are peculiar, and so shall perish where I first drew breath. Welcome, eternal rest! Olinska, dear Olinska, be thy well-loved name the last that murmurs from my expiring lips, and may thy angel prayers waft my racked soul to regions of repose and peace.

(*Music. The wild horse bears off* Mazeppa, L)

Scene 2. *A rude Tartar landscape. A marshy thicket, interspersed with shepherds' huts.*

Enter Oneiza, *through the wood.*

Oneiza. What ho! Koscar! Koscar! The sun mounts high in the heavens and chides thy sluggishness.

Koscar. (*without*) Hilloa! Here.

Enter Koscar.

Koscar. Ah, my sweet sister, thou abroad so early?

Oneiza. Our gods preserve thee! Some hours since, I led my herd to a secluded track amidst the mountain heights that look towards Poland. (*Looking off*) But here comes Kadac.

Enter Kadac.

What has raised thee, friend, from thy couch so soon?

Kadac. Oh, I have been to pay my morning tribute to our prophet-king, to beg his paternal blessing, and ask the assistance of his potent prayers.

Koscar. Prophet-king! Well, it's a strange mixture of trades. Most kings, I reckon, find enough to do without wandering out at nights upon the mountain tops, counting the stars and seeking wondrous visions.

Oneiza. Fie, Koscar, fie! How can you suffer your rude tongue to speak thus irreverently of him whom all our tribes revere? Ever was Abder Khan a mild and gracious monarch; but since that fatal time when on the fields of Poland he lost his only son, his mind has taken a strange and solemn turn. He is inspired by the gods of Tartary; in wondrous visions its future destiny's unfolded to his view.

Koscar. Visions, say you? Oh, I too see visions, if it comes to that. This very morn I have beheld a warning vision—horrible, most horrible!

Oneiza. Heavens, what do you mean, Koscar?

Koscar. Why, if my two eyes have the slightest knowledge of the business attached to their situation in my head, I have this very morning seen the Volpas.

Oneiza. You terrify me out of my senses. Koscar, what can you mean?

Koscar. I saw him sitting—or rather lying—on a furious wild horse, that bore him with more than lightning speed from rock to rock, o'er precipice, through stream, and plunged with him into the deep and foaming torrent of the Dnieper.

Kadac. Let us hasten to the Khan and ask his counsel; for by our old traditions the appearance of the Volpas has ever been the harbinger of wretchedness to our Tartar tribes. *(Music)*

Oneiza. Hark, hark! What mean those sounds?

Kadac. It is the trampling of a furious steed.

Koscar. (*looking off*) Ay, with more than mortal vigour. It is himself—the Volpas, the awful, accursed Volpas, who this way wings his flight. Hence, sister, hence! The Volpas! The Volpas!

(Exeunt, in the utmost terror)

Music. Enter the wild horse at full gallop, with Mazeppa. *He rushes across, and exit. Enter* Thamar, *with Tartar chiefs and soldiers, meeting* Zemba.

Thamar. I came to seek our king. Knowest thou where I may find him, gallant Zemba?

Zemba. Our king? Our prophet, rather say, my chief.

Thamar. Ay. Doting driveller, when he must needs take up one character, 'twere well he had laid down the other. A warlike people are not to be ruled by a seer of visions.

Zemba. At least they get little by it. Ever since he lost his infant son, he dreads the very name of Poland.

Thamar. The hour is at hand when the Tartarian sceptre shall be snatched by an arm that's bold enough to seize, and strong enough to wield it. This very day I will, in the name of our assembled tribes, demand that he proclaim his successor. There is but one he dare to name, and once pronounced his heir he shall soon find I will not tardily await the enjoyment of the power already dropping from his doting hand.

Enter hastily Koscar *and* Kadac.

Koscar. Help—help! Save me—save me!

Zemba. How now? What ails the man?

Koscar. I've seen him! I've seen him, I am sure I have!

Zemba. Whom have you seen, idiot?

Koscar. Why, the Volpas, to be sure—the dreaded Volpas!

Zemba. Driveller, what mean you?

Koscar. I mean, my lord, that I believe the evidence of my own two eyes. I saw him on a horse about twice as big as an elephant, who leaped from one rock to another a league apart! The whirlwind of dust that he kicked up reached to the skies——

Thamar. Dolt, weary not thus my patience, but assemble your shepherd tribes here in the valley. Our aged Khan has a revelation to make of the utmost importance. Obey me quickly, and await your monarch's bidding.

Koscar. We shall do so, my lord.

Music. Exeunt Thamar, Zemba, *chiefs and soldiers* L; Koscar *and* Kadac R.

Scene 3. *The plains or steppes of Tartary, bounded by rocky eminences, the last of a chain that separates it from Poland. Rocky pathways, broken by cataracts over which are thrown rude Alpine bridges; and in the foreground are marshy plants, brushwood, and a few scattered trees.*

Music. Shepherds *discovered reposing, whilst their steeds are grazing.* Abder Khan *discovered on one of the mountain eminences, attended by three* Elders.

Khan. Hail, glorious orb of day, that slowly rising from wide ocean's bosom, sheddest thy bright beams over animated nature, awakening all its creatures into life and chasing night's dark shadows far away, spreading light and peace around!

Music. He descends to the front, attended by the Elders.

First Elder. How fares our honoured master? What anxious cares have occupied his thoughts through the past night, and from his tent led his adventurous steps?

Khan. Deep thoughts for my loved people's welfare; and oh! in those wild regions I have visited, such mighty revelations from the skies have on my wrapped soul descended——

First Elder. Yet be not cast down, for threatened evils often pass away; nor shed one drop of bitterness on our protected heads.

Khan. Not for myself I fear, but for my people; for hope and fear to me have been denied since my loved child was lost. For Tartary alone I live, and, would it win her happiness, for Tartary with eager joy I'd die.

Second Elder. You yet believe he lives?

Khan. I do, I do! In hallowed visions constantly I see him, my diadem encircling his brow. Like a celestial halo does that blessed thought shed a bright gleam of comfort o'er my soul. Mazeppa shall return, shall be the joy of his long-sorrowing sire and the glory of his rescued people. (*Rural music heard at a distance*)

First Elder. See, sire, where the shepherd tribes approach, to lay their morning homage at your honoured feet.

Khan. Be their humble repast prepared. Their simple wants, at least, their king can yet supply; and to avert each threatened danger, they shall not need his prayers.

Music. From a tent the Elders *set out bowls of milk. The rural music approaches. Enter* Koscar, Kadac, *and a body of shepherds and shepherdesses at the back, whilst* Thamar *and his warriors advance in the front.*

Thamar. Sovereign of Tartary, thy people, deeply sympathising with thy childless loneliness, have yet a care for their own future peace and happiness. They expect that thou wilt name one of thy chiefs, whom thou deemest worthy, to succeed thee on the throne.

Khan. Doubt not I shall do my people justice. A solemn warning from above was last night whispered to my soul. Yes, yes, I feel this very day the will of heaven shall be declared, the name of my successor be breathed even from the skies. Again I will entreat the gods in prayer, in yonder tent for a few moments beg again their blessing. Do thou and all my chiefs and people await me here; anon I will rejoin you and proclaim my will. Doubt not, good Thamar, the successor I shall proclaim will be one who will meet thine and all my people's approbation. *(Music. Retires among the rocks)*

Thamar. (aside) Ha! Then the glorious prize indeed is mine; he dares not name another. Now to assemble all the chiefs and forces who are favourable to my views; and, should the rabble dare to murmur aught of discontent, we may crush all idle opposition and awe them to obedience. *(Music. Exeunt* Thamar *and warriors)*

Kadac. Well, as I have heard that music after meals is good for digestion, suppose old Zelos here gives us the song of the Volpas, whilst you, Koscar, accompany him on your pipe.

Koscar. What, that song of the Wild Genius of the Desert? The very thought of it gives me an indigestion.

Kadac. Psha, children's tales! You can't believe what they say of the Volpas! I thought you had more sense.

Koscar. Believe? I don't believe, but I know it. It never appears but at the forewarning of wonderful events. The very mention of the terrible Volpas turns all the milk I have been drinking into vinegar. The ravager! The destroyer!

Kadac. Come, come, no more talk, but the song of the Volpas.

Music. The pastoral groups form. Koscar *mounts a hillock and plays upon his pandean pipes. Three shepherds sing the song, with chorus, during which all the men and women figure a heavy dance, almost without stirring from their places, with extravagant movements of their heads and arms, terminating every time in grotesque and varied groups.*

Tartar Song

Shepherds. Across the wilds of Tartary there whirls a demon form,
His voice is not of this world, and mingles with the storm;
Through blasts of forked lightning his snorting courser dashes,

And death and terror, as his guides, smile grimly with the flashes.

Chorus. Let the lovely shepherd maid,
Most of all, his side evade.
Haste, haste! To your tents hasten back!
A pursuer is in your track.
Fly! Fly!
'Tis the Volpas that's coming; the Volpas is nigh.

Shepherds. His black and fiery courser's mane stands bristled by the blast,
And from his feet the dust in air is up in whirlwinds cast;
His wide and smoking nostrils dart before him fires of wrath,
And nothing that's of mortal born can live upon his path.

Chorus. Let the lovely shepherd maid, &c.

Shepherds. Oh, when that horse and rider come, the astonish'd earth and ocean
Shake and shrink with terror at the martial commotion;
Nature, as if she writh'd her last, heaves with the horrid pang,
And trumpets shriek in the troubled air their war-denouncing clang.

Chorus. Let the lovely shepherd maid, &c.

At the conclusion of the song, a storm comes on with immense fury. Lights down. Music. An universal scream of horror runs through the assembled multitude. Re-enter Abder Khan.

Khan. What means this wild alarm, my children, these screams of abject terror?

Shepherdess. Ah, sire, save us—save us! An awful visitation! The Volpas, the Volpas is at hand!

Khan. Dismiss this idle fear, and dread no fiend but that which vice has planted in the human heart. (*Music. Thunder*) The voice of heaven now surely speaks in the thunder of the elements. Its awful secrets shall this day be known; its pleasure and your future fate by my voice be declared. Chiefs and elders, attend me to assist me in my prayers. Do you, my children, secure your steeds from the fury of the elements; sound now your shells, and call them around you. Let the seats of our armed tribes be spread beneath the palm-grove, where I, with our chosen priests and elders, may consult the messenger of heaven. (*Aside*) But, oh, the peace I'd fain inspire in them is stranger to my soul. (*Music. Exit, with the* Elders)

Kadac. Koscar, call up the steeds affrighted and dispersed by the storm. Your sounding shells, pealing along the echoes, will bring them quickly around us. My friends, ascend to the mountain pastures and draw our flocks homewards to the valleys, for see! the storm increases.

Music. Thunder, lightning, rain. The shepherds sound their horns; their horses rush on from the adjacent pastures; they mount them and proceed in various directions. A large body of them on foot ascend the mountain eminence; as they ascend the rock, the storm redoubles. When they reach the summit, the heavens pour forth a continuous stream of fire. The shepherds, with a shriek of alarm, exclaim 'The Volpas! The Volpas!' *and rush forward and throw themselves on their faces. The wild horse, with* Mazeppa, *is seen furiously pursuing his course among the mountains, crossing first from* L *to* R, *backwards and forwards over the range of hills, till he reaches the front, and as he is crossing from* R *to* L, *a thunderbolt falls and strikes a fir tree* L, *which falls amongst the brushwood and hides him from view. The shepherds all rise up and rush off in horror.*

Mazeppa. (heard feebly exclaiming) Help, help! For heaven's sake, release me!

Music. Enter Oneiza, *rushing forward in dreadful alarm.*

Oneiza. Ha, what a dreadful conflict in the elements! Whither shall I seek for shelter? Ah, in this thicket I may find, perhaps, a momentary refuge from the storm. (*Music. She turns aside some of the brushwood and the branches of the fallen tree, which presents to view* Mazeppa, *extended motionless and apparently lifeless, upon the body of the exhausted horse*) What do I behold? A human being, apparently lifeless, yet bleeding, and bound by cruel thongs upon the body of a steed, exhausted, dead or dying! (*Leaning over* Mazeppa) He moves! He breathes! Oh, may I, under heaven, be the happy means of affording him relief! (*Loosening the cords which bind him*) I will unbind these blood-soaked cords, and plants of soothing virtues shall allay the anguish of their wounds. (*Rises and gathers leaves*) From this flask the cool refreshing stream shall shoot new vigour through his wearied frame.
  (*Giving him drink from her water-bottle, and binding his wounds with leaves*)
Mazeppa. (rising up a little) Ah, have the cords that bound my aching limbs at length bursted? Save—save me, or I die!
(*He sinks back, from exhaustion*)
Oneiza. Ah, he is not one of our tribes. Let me hasten to our Prophet-Khan, whose mild benignant spirit will lavish more effectual succour than my weak aid can offer. (*Music. Exit hastily*)

Re-enter Koscar, Kadac, *and some of the shepherds, cautiously.*

Kadac. What meant that strange and fearful vision which, amidst the flashes of the storm, gleamed on our affrighted view?
Koscar. Why, what should it be but the Volpas, as I told you. Ah!

What do I behold? There lies the wild horse sunk in death, and on his back a form that seems like mortal.

Kadac. Perhaps it is a fellow creature.

Koscar. It must be the Volpas. He's only taking a nap, and will wake up more savage than ever. I'll take care how I go nigh him. Back, the Khan approaches.

Music. Enter Abder Khan *attended by* Oneiza, *and followed by* Thamar *and suite.*

Khan. Where is the wounded and exhausted stranger? Why stand ye idle and indifferent when, perhaps, your cares might succour human woe?

Koscar. Human woe? Oh no, please your highness, it's no human woe, but that horrid, inhuman beast, the Volpas.

Khan. Assist me, friends, to raise the object of our pity and convey him to a timely shelter. (*Music. The shepherds remove the tree; the* Khan *advances and bends over the body of* Mazeppa. *He points to the name* 'Mazeppa' *engraved in Arabic letters on his right arm* [1]) Ah! What signs and characters now meet my sight? Like the bright lightning's blaze, it flashes on my soul. (*Rising and advancing to* Thamar) Thamar, my friend, behold and join with me in gratitude to heaven. A miracle has been wrought! Read, read, brave chief, those words of gladdening power. Mazeppa! Yes, mark thou that honoured word. It is my son —my son—my long-lost child! (*Music. Kneeling*) Eternal heaven, receive an old man's thanks, nor suffer the full tide of joy to over-whelm my soul.

Thamar. (*approaching* Mazeppa) I mark the characters, my liege. May they not be the work of an impostor?

Khan. (*approaching* Mazeppa) Saidst thou an impostor? This is the triumphant answer. Behold this jewelled star, the badge and emblem of our noble tribe! Myself affixed it there; and, glittering now upon his bosom, it flashes sweet conviction on my soul. It is indeed my child. See—he revives, he moves!

Mazeppa. Loose those dreadful cords, I say. See, see the gushing stream that mingles with the flood is draining from my heart! Why do those gnarling wolves howl on so hideously? They are upon us! Their ravening tusks tear off my flesh! Ha! That precipice! That must be swift destruction. We reach its brink—Lost! Lost for ever?

(*He again sinks back in exhaustion*)

Thamar. Methinks this wild delirium speaks ill for his recovery.

Khan. Peace, thou malignant fiend, whose withering breath would blast my new-born hopes! See, the pallid hue of death now brightens

---

[1] *He points . . . arm* not in Milner's text, but supplied from Cuvelier and Chandezon's *Mazeppa* (Paris, 1825).

into health. Raise him with care, and be he to yon foremost tent conveyed, henceforth the seat of royalty.

Music. Four shepherds enter with bier and cloth. Mazeppa *is placed upon it.*

Thamar. (*aside, whilst the assistants are raising* Mazeppa *on a litter*) Make not too sure of that. Delusion—miracle—imposture? What it will, my hopes and high ambition are not to be o'erthrown thus by a single blow.   (*Music.* Mazeppa *is raised on a bier*)

Khan. (*pointing to the wild horse, which still lies extended on the earth*) That noble steed claims our assistance, too. Of mortal mould it cannot be, but the choice instrument of heaven to restore to Tartary a sovereign, to a doting sire a long-lost son. (*Music. The shepherds raise the horse*) Ye priests and people, raise aloud your voices! Implore of heaven it will not leave its glorious work unaccomplished, but that, restored to vigour, my son may bless alike his father and his people.

The priests and people join in the chorus. The Khan, *with a mixture of anxiety, tenderness, and exultation, watches his son, while* Thamar *with his associates, aside, evince their rage and disappointment.*

Chorus.   Powers benignant, now look down,
                 A father's hopes with mercy crown!
                 Listen to a people's prayer,
                 Bless, oh bless, our tender care!

                 Gracious powers, whom we adore,
                 Our future monarch now restore;
                 That our triumphant shouts may raise
                 In songs of gratitude and praise.   (*The scene closes*)

Scene 4.   *A Tartarian landscape, adjacent to the great encampment, which is seen in the distance.*

Music. Enter Thamar, Zemba, *and warriors.*

Thamar. In vain does yonder hoary dotard dream his new-found fondling shall defeat my purpose and enjoy the throne. Too long have we been slaves—the grovelling slaves of superstition. You all have sworn to see your leader on the throne; nor can I fear the firm determination of such gallant warriors can be diverted by so poor an artifice. Will you uphold me still?

All. We will! We will!

Thamar. Then am I still the sovereign of Tartary. For this poor impostor—my dagger shall quickly remove that trivial obstacle. To me the guard of the royal tent has been confided. Soon will I teach the Prophet-Khan to know that his weak delusions can never turn from his affirmed resolve the unshrinking soul of Thamar. On to our purpose, warriors!   (*Exeunt. Music*)

Scene 5.   *The interior of a rude Tartar tent, hung with characteristic arms and armour; on the flat hangs a large metal shield, used to strike signals on.*

Music. Mazeppa *discovered sleeping on a low pallet, the* Khan *watching over him with intense anxiety. An* Elder *in attendance.*

Khan. Let all our armed tribes at earliest dawn be assembled around my tent, that of the prince's first returning sense I may apprise them, and proclaim him to my people. (*Exit* Elder *through the tent*) Sleep on, my boy. The camp is silence all, save where the trusty sentinel paces his little round. The tent is guarded by my choicest warriors, but here thy father shall maintain his post; and, till thy slumber breaks, thy foremost safeguard be thy father's heart.

Music. He lies down at the foot of the couch near Mazeppa, *and shortly falls asleep. Enter* Thamar *and* Zemba, *cautiously.*

Thamar. Thanks to the guard I chose for their protection, our entrance hither has been easy and noiseless. Fate favours our design. They sleep. Myself will strike the blow; my dagger's thirsty for the stripling's blood.   (*Music. He approaches the couch of* Mazeppa)
Mazeppa. (*in his sleep*) Off, tyrant, off! Thy bonds shall not withhold me. The energies of such a soul as mine shall burst thy puny cords, and in the power of vengeance I shall stand terribly before thee.
Thamar. He raves; he wakes. Back, back. Delay our purpose, till returning slumber render it secure from all alarm.
                                        (*Music.* Thamar *and* Zemba *retire*)
Mazeppa. (*awaking*) Still do those cruel lashings press upon my flesh, and eat into my bone. Ah, this limb is free; so are all. (*Music. He rises and advances to the front*) Again I stand erect, again assume the god-like attitude of freedom and of man. Though weak and tottering, still these limbs are freed from galling bonds and own no tyrant's chain. Where can I be? My confused ideas and broken memory serve not to recall the incidents of the past hour. Something I do remember of a venerable form, that hung in pity o'er my prostrate wretchedness and with compassion's tears did wash my wounds. (*Music. He traverses the tent and looks out at the opening*) The canopy of heaven, studded with glittering fires, spreads its broad expanse around; and, by their light, long avenues of tented habitations show that I am treading on the field of war. Ah, at that bless'd idea my soul swells high, my energies are strung with new-recovered vigour, and I feel sufficient yet to conquer my own glory. Let me

observe; and lest around this friendly shelter malice should lurk, or any hostile arm (*Seeing a shield and sword hanging up*), thou friendly steel, I'll borrow thy assistance.

Music. He takes down a sword and shield, and goes out at the back of the tent. Thamar *and* Zemba *advance.*

Thamar. Another and a surer plan has glanced across my mind. The Khan himself shall perish. The crime, charged on this new-found stranger, hurls him at once to irretrievable ruin; and who can then dispute the throne with Thamar?

Khan. (*awaking*) My boy—my child—where art thou? Misery and despair! Sure, treason is abroad. (*Music. Rises and comes forward*) Thou here, Thamar, at this unwonted hour? The truth at once flashes upon my horror-stricken soul. Pernicious miscreant! Thou hast destroyed my child!

Thamar. Thy child, fond dotard? The easy dupe thou art to yonder rash impostor proves thee unfit to reign. Think not the destiny of Tartary is thus to be surrendered to thy childishness, or yon adventurer's audacity. The chiefs of Tartary would have a warrior king! 'Tis me they have selected. And, ere I snatch—somewhat too rudely, perhaps—the tottering crown that trembles on thy aged brow, wisely surrender it.

Khan. To thee, insidious monster? Never! I have now an heir to prop the drooping glories of my house, and ere I would surrender one tittle of his just rights, traitor, thou shouldst hew me piecemeal! Least of all would I abandon my beloved people to the ambitious fury of such a wretch as thou art!

Thamar. Yet, ere our daggers drain thy aged veins of all their poor remains of life, be wise and yield. Affix thy seal to this parchment, renouncing all title to the throne and stamping him thou callest thy son a foul impostor—do this, and live. And oh, be sure thy death is but the prelude to that foundling boy's, who never shall dispute with me the crown.

Khan. Your threats I scorn. The spirit that has often led me on to victory shall nerve me still; nor do I dread to meet a host of coward traitors such as Thamar.

(*Music. Snatches up a sword, and places himself in an attitude of defence*)

Thamar. Thou hast pronounced thy doom.

Music. The Khan *rushes towards the entrance of the tent as if to strike the shield. As he does so, on a signal from* Thamar, *two other conspirators rush forward, meet him, and drive him back.*

Each sword that gleams around is sworn to do my bidding.

Khan. Thy king defies thee still. I strike for my own right and for my boy's, and heaven will assist my arm.

Music. Combat of three. Thamar *and* Zemba *rush on him, the other two conspirators guarding the entrance to the tent and keeping the curtain down. After a short contest, the* Khan *is overpowered, and falls.* Thamar *and* Zemba *stand over him with uplifted weapons. Picture.*

Thamar. Yet ere our weapons drink thy blood, sign this and save thyself.

Khan. I never will!

Thamar. I'll hear no more. Comrade, let both our points strike deep into one wound, and end the dotard's clamour for ever!

During this, a sort of struggle has been perceived at the entrance of the tent, as of someone endeavouring to force his way in, which is successfully resisted by the two Tartars placed there. At the moment when Thamar *and* Zemba *are on the point of striking their weapons to the heart of the* Khan, *the tent is slit up in another place by a sword, and* Mazeppa *darts through the opening with his sword and shield, catches the blow on his shield, and stands in a protecting attitude over the prostrate* Khan. *Picture.*

Mazeppa. Cowards and villains! And in the garb of Tartar warriors —and two of you against an aged, feeble man! He, too, whose kindness rescued me from death, and soothed my sufferings! In such a cause, I'd brave a world in arms.

Music. The four conspirators now furiously attack the Khan *and* Mazeppa. *In the course of the conflict several interesting pictures are formed by the mutual efforts of father and son to save each other. They overpower the conspirators.* Elders *rush on.*

Thamar. Yet do I laugh thy power to scorn, for hundreds now without await but my nod to shed their life-blood in my cause.

Khan. Millions will strike in mine!

Strikes the shield with his sword. The curtains of the tent are drawn up, and the whole Tartar army is discovered in battle array.

Tartars, behold the traitor who has sought your sovereign's life! (*A party of guards seize* Thamar *and his confederates*) Away with them to punishment!

Music. They are taken back. Thamar *breaks away, and is rushing on* Mazeppa *with dagger. 'Tis struck from his hand by one of the* Elders. *He is seized, and exit.*

And now, young hero, in the aged man you have preserved, embrace and own a fond, a doting father.

Mazeppa. A father! How does that sacred sound, like heaven-descended dews, speak comfort to my heart! (*Embraces the* Khan)

Khan. No longer must the glad, the important, task be now delayed. Assembled Tartars, priests, warriors, people—behold and mark me:

in this brave youth, who has even now saved your sovereign's life, know and revere Mazeppa, my long-lost, only son, your sovereign prince! Hail my boy, Mazeppa, King of Tartary!

All kneel before Mazeppa. General shout. Music. Mazeppa is conducted off. The curtains of the tent fall. The Khan motions his officers to assemble the people; they go out in various directions. The Elders bring him his shield and staff of office. Exeunt Abder Khan and attendants, exultingly.

Scene 6. *Extensive Tartar encampment.*

Music. The whole Tartar army with their chiefs assembled. Enter the Khan leading on Mazeppa. The people kneel and receive him with acclamations.

Mazeppa. (*whose surprise has been momentarily increasing*) I, King of Tartary! Where am I? What has happened? After a doom beyond expression awful—bound to a wild horse, whirled o'er torrents, deserts, precipices, on all sides danger and destruction—I ceased to feel. Have I then passed the realm of death? And do I wake to new life and other being? I find myself free, beneath a strange sky, a prostrate people hailing me their king! Say, say, do I dream? Do I still exist?

Khan. Heaven has restored thee to thy native land, and to the throne which thou wast born to fill. Reign o'er thy land, which welcomes thee, Mazeppa. Be powerful, and be happy!

Mazeppa. Happy! I, happy without my loved Olinska? Never—ah, never! I renounce glory Olinska shares not. I but accept the sovereign sway to right my people's wrongs and to revenge my own; to retrieve the honour of the nation, wrecked on the fields of Poland; to hurl swift vengeance on our foes, and rescue my dear Olinska.

Khan. If thy love be worthy of your love, then head our tribes and tear her from thy rival.

Mazeppa. Thou shalt behold and share my joyous triumph. I fight for my Olinska and my love.

Khan. I, for my much-loved child and my revenge. (*Music. The horse is brought on*) Behold the steed, fated by heaven to bring you to your native land and throne, again awaits you. He bore you to my arms; let him now bear you to your triumph.

Mazeppa. He was the instrument of torture; let him now be the messenger of vengeance. (*Music*) On to the Polish frontier! I cannot know repose whilst my Olinska's fate's uncertain. I can feel no glory till from a rival's power I've conquered her.

Khan. Then with tomorrow's dawn the march begins. Drive all our cattle within the lines. Be every soldier ready at his post; for ere two suns have set behind those Polish mountains, our force shall beneath

the tyrant's wall make him to tremble in his stronghold of power,
and rue the day he injured child of mine.

Away, Away!

Eager we seek the foe at dawn of day.

Music. A superbly caparisoned steed has been led on for the Khan. *They mount. A general parade and movement of the army takes place, on which the drop falls.*

ACT III

Scene 1. *A gothic chamber in the castle of the* Castellan, *in Poland.*

Music. Olinska *discovered, pale and dejected, seated at a rich toilet, attended by a female.*

Olinska. Bid my nurse come to me. (*Exit attendant*) The victim's adorned not for the altar but the tomb. (*Rises and advances*) This day is the last whose light will shine on the poor Olinska. (*She approaches the toilet and moves a little casket concealed beneath the drapery, opens it, and takes out a portrait on which she gazes with the liveliest emotion*) Cassimir, my beloved—murdered—mangled! Can I, ought I, to survive thy horrid death? (*Takes from the casket a dagger, which she pushes from her with a shudder*) Father, I have given you my oath to be the bride of Premislas. My oath shall not be broken; the honour of our house exacts the sacrifice. (*Takes the dagger and hides it in her dress*) One awful means is left of obedience and fidelity. Yes, this night, this very night, restores me to my lover, in the tomb. (*Placing her hand upon the dagger*)

Enter Agatha.

Agatha. See, lady, where your father comes.
Olinska. Quickly, conceal that packet.

Music. Enter the Castellan. Agatha *conceals the casket.*

Castellan. Olinska, your imprudence might have caused the ruin of your father; but Count Premislas, restored to life, has deemed the act of Cassimir merely a presumptuous vassal's crime, without your sanction. But the pretender has been punished. And now, Olinska, I trust I may confide in your entire submission?
Olinska. Implicitly.
Castellan. That pledge disarms my wrath. My child, the past is all forgiven, forgotten. Come to thy father's arms, who now can call thee once again his daughter.

As she is dropping on her knees, he catches her to his bosom.

Olinska. Father!

Castellan. My child, my dearest child. May heaven's peace attend thee!

Olinska. May thy prayer be heard, my father. Ere long, thy child will
cease to suffer.   *(Trumpets heard without)*

Castellan. Hark thee, my child! Yon trumpets speak the bridegroom
ready, the cortège prepared. Throughout my castle's precincts, this
day all wears one universal face of joy.

Olinska. All except one. Oh, in the journey I'm about to undertake—
gloomy and dark it may be—let me receive the sacred consolation
that a father's blessing shall attend his child!

Castellan. Heaven for ever bless thee, sweet Olinska! Come, come my
child; away with thoughts of gloom! Share thou the triumph which
on every side courts thy acceptance.

Olinska. Father, again thou'st blessed me. I can bear it all.

Music. They embrace and exeunt, Olinska R, Castellan L.

Scene 2.   *A hall of the castle of Laurinski.*

Music. Enter Drolinsko.

Drolinsko. I am clean an altered man. I feel myself already puffed up
and swelling with my new dignity, even as I hope ere long my body
shall be stuffed and swelled with the perquisites of office. I was a
huntsman; I am a cook. I'll never look another live head of game in
the face again. I'll commit no murder on hares, pheasants, bears,
stags and partridges more. No; I'll leave off executioner and be a
kind of undertaker—that is, I'll dress them up in a proper manner to
be sent to their graves, the throats of gormandizers.

Enter Zemila.

Zemila. Ah, Mr Drolinsko! You look quite a different person from
what you used to be.

Drolinsko. And I am a different person too, Mistress Zemila. Know
that I am placed at the head of the victualling department, that I am
chief officer of the mouth and general purveyor for the belly. I've got
you all under my thumb now. Only look as I would not have you,
and I clap you all on short allowance; offend me, and the soup's all
turned over; insult my dignity, and all the fat's in the fire. I shall
astonish you all.

Zemila. No absurdity that you can commit can possibly astonish me.

Drolinsko. Oh, I'm a clever fellow at nosing out a good thing. There was
I, early this morning, wandering out into the wood beyond the castle,
my teeming brain on fire with the grand devices which this day shall
produce—what should I meet with, but a group of wandering

Tartars! I've engaged them to come to the festival. What do you think of that, now?

Zemila. Why, that my lord will break your head and have you kicked out of the place. You know he hates the very name of Tartar.

Drolinsko. These are jovial fellows, innocent as lambs. For a mouthful of broken victuals they'll dance such dances, and show us such singular manœuvres and evolutions—I mean it to be the principal feature of the whole festival. (*Music*) Here they come.

Zemila. Then here I go. (*Exit*)

Music. Enter Abder Khan, Mazeppa, *and a* Tartar Chief, *in close disguise as Tartar peasants.*

Drolinsko. Well, now you've filled your bellies, I hope it has relieved your imaginations.

Mazeppa. Trust us, sir; we do not need excitement.

Drolinsko. Well now, I suppose you've made up your minds to do something a little out of the way on this occasion?

Khan. Be sure we shall astonish you.

Drolinsko. Well, do so. I like to be astonished, and on this occasion I wish everything to be new and uncommon. I should like the very walls to caper.

Chief. Caper? They shall fly!

Drolinsko. Come, come, none of your nonsense now; you are going too far! I'm not so soft as all that comes to.

Khan. 'Tis necessary you should furnish me with the key of the great gates. My two comrades here I leave with you; I will hasten to rejoin the rest, hold ourselves in readiness adjacent to the castle, and on your signal rush forward to effect the grand tableau.

Drolinsko. I'll go and fetch you the key. You're a jolly old blade you are, too—no chicken—but there seems stuff in you yet. I'll be with you again in the spitting of a partridge. (*Exit*)

Mazeppa. Haste thou to our bands, good father. Marshal them in yonder forest, and when I give the signal let them, like a mountain torrent, rush—o'erwhelming all resistance—to the aid of those that are within. I will be on the spot, and at the moment when the perjured fair would offer her unhallowed vows upon the sacred altar, my steel shall drink the life-blood of them both and their mingled gore proclaim the vengeance of my outraged love. (*Music heard without*) See, see, where the traitress comes! Down, down, struggling spirit! The moment of thy triumph is not yet arrived.

Enter Drolinsko, *with a key.*

Drolinsko. Back, fellows, back. See where the bride approaches.

Music. Enter Olinska *attended by* Agatha, *preceded by* Rudzoloff *and followed by attendants.*

34

Agatha. Cheerly, cheerly, lady; this is not the countenance you should exhibit on your bridal morn.

Olinska. It well befits a bridal such as mine. My hopes are buried in another's tomb; soon, soon, may I go seek him there!

Agatha. But this dejection scarce fulfils your promise to your father. All was to be submission.

Olinska. It is submission, nurse—submission I have learned by trampling on every feeling of my heart. I shall obey my father; let him not require more than I can perform.

Drolinsko. (*approaching* Olinska) Lord love your beautiful ladyship, you'll be delighted when you see the preparations for the fête, solely contrived by me, Drolinsko. Why, it's worth while being married if only to see such a tasty set-out! You'll be half inclined to love me for the cultivated fancy I have displayed.

Rudzoloff. Who are those strangers?

Drolinsko. Ah, that's another of my contrivances that you'd never suspect, godfather. Those? Why, those, bless you, are wandering Tartars introduced by me.

Rudzoloff. Tartars! Introduce Tartars here! Why, it's more than your head's worth—let but the Castellan know it.

Drolinsko. Ay, it's plain to see you're a fellow of no pith and enterprise. He may think what he likes about Tartars, but if these fellows don't caper him into good humour, he's a sulkier dog than I take him for.

Khan. Doubt not that we will overcome all his displeasure.

Mazeppa. (*approaching* Olinska) Deign you, fair lady, to cast an eye of approbation and encouragement.

Music. He is close to her. She turns to look at him. He throws aside part of his disguise, so that she recognizes him.

Olinska. (*with a scream of astonishment*) Cassimir! (*All start, surprised. He hastily resumes his disguise, and* Olinska, *by a great effort, assumes an appearance of composure*) Cassimir, some time a page of this household, was a countryman of yours, I believe?

Mazeppa. Belike, fair lady. I do bethink me of a tale of a poor Tartar lad, bred up in Polish climes, who rashly loved a noble lady. 'Twas a fault in him. But oh, whoever looked upon that fair one's beauty and her worth must have forgiven him, knowing that to see and not to love was scarcely possible. Her father found it in him a crime not to be pardoned, and sentenced him to a most cruel death.

Olinska. (*muttering*) It was, indeed, most horrible.

Mazeppa. By miracle he was saved and, like the polar needle, true to his first affection, back he rushed, impatient still to lay his homage at the adored one's feet. But oh, death-blow to his hopes! Torture more cruel than all before he'd suffered! He found her perjured, faithless, voluntarily about to give her hand unto another.

Olinska. Ah, had he known her tears, her anguish, the silent calm despair with which—unable to resist—she yielded to her parent's harsh commands, enforced under the penalty of his awful curse, how like a victim to the sacrifice she did approach the altar—he would not, could not, dare not, to condemn her!

Mazeppa. Had she then no remedy to save herself from such accursed pollution?

Olinska. Yes, and a noble one; which, rather than betray her first fond vows, she's resolute to clutch at——

(*Draws a dagger from her bosom and shows it to* Mazeppa)

Mazeppa. (*with a burst of triumph*) Ha! She was a heroine worthy a sovereign's love!

The attention of the bystanders is excited. Mazeppa *and* Olinska *are compelled to control their feelings.*

Drolinsko. Zounds! This Tartar gipsy has contrived to astonish my lady already.

Khan. The tales of our country have a wild and wondrous force, well calculated to awake the feelings thus.

Rudzoloff. Your pardon, lady. Had we not better on?

Olinska. I attend you, Rudzoloff.

Mazeppa. (*to* Olinska) Doubt not, fair lady, all shall be accomplished; your smallest wish most scrupulously obeyed.

Music. Exit Olinska, *preceded by* Rudzoloff *and supported by* Agatha, *exchanging significant glances with* Mazeppa.

Drolinsko. (*giving the key*) Now mind, you fellows; be at your posts.

Mazeppa. The dearest feelings of our hearts are pledged to be so. (*Exit* Drolinsko) Ah, father, what a weight's removed from off my heart! Olinska yet is mine! Your son shall yet be happy.

Khan. He shall—he shall! Oh, to attain that end, how joyfully thy father would shed his latest crimson drop!

They embrace and exeunt, Abder Khan R, Mazeppa L.

Scene 3. *The Gardens of Laurinski, closed in at the back by terraces, the last of which is entered through a spacious gate of golden bars; its other end communicates with a wood. The whole extent is bounded on the L by the buildings of the castle. From the topmost terrace, near the great gate, a spacious flight of steps which leads down to the stage.*

Music. Enter Mazeppa. *He advances cautiously, ascends the steps, and beckons on* Abder Khan, *who advances from the building.*

Mazeppa. Now, honoured father, how speeds the glorious work?

Khan. Even as should the deed on which depends thy happiness. Our troops are all at hand and eager for the attack. Yes, my son, thy triumph is assured. Here, on the haughty despot's battlements, he shall surrender thee thy love, or thou shalt tear her from his arms amidst their blackened ruins.

Mazeppa. All is prepared for the ceremony. I will be on the spot. When I give the signal, let them sweep all opposition into dust. (*The music of the procession is heard*) They come, they come!

Music. Abder Khan retires up the steps and along the terrace. The nuptial procession advances from the building L, through the great gate and down the steps. It is composed of the entire household of the Castellan, headed by Drolinsko. Rudzoloff immediately precedes Olinska, who is led by the Castellan and Premislas and followed by Agatha. They come down. The guards, banners, &c. countermarch and form on the R side and on the terraces. The nuptial party sit on a throne L, surrounded by their attendants. On a signal from Drolinsko, a tribe of Tartar youths and maidens appear on the upper terrace and descend the staircase.

MILITARY CHARACTERISTIC BALLET

At the conclusion of the ballet, a small altar is placed on the lower terrace. The priest advances. Olinska, led by Premislas and the Castellan, approaches the altar. The priest commences the ceremony, when Mazeppa, still disguised, appears suddenly on the terrace and thrusts the priest aside.

Mazeppa. Hold! I forbid such sacrilegious vows! They are offensive in the sight of heaven. This maid, in heart and spirit, and by long previous vows breathed from the very bottom of her soul, is mine; and any other union, by tyranny accomplished, is perjury—pollution!

Castellan. What insolent intruder dares thus to break, with barbarous scoffings, on our solemnity?

Mazeppa. One whom thou shouldst remember. Tyrant, behold thy victim!   (*Throws off his disguise. Music*)

All. Cassimir!

Mazeppa. Cassimir—Mazeppa—one. Thy vengeful tyranny but doomed me to my glory. The wild horse bore me to the throne of Tartary; and now Mazeppa, King of Tartary, proudly returns to claim his early love.

Castellan. Impostor! Barbarian! Traitor! Wert thou the king of half the eastern world, the scorn in which I hold thee were not lessened. Bear him away! A death more certain this time punishes his presumption.

Music. Some of the household advance to seize Mazeppa. The Tartar youths and maidens form a rampart in front of him, and the Khan, followed by Tartar soldiery who occupy the upper terrace, appears at the head of the staircase.

Khan. Stay, monsters! Stay your uplifted hands! Let but one hair of his head be injured, and your castle quickly is a heap of ruins soaked in your blood—for every soul shall perish. Your castle is invested.[1] On every tower, buttress and pinnacle clings a Tartar, awaiting but my word, when havoc is let loose and fierce destruction ravages half Poland. Speak but one word, and let Olinska be the pledge of peace.

Premislas. (advancing) I will not wait to hear the Castellan's answer. Olinska is my bride in sight of heaven, my wife. My troops now man these walls, and to my last red drop I will defend her.

Mazeppa. Then let revenge and slaughter be our word of battle! And let ruined Poland speak Mazeppa mounted to the throne of Tartary!

The Polish troops in the garden fire at the Tartars on the terraces. The latter charge down the steps. A general conflict ensues. A charge of Tartar cavalry is made along the upper terrace; they are met by the Poles, issuing from the principal portal. The attendants endeavour to force Olinska *through the tumult into the castle. The cavalry appear in front, and after skirmishing off on both sides, a charge in line from* L *to* R *is executed by the Tartars. The front then becomes occupied by pairs of combatants.* Abder Khan *is on the point of cutting down the* Castellan, *when* Olinska *rushes in and interposes. She is followed by* Mazeppa, *to whom the* Castellan *resigns her, which is the pledge of peace.* Premislas *has been meantime overcome by a Tartar warrior, and the Poles altogether vanquished.* Abder Khan, Mazeppa, *the* Castellan, *and* Olinska *hasten to mount the steps to stop the slaughter, and on the top form a group. The females line the terraces. Subdued Poles and triumphant Tartars fill the scene, which is lighted by the conflagration of the forest; and on the general picture the curtain falls.*

[1] *invested* besieged

The Factory Lad

A DOMESTIC DRAMA IN TWO ACTS BY JOHN WALKER

First performed at the Surrey Theatre, London, 15 October 1832

CAST

GEORGE ALLEN		Mr Waldron
FRANK WILSON		Mr Lee
WALTER SIMS	lately discharged from the factory of * * * * *	Mr Brunton
JOE SMITH		Mr Gardner
JACK HATFIELD		Mr C. Hill
WILL RUSHTON, an outcast		Mr Stuart
SQUIRE WESTWOOD, master of the factory		Mr Dibdin Pitt
TAPWELL, landlord of 'The Harriers'		Mr Young
JUSTICE BIAS		Mr Clarkson
CRINGE, his clerk		Mr Smith
JANE ALLEN, wife to George		Mrs W. West
MARY, her eldest child, about eleven		Miss H. Pitt
MILLY, her second, about six		Miss Clarke
A CHILD IN CRADLE		

Officer, servant to Westwood, constables, soldiers

The Surrey playbill also includes

CAPTAIN FENTON	Mr Maitland
GRIMLEY	Mr Banister

and Duncombe's cast list adds

CRIER	Mr C. Pitt

Fenton and the Crier are not mentioned in any text; Grimley appears with Westwood to arrest George Allen in II. ii.

The action takes place in the neighbourhood of Bury, near Manchester.
Period: 1832

JOHN WALKER

Life unknown. Active melodramatist at the minor theatres between 1825 and 1834. Cashed in on the craze for European Gothic with *The Wild Boy of Bohemia* (1827), with Countess Czartoryski, Baron Leitzimer, and a castle overlooking the mountains of Carpathia. Then came *Louis Chaumont* (1828), *The Outlaw's Oath* (1828), and *The Wizard Priest* (1833). Attempted costume comedy in *Napoleon* (1828) and *Nell Gwynne* (1833). None of the published plays suggests the author of *The Factory Lad* (1832); closest in tone is *Ellen Wareham* (1834), a domestic drama sometimes attributed to William Evans Burton.

THE FACTORY LAD

This Evening, Monday, October 15, 1832, will be produced an entirely new and original Domestic Drama, of deep interest, and founded on Passing Events, called *The Factory Lad: or, Saturday Night* . . . EXTERIOR OF LARGE FACTORY . . . The interior lighted with gas. Determination of the men to resist the introduction of Steam and Manufactory by Power Looms. Fatal Consequences of Combination, &c. Destruction of the Factory by Fire! Romantic View by Moonlight, with Factory in the distance, still burning. The Interposition of the Soldiery to quell the rioters—their Capture—Examination—Commitment for Trial, &c. &c.

So ran the playbill pasted up outside the Surrey Theatre in Blackfriars Road. Obviously, it was a cheap production mounted from stock scenery, played in modern dress, and cast from the stock company and their children. Mrs West, who had appeared at Drury Lane with Kean, now led the Surrey company as Jane. Young Stuart was Will Rushton, and Dibdin Pitt—the future dramatist of *Sweeney Todd*—combined the roles of villain and stage manager. Despite their skill, *The Factory Lad* refused to set the Thames on fire; it played throughout the week and was withdrawn on Saturday after six performances. No revivals are recorded, though publication of the text in both Duncombe's British

Theatre and Dicks' Standard Plays suggests it had some later acting
life, most probably with working-class play reading groups or amateurs
in search of social propaganda. In 1833, Duncombe's text was advertised in the pages of a radical weekly called *The poor man's guardian*. As a
social document of considerable value, the play would stand up well to
serious revival, and might provide a useful text for teachers working on
the Luddite riots and the massacre of Peterloo. The present text is
based on Duncombe; misprints have been corrected, and a few stage
directions amplified to clarify the action.

ACT I

Scene 1. *Exterior of a factory, lighted.*

As the curtain rises the clock strikes eight, and the men, including Allen, Wilson, Smith, Sims *and* Hatfield, *enter from factory.*

Allen. Now my lads, the glad sound—eight o'clock, Saturday night. Now for our pay, and for the first time from our new master, the son of our late worthy employer.

Wilson. The poor man's friend.

Hatfield. And the poor man's father, too!

Allen. Ay; who, as he became rich by the industry of his men, would not desert them in a time of need, nor prefer steam machinery and other inventions to honest labour.

Wilson. May his son be like him!

Allen. Ay; he was a kind man, truly. Good as good could be, an enemy to no man but the slothful. Ah, a tear almost starts when I think of him. May he be happy, may——. He must be as happy above as he made those on this earth. But come, come, we won't be melancholy. Saturday night! We won't put a dark side upon things, but let us hope his son, our present master, may be like his father, eh?

Hatfield. Ah, half like, and I shall be content.

Wilson. And I—and all of us.

Allen. Hush! he comes.

Enter Westwood, *from factory.*

Westwood. Gentlemen!

Hatfield. (*aside to* Allen *and rest*) Gentlemen! There's a pleasing way.

Allen. Gentlemen, sir? We're no gentlemen, but only poor, hard-working men, at your honour's service.

Hatfield. Hard-working and honest, we hope.

Westwood. Well, well; gentlemen or hard-working men, it's not what I've come about.

Allen. No complaint, I hope? Work all clean and right?

Westwood. It may be.

Hatfield. It may be! It is, or I'll forfeit my wages. Your father, sir, never spoke in doubt, but always looked, spoke his mind, and——

43

Westwood. And that's what *I've* come to do—I've come to speak my
mind. Times are now altered!

Allen. They are indeed, sir. A poor man has now less wages for more work.

Westwood. The master having less money, resulting from there being
less demand for the commodity manufactured.

Allen. Less demand!

Westwood. Hear me! If not less demand, a greater quantity is thrown
into the markets at a cheaper rate. Therefore, to the business I've
come about. As things go with the times, so must men. To compete
with my neighbours—that is, if I wish to prosper as they do—in
plain words, in future I have come to the resolution of having my
looms propelled by steam.

Allen, Hatfield and *Wilson.* By steam!

Westwood. Which will dispense with the necessity of manual labour,
and save me some three thousand a year.

Allen. And not want us, who have been all our lives working here?

Westwood. I can't help it. I am sorry for it; but I must do as others do.

Allen. What! and turn us out—to beg, starve, steal, or——

Hatfield. Ay, or rot, for what he cares.

Westwood. 'Turn you out' are words I don't understand. I don't want
you, that's all. Surely I can say that? What is here is mine, left me by
my father to do the best with, and that is now my intention. Steam
supersedes manual labour. A ton of coals will do as much work as
fifty men, and for less wages than ten will come to. Is it not so?

Allen. It may be as you say, sir; but your poor father made the old
plan do, and died, they say, rich. He was always well satisfied with
the profits our industry brought him, he lived cheerful himself and
made others so; and often I have heard him say his greatest pleasure
was the knowledge that so many hard-working men could sit down
to a Sunday's dinner in peace, and rear up their children decently
through his means.

Wilson. Ah, heaven bless him!

Hatfield. Heaven has blessed him, I trust, for he was a man—an
Englishman—who had feeling for his fellow creatures, and who
would not, for the sake of extra gain, that he might keep his hounds
and his hunters, turn the poor man from his door who had served
him faithfully for years.

Westwood. I hear you, and understand you, sir. Sentiments in theory
sound well, but not in practice; and as you seem to be the spokesman in this affair, I will—though I consider myself in no way compelled—reply to you in your own way. Don't you buy where you
please, at the cheapest place? Would you have bought that jerkin of
one man more than another, if he had charged you twice the sum for
it, or even a sixpence more? Don't you, too, sow your garden as you
please, and dig it as you please?

44

Hatfield. Why, it's my own.

Westwood. There it is! Then have *I* not the same right to do as I please with *my own*?

Allen. Then you discharge us?

Hatfield. Oh, come along! What's the use of asking or talking either? You cannot expect iron to have feelings!

Westwood. I stand not here to be insulted; so request you'll to the counting house, receive your wages, and depart.

Allen. And for ever?

Westwood. For ever! I want you not.

Allen. Will you not think of it again once more?

Westwood. I'm resolved.

Allen. (*aside*) My poor wife and children! (*To* Westwood) No, no; not quite—not quite resolved! Things, mayhap, may ha' run cross, so you be hasty. Think, think again! (*Kneels*) On my knees hear a poor man's prayer.

Westwood. It is useless. I *have* thought and decided.

Allen. (*rises*) My wife! my children!   (*Rushes off*)

Wilson. Poor fellow!

Hatfield. Then, if ye will not hear a poor man's prayer, hear his curses! May thy endeavours be as sterile land which the lightning has scath'd, bearing nor fruit, nor flower, nor blade, but never-dying thorns to pierce thee on thy pillow! Hard-hearted, vain, pampered thing as thou art! Remember, the day will come thou'lt be sorry for this night's work. Come, comrades—come!

Hatfield, Wilson, Sims *and* Smith *exeunt.* Westwood *into factory, sneeringly.*

Scene 2.   *A country lane. Dark.*

Enter Rushton, *cautiously, with snare, bag and gun. Sets a snare.*

Rushton. That be sure for a good 'un—ha, ha! The Game Laws, eh? As if a poor man hadn't as much right to the bird that flies and the hare that runs as the rich tyrants who want all, and gripe and grapple all too! I care not for their laws. While I have my liberty, or power, or strength, I will live as well as the best of 'em. (*Noise without*) But who comes here? Ah, what do I see? Some of the factory lads, and this way too! What can this mean? I'll listen.   (*Stands aside*)

Enter Hatfield, Wilson, Sims *and* Smith.

Wilson. Well, here's a pretty ending to all our labours, after nine years, as I've been——

Sims. And I, ten.

Smith. And I, since I was a lad.

Hatfield. And I, all my life; but so it is. What are working men like us but the tools that make others rich, who, when we become old——

Omnes. Ah!

Hatfield. We're kicked from our places like dogs, to starve, die and rot, for what they care!

Sims. Or beg!

Hatfield. Ah, that I'll never do!

Wilson. Nor I!

Smith. Nor I, either!

Sims. Then rob, mayhap?

Wilson. That may be!

Hatfield. Ay! Be like poor Will Rushton—an outcast, a poacher, or anything!

Rushton. (*starting forward. The others stand amazed*) Ay, or a pauper, to go with your hat in your hand, and after begging and telling them what they know to be the truth—that you have a wife and five, six, or eight children; one, perhaps, just born; another, mayhap, just dying —they'll give you eighteen pence to support them all for the week; and if you dare to complain—not a farthing, but place you in the stocks, or scourge you through the town as a vagabond! This is parish charity! I have known what it is. My back is still scored with the marks of their power. The slave abroad, the poor black whom they affect to pity, is not so trampled on, hunted, and ill-used as the peasant or hard-working fellows like yourselves, if once you have no home nor bread to give your children.

Wilson. But this I'll never submit to!

Sims. Nor I.

Smith. Nor I.

Hatfield. Nor I. I'll hang first!

Wilson. Thank heaven, I have no children!

Smith. Nor more have I, nor Sims; but some have both wives and children.

Wilson. 'Tis true. I have a wife, but she's as yet young, healthy, and can work—and does work. But think of poor Allen, with a wife and three small children and an aged mother to support.

Rushton. What! And is he discharged too? What, Allen—George Allen?

Hatfield. Ay, along with the rest. Not wanted now!

Rushton. My brother George, as I do call him still—for though my poor wife be dead and gone, she were his wife's sister. Ah, but let me not think of that. Where—where be poor George? He be not here!

Wilson. He rushed off home, I do believe, like to one broken-hearted.

Rushton. Ah, to his poor wife and children! There will I go to him, and say though all the world do forsake him, Will Rushton never will! No; while there be a hare or bird he shall have one; and woe to the man who dare prevent or hold my hand!

Hatfield. You're a brave and staunch fellow.

Rushton. Ay, and a desperate and daring, too.

Wilson. Give me your hand.

Hatfield. And here's mine. What say you? Suppose we go to 'The Harriers', and, in the back room by ourselves, just ha' a drop of something and talk o' things a bit.

Wilson. We will go.

Smith. Ay, we will.

Hatfield. (*to* Rushton) And you to George, and say where we are.

Rushton. I will—and bring him with me! But he'll not want asking. These times cannot last long. When man be so worried that he be denied that food that heaven sends for all, then heaven itself calls for vengeance! No; the time has come when the sky shall be like blood, proclaiming this shall be the reward of the avaricious, the greedy, the flinty-hearted, who, deaf to the poor man's wants, make him what he now is, a ruffian—an incendiary!

Wilson. Remember Allen. Yet stay! Now I think again, will it not alarm his wife to see *you*?

Rushton. (*approaches* Wilson) Ah!

Hatfield. And bring things to mind that must not be—I don't mean *together*, but—you know—not thought of just now.

Rushton. Ah, my wife——

Hatfield. Was her sister. So, suppose Smith here goes instead. She do not know him—does she, Smith?

Smith. But bare—perhaps not. I ha' passed her once or twice.

Hatfield. 'Twill do then. You go then and whisper in his ear where we are.

Smith. Ay; 'The Harriers'.

Hatfield. (*to* Rushton) What say you, isn't it better so?

Rushton. Ay, ay!

Wilson. 'Tis much better.

Hatfield. Remember, then. To 'The Harriers'!

Rushton. And shall I be there?

Smith. To be sure.

Wilson. But won't our all meeting in a room by ourselves, and Will with us too, excite suspicion?

Hatfield. That's well thought again. Then we'll drop in one by one, or two together so—and, Will, you can look in too, as 'twere by accident, for a drink o' summat—that way.

Rushton. I care not how, lads. In Will Rushton you see one who has been so buffeted he thinks not of forms; but be it as you will. To the

last drop I have, I'll be your friend—ay, the friend of poor George
Allen!

Hatfield. George! Away—away!

Music. They shake hands earnestly, and exeunt.

Scene 3. *Interior of* Allen's *house. Fireplace, with saucepan on. A clock—time twenty minutes past eight. A cradle with child.* Jane Allen, *and* Mary *and* Milly *assisting her in pearling lace and drawing ditto.*

Mary. I've done another length, mother, and that makes five, and
sister hasn't done four yet.

Jane. Never mind! She does very well. You're both very good
children! Only now you may lay the cloth, and get out the supper.
It's past eight, and your father will be coming home, and he'll be
very tired, I dare say, and hungry too, and at the end of the week a
bit of supper and a draught of ale is a thing he looks for. And, his
family around him, who so happy as George Allen?

Mary. And you too, mother, and me too, and sister too, and little
brother in the cradle.

Jane. All, all, bless you and thank heaven!

Mary. Then I'll not begin another, mother?

Jane. No; but make haste and lay the cloth.

Milly. And shan't I finish mine neither, mother?

Jane. No, never mind, that's a good girl. Get out the bread and be
quick. (*Clock chimes half-past*) Hear! It's half-past. A fork—the
potatoes must be done.

Mary. Yes, mother.

Hands fork. Jane *goes to fire, and* Milly *gets bread out.*

Jane. Oh, I think I hear him!

Mary. And so do I, mother—I can hear him! But oh dear, how he's
banging to the gate!

Enter George Allen, *who throws himself in a chair, fretfully.*

Jane. Why, George, what's the matter? Dear me, how pale you are!
Are you not well, George? You seem feverish.

Allen. I am, I am!

Jane. You'll be better after supper. Children, quick!

Mary. Oh, father, we've been so busy and done such a deal! See,
father!

Shows him lace. Allen *takes it, throws it down, rises, and stamps on it.*

Allen. Curses on it!

Mary. Oh, mother, mother! Father's thrown down all my work and
  has stamped on it, and I'm sure it's done very well!   (*Cries*)
Milly. Oh, mother, see what father's done!
Jane. George! Oh, tell me what means this?
Allen. It means that——
Mary. What, father? What makes you angry?
Jane. Say, George.
Allen. (*looks at his children, and then clasps them*) God—God bless you!
  (*Picks up the lace and gives it them*) There, there! You're good children!
                                                          (*Sits down*)
Mary. I'm sure, father, I never do anything to make you angry.
Milly. No more do I, father—do I?
Mary. Nor does mother, either?
Allen. No, no; I know she does not!
Jane. Then what is it, George? I never saw you thus before. You're so
  pale, and you tremble so. Why did you throw down the lace, that
  which is a living to us?
Allen. Because it will never be so again!
Jane. Not a living to us?
Allen. No! George Allen must beg now! Ah, beg or as bad—work
  and starve. And that I'll never do!
Jane. Oh, speak! Work and starve? Impossible!
Allen. Naught be impossible these days! What has ruined others will
  now ruin us. It's been others' turn first; now it be ours.
Jane. What, George?
Allen. That steam—that curse on mankind, that for the gain of a few,
  one or two, to ruin hundreds, is going to be at the factory! Instead
  of five and thirty good hands, there won't be ten wanted now, and
  them half boys and strangers. Yes, steam be now going to do all the
  work, and poor, hard-working, honest men, who ha' been for years
  toiling to do all for the good of a master, be now turned out
  o' doors, to do what they can or what they like. And you know what
  that means, and what it must come to.
Jane. Oh, dreadful—dreadful! But don't fret, husband—don't fret!
  We will all strive to do something.
Allen. (*again rising*) But what be that something? Think I can hear my
  children cry for food and run barefoot? Think I don't know what
  'twill come to?
Jane. But some other place will perhaps give us employ.
Allen. Ay, some foreign outlandish place, to be shipped off like
  convicts to die and starve! Look at Will Rushton, who was enticed
  or rather say ensnared there with his wife and four children. Were not
  the children slaughtered by the natives, who hate white men and live
  on human flesh? And was not his wife seized too, your own sister,
  and borne away and never returned—shared perhaps the same fate as

her children, or perhaps worse? And has not poor Will, since he
returned, been crazed, heart-broken, a pauper, poacher, or anything?
Jane. Oh, no, no! We shall meet with friends here, George.
Allen. Ay, Jane; such friends that if thou wert dying, starving, our
children stretched lifeless, and I but took a crust of bread to save
thee, would thrust me in a prison, there to rot. I have read, Jane—I
have seen, Jane, the fate of a poor man. And you know we have
nothing now, no savings, after the long sickness of father and
burying, and the little one we lost, too.
Jane. They are in heaven now, I hope!

Door opens and Smith *appears.*

Allen. Who's there?
Smith. It's only me, George.
Allen. Ah! (Smith *approaches and whispers in* Allen's *ear*) I will!
Jane. (*apart*) What can this mean?
Smith. Be secret.
Allen. As the grave!
Smith. (*whispers again*) . . . there, too!
Allen. He will?
Smith. As by chance, you know.
Jane. (*apart*) Heaven, what can it mean?
Allen. I'll be there.   (*Shakes* Smith *by the hand, who leaves at door*)
Jane. Oh, George—George, what is this, that your eyes roll so? Now
think!
Allen. I do think, Jane.
Jane. Sit—come, come, sit—sit down and have some supper, then
you'll be better. Remember, it is Saturday night. I know it is enough
to make you vexed; but think, George—think, and remember there is
ONE who never forsakes the good man, if he will but pray to him.
Allen. I will—I will; but I must now to see the lads that be like
myself, poor fellows—just to talk, you know—to think, as like—to
plan—e'es to plan—merely to plan.
Jane. But not yet. Sit awhile. Take some ale.
Allen. Why, I can get ale there, and I can't eat, my tongue and throat
be so dry. God bless you!   (*Going*)
Mary. Not going, father?
Milly. Not going, father?
Jane. See, George! Don't go yet.
Allen. (*kisses children*) I must! I must! Only for a short time, and it be
growing late.   (*Approaches door*)
Jane. Don't! Stay, George, stay!   (*Kneels and catches hold of him*)
Allen. I must—I must!

Rushes out. Music. Jane *falls.*

Mary. (cries) Mother, mother! Oh, father!

The children fall on their mother, and scene closes.

Scene 4. *An apartment in* Westwood's *house.*

Enter Westwood.

Westwood. I must be on the alert, and keep my doors well fastened, and have, too, an armed force to welcome these desperadoes, if they should dare to violate the laws well framed to subject them to obedience. I did not half like the menace of that fellow. However, I'll be secure, and if they dare, let them take the consequences. *(Muses, and repeats* Hatfield's *words)* 'The day will come, I shall be sorry for what I have done!' Ha, ha! Sorry! Fool, and fools! What have I to fear or dread? Is England's proud aristocracy to tremble when brawling fools mouth and question? No; the hangman shall be their answer.

Enter Servant.

Servant. The dinner's ready, sir.
Westwood. Is it eight, then?
Servant. Yes, sir.
Westwood. Is that old grumbler, my father's late housekeeper, gone, who dared to talk and advise, as she called it?
Servant. She went at six, sir. We trundled her out, sir.
Westwood. And the French cook, is he arrived yet?
Servant. He has sent his valet to say he'll be here in three days, after his excursion to Brighton. *(Exit)*
Westwood. What, because our fathers acted foolishly, shall we also plod on in the same dreary route? No; science has opened to us her stores, and we shall be fools indeed not to take advantage of the good it brings. The time must come, and shortly, when even the labourer himself will freely acknowledge that our improvements in machinery, and the aid afforded us by the use of steam, will place England on a still nobler eminence than the proud height she has already attained.
(Exit)

Scene 5. *A room in* 'The Harriers'.

Wilson, Sims, Smith *and* Hatfield *discovered at a table, drinking.* Tapwell, *the landlord, just entering.*

Tapwell. Another mug, did you say?
Hatfield. Ay, and another to that! What stare you at?

Tapwell. Eh? Oh, very well! (*Exit*)

Sims. Master Tapwell seems surprised at our having an extra pot.

Hatfield. Let him be. We care not, no more will he, if we have twenty, so he gets the money.

Wilson. He said he'd come, did he—Allen?

Smith. For certain.

Hatfield. His wife, no doubt, was there? Did you manage all well? Whisper secretly?

Smith. Not a word out.

Hatfield. That's well, for women are bad to trust in these things. I've read in books where the best plots have failed through women being told what their husbands or their fathers were going to do, though it was to free a nation from the yoke of tyranny.

Wilson. Ay, right! And so have I.

Re-enter Tapwell, *with beer.*

Tapwell. The beer. (*Holds out his hand without delivering it*)

Wilson. What's that for?

Tapwell. Another mug, and you didn't pay for the last, which makes one and fourpence.

Hatfield. What, you know, do you, already, that we're discharged?

Tapwell. Why, yes, if truth must be told, young Squire——

Hatfield. Young who?

Tapwell. Young Squire—Master Westwood.

Hatfield. Young damnation! Squire such a rascal as that again while we're here, and this pot with its contents shall make you call for a plaster quicker than you may like. Squire Westwood? Squire Hard-heart! No man, no feeling! Call a man like that a squire! An English gentleman—a true English gentleman—is he who feels for another, who relieves the distressed, and not turns out the honest, hard-working man to beg or starve, because he, forsooth, may keep his hunters and drink his foreign wines.

Sims. Ay, and go to foreign parts. Englishmen were happy when they knew naught but Englishmen; when they were plain, blunt, honest, upright and downright—the master an example to his servant, and both happy with the profits of their daily toil.

Allen *enters at door.*

Smith. Allen!

Hatfield. (*to* Tapwell) Off, thou lickshoe! There, take that. (*Throws him down a crown piece on the floor*) That will do, I suppose, for another pot, or a gallon?

Tapwell. Oh, certainly, Master Hatfield—certainly, gentlemen! Another pot now, did you say?

Smith. Off! (*Thrusts him out and shuts the door*)

Hatfield. (*to* Allen) Come, come, don't look so down—come drink!

Wilson. Ay, drink!

Allen. Nay, I——

Hatfield. Not drink? Not 'Destruction to steam machinery'?

Allen. Destruction to steam machinery! Ay, with all my heart!
(*Drinks*) Destruction to steam machinery!

Hatfield. Ay, our curse—our ruin!

Wilson. Ay, ay; we've been talking about that, and one thing and
t'other like, and about what we shall do, you know——

Allen. Ah!

Sims. I say poaching.

Allen. And for a hare, to get sent away, perhaps, for seven long years.

Smith. So I said.

Sims. But we mayn't be caught, you know, not if we are true to each
other. Four or five tightish lads like us can't be easily taken, unless
we like, you know!

Allen. And if we carry but a stick in our defence, and use it a bit, do
you know the law? Hanging!

Hatfield. Right! Hanging for a hare!

Sims. Not so—not hanging. Don't Will Rushton carry on the sport
pretty tidishly, and has only been——

Allen. In the stocks twice, whipped publicly thrice, and in jail seven
times. And what has he for his pains? Not a coat to his back worth
a groat, no home but the hedge's shelter or an out-house, and himself but to keep. What would he then do had he, as I have, a wife and
three young children to support? Besides, isn't he at times wild with
thinking of the past—of his lost wife and murdered children? He,
poor unhappy wretch, cannot feel more or sink lower—the jail to
him is but a resting-place.

Hatfield. 'Tis true, indeed. I remember him once a jovial fellow, the
pride of all that knew him; but now——

Allen. Ah! (*To* Smith) But said not you he would be here?

Wilson. Ay, as by accident.

Rushton *partly opens door, when* Tapwell *stops him.*

Allen. Ah! 'Tis he.

Wilson. (*to* Allen) Be not over anxious.

Tapwell. No, you can't. You remember the bag you left here the last
time, and the scrape it got me into?

Rushton. But only a minute or so.

Tapwell. Not for half a minute.

Hatfield. (*to* Allen) Shall I cleave the dastard down?

Allen. Leave it to me. (*Approaches* Tapwell) Come, sir landlord,
mercy a bit; though you may not like his rags, and for bread he
snares a hare now and then, he may wear as honest a heart as many

who wear a better garment; therefore, let him in. The outcast should sojourn with the outcast. Come, another gallon, and take that.

(*Gives* Tapwell *money*)

Tapwell. Oh well, certainly, if you have no objection, gentlemen, and he has no game or snares about him.

Hatfield. Off! (*Exit* Tapwell)

Allen. Rushton!

Rushton. Allen!

Allen. Thy hand!

Rushton. 'Tis here, with my heart.

Allen. (*gives beer*) Drink.

Rushton. Thanks! Many's the day since I was welcomed thus.

Sims. Not since, I dare say, you lost your poor wife.

Rushton *stands transfixed.*

Allen. That was foolish to mention his wife.

Sims. I forgot.

Rushton. Who spoke of my wife? Ah, did she call? Ah! She did! I hear her screams! They are—are tearing her from me. My children, too! I see their mangled forms, bleeding, torn piecemeal! My wife—my children! (*Subsides*) My wife—my—— (*Looks about*) Where, where am I? (*Sees* Allen) Allen, Allen!

Allen. To be sure—George Allen! Don't you know me? Your brother, your friend George, who——

Rushton. I know. Sent me food while I was in prison! (*Clasps* Allen's *hand and sobs*) Heaven—heaven bless you!

Allen. Come, come, an end to this! I am now like thyself, an outcast— one driven, after years of hard toil, upon the world. These the same! (*Pointing to his comrades*) Come now, say honestly, as a man who has seen much and whose hairs are grey, what would you advise us to do?

Rushton. I know all. You are discharged.

Wilson. Ay, from where we've worked since lads, nearly, if not all, and our fathers before us.

Hatfield. And we are turned beggars on the world, for no reason but to make room for that which has ruined hundreds, to suit the whims and finery of a thing unworthy the name of man!

Rushton. (*stands absorbed awhile*) I would, but I dare not advise, for my blood now boils, and my flesh is gored with the lash of power. Hush! Hither! (*Beckons them round him*) A word! Are you all good here? (*Touching his heart*) Sound? Prime?

Hatfield. Who dare to doubt?

Rushton. Enough. Hush! (*Whispers in their ears, and ends with*) . . . dare you?

Hatfield. I dare!

Smith. And I!

Wilson. And I!
Sims. And I!
Allen. And I!
Rushton. 'Tis well. (*Shakes them by the hand*) Now then, come lads, the
time answers. Hush!

Music. Exeunt omnes out of door.

Scene 6. *A country lane. Dark.*

Enter Rushton, Allen, Wilson, Sims, Smith *and* Hatfield, *armed
variously.*

Rushton. Steady! Steady, lads, and resolute!
Wilson. 'Tis well; no one crosses our path.
Hatfield. What if they did?
Allen. My heart almost begins to sicken; a fear, ever unknown to me,
seems to shake me from head to foot.
Rushton. Pshaw, fear? Fear is the coward's partner and the companion
of the guilty; not of men who are about to act in their own right and
crush oppression.
Wilson. 'Tis true, we are oppressed.
Smith. We are!
Sims. Ay, we are!
Hatfield. And we'll be revenged!
Sims. Ay, revenged!
Allen. But if we meet with resistance—I mean if they attack us?
Rushton. Return their attack—blow for blow, if they will have it; ay,
and blood for blood. Give in, and you're lost for ever! You'll have
no mercy. Look at me, Will Rushton, honest Will Rushton that was
once—hard-working Will Rushton. You know my fate—torture upon
torture; the insult of the proud and the pity of the poor have been
my lot for years. Trampled on, crushed, and gored to frenzy! My
blood boils now I think on't! The pale spectre of my wife, with my
slaughtered children, now beckons me on! Revenge, revenge! Come,
revenge!

Takes Allen's *hand and exeunt.*

Hatfield. Ay, revenge—revenge!
Wilson and The Rest. Ay, revenge!

They follow Rushton *and* Allen.

Scene 7. *Exterior of the factory. Dark.*

Enter Rushton *with a torch, followed by* Allen, Wilson, Sims, Smith *and* Hatfield.

Rushton. Now to the work—to the work! Break, crack, and split into ten thousand pieces these engines of your disgrace, your poverty, and your ruin! Now!

Hatfield. Ay, now destruction!

Wilson. Ay, spare not a stick! Come, come, Allen!

Rushton, Wilson, Sims *and* Smith *rush into the factory. The factory is seen blazing.* Westwood *rushes in, followed by* Constables.

Westwood. Ah, villains, stay! It is as I was told; but little did I think they dared. Seize them!

Hatfield. Ah, surprised!

Rushton *comes from the factory, with firebrand, followed by his comrades.*

Westwood. Submit, I say!

Rushton. Ah!

Seizes him by the throat, hurls him to the earth, and waves the lighted ember above him in wild triumph.

ACT II

Scene 1. *Moonlight. Open country, with view of factory burning in the distance.*

Enter Rushton, *with firebrand.*

Rushton. Ha, ha! This has been a glorious night—to see the palace of the tyrant levelled to the ground, to hear his engines of gain cracking, to hear him call for help, and see the red flame laugh in triumph! Ah, many a day have I lain upon the cold, damp ground, muttering curses; many a night have I called upon the moon, when she has frenzied my brain, to revenge my wrongs. For days and nights I have never slept—misery and want, and the smart of the lash, with visions of bygone days, have been like scorpions, rousing me to revenge; and the time has come. I have had partners, too, in the deed—men who, like myself, glory in the act. But where can Allen be, and the rest? They must away now. I'll to his cottage, and if the minions of power dare but touch a hair of his head, this brand shall lay them low.   *(Exit)*

Scene 2. *Interior, as before, of* Allen's *house. The casement open, and the blaze of the factory seen in the distance.*

Jane *watching at the window.* Mary *and* Milly *near her.*

Jane. Oh, horror—horror!
Mary. It's not out yet, mother; it seems as if some other house was on fire.
Milly. See, mother!
Jane. 'Tis too true, child. Oh, mercy—mercy! The flames have caught the farm next to it. I can no longer look. The worst of thoughts crowd upon my brain: my husband's absence—his wild and distracted look—the factory in flames!

Enter Allen, *hurriedly.*

Ah, my husband! Oh, say, George, where—where is it you have been?
Allen. Jane—my children! (*Embraces them in silent anguish*) Some ale, water, or something! My throat is parched!
Mary. Some ale, father?
Jane. You've seen the fire?
Allen. Yes, yes. Some ale, I said.
Mary. Here it is, father.   (*Gives jug.* Allen *drinks*)
Allen. Ah, that be sweet. (*To his wife in an undertone*) Hush! Here, here, take this (*gives money*)—it be all I have, and this too (*gives watch*). There be, too, a little up-stairs. Take care of thyself, Jane, and of children.
Jane. Oh, George, say not that! You would not leave your Jane, who has ever loved you, and ever will?
Mary. Oh, mother, don't cry.
Allen. Mother's not crying. (*Standing before her*) See to the child, it wakes. (*Fire blazes vividly.* To Jane) See you that? All be broken and burnt now. Say, if they come, you ha' not seen me, you know. They cannot harm thee.
Jane. Oh, George! Say, for mercy's sake, you've had no hand in this!
Allen. What be done, Jane, cannot now be altered.
Jane. Oh, George, bad advice has led you to this. I know you would not have done so of yourself.
Allen. It matters not, now, Jane. It be done, and I must away; but you shall hear from me, Jane, where'er I be. I will send thee all I get.

A noise without.

Jane. Ah, that noise——
Allen. It be they come—come to take me.
Jane. Fly! Fly!

Allen *rushes towards the door, when* Westwood *and* Constables *appear at the window.*

Allen. Ah, 'tis useless!
Westwood. He's here.

Enter Westwood, *followed by* Constables.

Seize him! (*They seize* Allen)
Jane. (*kneels*) Oh, mercy, mercy! Spare him—spare my husband!
Mary. Oh, spare my father!
Milly. Don't hurt father!
Jane. He is not guilty; indeed he's not.
Westwood. Not guilty! When I saw him with the rest?
Jane. But he did not set fire the place. I know he did not—he would not.
Westwood. What matters what hand did the deed? Is not all a heap of ashes—all burnt and destroyed?
Jane. Yet mercy!
Westwood. Mercy! What mercy had he to me? Cast thy eye yonder, and petition to the flames.
Jane. Oh, George! George!
Westwood. Away with him. Now for the outcast!

Enter Rushton, *frantically, with a piece of burnt machinery in his hand.*

Rushton. Who calls for the outcast? Stay! What are you about? Seizing an innocent man? Here stands the incendiary! I, Will Rushton, the outcast, the degraded—ha, ha! yes, and the revenged! 'Twas I led them on, and this hand lit the firebrand, and I am satisfied.
Westwood. Seize him! 'Tis the instigator—the ringleader!

They attempt to seize him.

Rushton. (*in a menacing attitude*) Approach not, or your grave is at my feet!

They retreat, intimidated.

Westwood. Cowards, do you fear a madman? Surrender, idiot, fiend, wretch, outcast, or this shall tame thee! (*Presents a pistol*)
Allen. Rushton, you escape; I care not.
Westwood. Ah! Then stir but one foot, and——
Rushton. And what? (*Seizes him by the collar and hurls him to the ground,* Westwood *firing the pistol*) Away, I say!
Jane. Oh, fly—fly, George!

Westwood *attempts to rise.* Rushton *stands over him and, waving the ember, secures the retreat of* Allen. *As he is rushing out, the scene closes.*

Scene 3. *Exterior of an out-house or hovel, in lane. Moonlight.*

Enter Allen, *frantic, as if pursued.*

Allen. Where shall I fly? My brain is giddy, my legs feeble. I can no further. Oh, my wife—Jane, Jane—my children, too! (*Falls exhausted*)

Wilson *and* Hatfield *look out from hovel.*

Hatfield. It was Allen's voice, I'm sure, yet I see no one.
Wilson. See, who lies there?

They come out.

Hatfield. Ah, it is he!
Wilson. What is this? Not dead—killed himself? (*Calls*) Allen! Allen!
Hatfield. Allen, lad!
Allen. (*starting*) Ah, who calls on Allen? Was't my wife—my children? I'm here—don't you see me? What—what's—— (*Looks about wildly*)
Wilson. Allen, it's but us, your old friends, Wilson and Hatfield. Don't you know us?
Allen. Ah! Is it? (*They assist him to rise. He clasps their hands earnestly*) Have you seen my wife—my children?
Hatfield. I thought you'd been to see them.
Allen. Ah, I remember. Like a wild dream it comes across my brain. But where—where's the rest? Smith and——

Voices without cry 'This way—this way!'

Ah, they come!
Hatfield. In—in there! Would you be taken?
Allen. I care not. Ah, 'tis he—'tis Rushton! Never will I fly. He who would desert his comrade in the hour of peril is worse than coward.

Enter Rushton *in haste, followed by* Westwood *and* Soldiers.

Westwood. Ah, here are the rest. Seize them all and spare none!
Rushton. Hell-hound, would you murder the poor wretches you have deprived of bread?
Westwood. Villain, have you not deprived me of bread, and set fire to my dwelling, reckless who might perish in the flames?
Rushton. That *you had*, then justice had been done and my revenge satisfied!
Westwood. Officer, your duty. Let them not escape!
Officer. In the King's name, I desire you to yield!
Hatfield. Never!
Rushton. That's right, my lads—never yield!

They stand on the defensive.

Officer. Then at your peril!

Presents pistol. Soldiers *advance, and a confused combat ensues, ending in the disarming of* Hatfield *and* Wilson, *and capture of* Allen *with a wound across his forehead. At that moment,* Jane Allen *enters, distracted. She screams on seeing her husband wounded and taken.*

Jane. Oh, mercy—mercy! My husband! Do not—do not murder him! Oh, George!   (*Kneels and clasps him round the knee*)

Allen. Who calls on George Allen?

Jane. It is thy wife! Don't you know me? Thy wife, you know, George. Jane, Jane, thy wife!

Allen. Ah, Jane, my doom is fixed! Leave me, and clasp those who are helpless—my little ones!

Rushton. There, monster, dost thou see that? Thy doing.

Westwood. 'Tis false! Liar, fiend, reprobate!

Rushton. 'Tis true! Liar, fiend, and reprobate again! Didst thou not turn these poor men from their honest employ to beg, steal, starve, or do as they have done—be revenged?

Allen. Peace, peace; it is over now. Jane, I feel my life fast ebbing. Home—home!

Westwood. Away with them!

Jane. Oh, pity, mercy! Tear him not away from me.

Officer. The law's imperative!

The Soldiers *march them off.* Jane *falls fainting.* Jane *is lying senseless.* Mary *enters.*

Mary. Mother, mother, where are you? Oh, what do I see on the cold ground? It can't be mother? Mother! (*Approaches nearer*) Mother! Oh, it can't be my mother—she would hear me—yet it looks like my mother. Oh dear, it is, I know it can be no other! Mother, mother! (*Cries and falls on her mother*) Mother, why don't you speak? Mother!

Kneels and kisses her. Jane, *recovering, looks about her in wild disorder.*

Jane. Where am I?

Mary. Here, mother, on the cold ground!

Jane. (*seeing her child*) Ah, my child! Bless you, bless you! But what are we doing here in the open air?

Mary. You came out after father, mother.

Jane. Your father! (*Screams*) Ah, I now remember all. They are tearing him from me, to take him to a loathsome dungeon! All now crosses me like a wild dream. The factory—the red sky—flames whirling in the air! My eye-balls seemed cracked—my brain grows dizzy—I hear chains and screams of death! My husband—they shall not tear him from me!

Mary. Mother, mother, where are you going?

Jane. To thy father—to the jail—they will not refuse his poor, weak, and broken-hearted wife!

Mary. Nor me either, will they, mother?

Jane. (*takes her up*) Bless you, bless you! Never, never shall they part us! (*Exeunt*)

Scene 4. *Interior of a Justice Room.*

Justice Bias *and* Clerk *discovered seated at table.* George Allen, Sims, Wilson *and* Hatfield *discovered handcuffed.* Westwood, Constables, Officer *and* Soldiers *dragging in* Rushton, *struggling.*

Rushton. Why do you drag me thus? Do you think I'm afraid? Do you think I fear to own that I was the man who led them on? No! I glory in the act—'twas the sweet triumph I've oft longed for!

Bias. Silence, sirrah!

Rushton. I speak or am silent as I please. Talking is not hanging, is it? What are you more than I am? I remember when you were over-seer—the man appointed to protect the poor.

Bias. And what has that to do with the present business?

Rushton. It has this: to show that an honest man at least should sit in that seat, and not one who has crept into it by robbery and oppression.

Bias. Maniac!

Rushton. Ay; but I was not so when the cart, laden with provisions for the workhouse, by your order stopped at your own door to pretend to deliver some articles ordered for yourself, but which belonged to the poor famished creatures who had no redress but the lash if they dared to complain.

Bias. It is false!

Rushton. Is it false, too, that through your means alone, when but seven years of age, I was condemned to six weeks' hard labour in a prison for stealing—as you called it—but a handful of apples from your orchard?

Bias. 'Tis false, or why not have made your charge before? Is it to be supposed one so vindictive, a common thief, an incendiary, would have concealed this so long? The law is open to you, is it not?

Rushton. No; I am poor.

Bias. And what of that? The law is made alike for rich and poor.

Rushton. Is it? Why, then, does it so often lock the poor man in a jail, while the rich one goes free?

Bias. No more of this. Clerk, draw out the commitment.

Rushton. Commitment! Who would you commit? Not these poor men. 'Twas I broke into and destroyed the engines of power. 'Twas I set

61

fire to the mass, and reduced to ashes what has reduced others to beggary. Think you I regret—think you I fear? No; I glory in the act. There! I have confessed; and as in me you see the avenger of the poor man's wrongs, on me and me alone heap your vengeance.

Bias. Clerk, record the prisoner's confession; and Charles George Westwood, proprietor of the factory and buildings joining thereunto, lately burnt, stand forth and make your further allegations, and name the prisoners charged in this atrocious act.

Westwood. I charge all the prisoners now standing here as being concerned in the destruction of the factory, dwelling house, and out-houses. First, their leader there, William, or Will Rushton, as I believe he is called; second, John Hatfield; third, Walter Sims; fourth, Francis Wilson; fifth, Joseph Smith, not here through being wounded; sixth and last, George Allen.

Bias. And this you are willing to swear?

Westwood. I am.

Bias. Prisoners, you have heard the charge. Have you aught to say?

Hatfield. No; if it is to be, let it be. We may as well die on a scaffold as be starved!

Wilson. Don't look down, George; let's bear it up like men.

Allen. Yet my wife and children!

Bias. 'Tis well; this silence shows a proper sense of shame. 'Tis written, they who defy the law must suffer by the law. Prisoners, though it is not my duty to pronounce judgment, still I deem it so to apprise you of the fate likely to await you. Tomorrow will commence the assizes at the neighbouring town, where you will be removed and arraigned before a tribunal, which will hear your defence and give the verdict according to the evidence produced. Further, I have naught to say. Officer, remove the prisoners.

Jane. (*without*) Unhand me, I will enter!

She enters. Allen *conceals himself.*

Jane. He is here—must be here! Is it that agony has dimmed my sight, or that reason has left her seat and madness mocks me? (*Sees him*) Ah, he's there! Oh, George, is this the end of all our former bliss? Torn from me, and for ever? My husband—he whom I have pressed to my breast—my heart's blood—the father of my children—oh, horror, horror—exposed like a common felon to the gaze of thousands on a gibbet? Hung? Oh, my heart sickens! No, no, it cannot be—must not be! Never shall it be said that my husband, George Allen, died like a felon, a common robber, a murderer!

Bias. Seize this frantic woman, and let her be removed!

They approach to take her.

Jane. Oh, touch me not! Off—off, I say! Yet have pity on me, I know not what I say. A whirlwind rushes through my brain! (*Falls at* Westwood's *feet, clasping his knees*) Mercy—mercy! To you I kneel; pity my poor husband, and I will pray for thee, work for thee; my children, all, all, shall be your slaves for ever—ever, but spare him!

Westwood. Cling not to me Justice shall have its due!

(*Spurns her from him*)

Rushton. Spurn a helpless and imploring woman, whose heart is broken—whose mind is crazed? If her *voice* is weak, my *arm* is not. Justice shall have its due. Die, tyrant! Quick, to where water quencheth not!

Fires. Westwood *falls, and the curtain drops on picture of* Rushton *standing in centre, laughing hysterically, pointing at* Westwood. Jane *in the arms of* Allen. Hatfield, Sims *and* Wilson *in an attitude of surprise. The* Soldiers *with their muskets levelled at* Rushton.

Nick of the Woods

A DRAMA IN THREE ACTS BY MISS L. H. MEDINA

First performed at the Bowery Theatre, New York, 5 February 1838

CAST

at the Bowery Theatre, 6 May 1839

NATHAN SLAUGHTER, alias REGINALD ASHBURN, alias THE JIBBENAINOSAY	Mr Joseph Proctor
ROLAND FORRESTER	Mr Bannister
RALPH STACKPOLE, the ring-tailed screamer	Mr Gates
COLONEL BRUCE, in command of the Bruce-town station	Mr J. B. Rice
BIG TOM BRUCE ⎫	⎧Mr Nickinson
YOUNG TOM BRUCE ⎬ his sons	⎨Mr Foster
LITTLE TOM BRUCE ⎭	⎩Master G. Lewis
RICHARD BRAXLEY	Mr Bellamy
ABEL DOE, alias JACK ATKINS, his tool	Mr J. H. Hall
WENONGA, chief of the Shawnees	Mr Lewis
PIANKESHAW	Mr Addis
EMIGRANTS	⎧Mr Fagan ⎨Mr Price
EDITH FORRESTER, cousin to Roland	Mrs Proctor
TELIE DOE, adopted by Abel Doe	Mrs Shaw
MRS BRUCE, wife to Colonel Bruce	Mrs Jones
PHOEBE BRUCE ⎫ her daughters	⎧Mrs Penson
NELL BRUCE ⎭	⎩Mrs Williams

Indians, male and female emigrants and settlers

The Bowery cast list also includes

EMPEROR, a negro	Mr Jackson
NEHEMATTALAH ⎫ Indians	⎧Mr Barnett
TIANESKA ⎭	⎩Mr Beckwell
PATIENCE SEATON	Miss Verity

None of these is mentioned in the text of Miss Medina's play.

The action takes place in the border wilderness of Kentucky.

Period: 1782

LOUISA HAMBLIN, *née* MEDINA

Third wife of Thomas Sowerby Hamblin, leading man and manager of the Bowery Theatre from 1830 to 1848. Dramatized Bulwer-Lytton's poem *O'Neill the Rebel* (1827), and then turned to his novels: *The Last Days of Pompeii* (1834), *Rienzi* (1835) and *Ernest Maltravers* (1837). Wrote several Indian melodramas, including *Kairrassah*, *Wacousta* (1833) and, of course, *Nick of the Woods* (1838). Died in New York, 12 November 1838.

NICK OF THE WOODS

Robert Montgomery Bird's fine novel, first published in 1837, was dramatized on both sides of the Atlantic. John Haines' version for the Vic (1839) lynched Stackpole in Act One and introduced a down-east Yankee by the name of Pardon Dodge. Two later adaptations played at Edinburgh (1841) and Leeds (1844). The first American production launched Medina's text at the Bowery on 5 February 1838; Charles S. Porter was a giant-like Stackpole, with Mrs Flynn as Telie Doe. Their triumph was cut short a fortnight later, when the theatre and its contents, for the third time in ten years, were totally destroyed by fire. The rebuilt Bowery opened under Hamblin's management on 6 May 1839. The play, perhaps in memory of his late wife, was *Nick of the Woods or The Renegade's Daughter*, and the cast was led by Joseph Proctor, making his début as Nick, and Mrs Shaw, making hers as the renegade's daughter. *Nick* was again a great success, and stayed on at the Bowery for many seasons. So did Mrs Shaw, who repeated Telie for her benefit in 1841, went on to play Hamlet and Jack Sheppard, and eventually retired as Mrs Hamblin IV. Proctor, meanwhile, took the play to many other theatres, re-creating Nick across the eastern seaboard from Boston in 1843 (when his Braxley was 'Mazeppa' Cartlitch) to Brooklyn in 1879. The last revival I have traced was given at the Germania Theatre, New York, on 13 August 1886.

The present text is based on that in French's Standard Drama, which is virtually reprinted in Dicks. One or two stage directions have been expanded to clarify the action.

ACT I

Scene 1. *Forest glade and log hut, cattle grazing, trees lying about; sunset.*
Emigrants, *male and female, discovered, as if just come to a halt. Music.*

Emigrants.   CHORUS
>   Wanderers from our native hearth,
>   Exiles from our homes of birth,
>   Weary, faint, and wasted, we
>   With joy our place of refuge see.

At end, all shout as Roland *enters, leading* Edith.

Roland. Friends, companions, our weary march is almost ended, for
lo! before us lies the station of our refuge. Here, then, let us join the
hand of fellowship, and offer our prayers to that power who has led
us safely through the pathless wilderness. That we have suffered,
toiled, and bled, is to us who are men, nothing; but women, gentle
and delicate women, have suffered too. Therefore, let each lead his
weary companion to the welcome resting-place. Tomorrow, with
strength repaired and energies renewed, we will resume our march.

Music. The chorus is resumed and all Emigrants *exeunt, leaving* Roland
and Edith.

Edith. Cousin, will you not forward and salute the friends who are
waiting to give us welcome?
Roland. Us? Where shall we look for friends to give us welcome?
Edith. Here, among the inhabitants of these woods. A kinder or more
hospitable people exists not on the earth.
Roland. I know it, Edith. But to see you—the favoured offspring of
luxury and wealth—thrown thus upon a savage wild, galls my soul.
Are these rough people fit companions for the tender Edith
Forrester?
Edith. They are, Roland. Honesty should be the welcome companion
of all. Shall we despond, because the treachery of a villain induced
our uncle to disinherit us, and who has sent us forth to wander as
exiles in a strange land? No! Trust me, dear Roland. I feel more
pride to be allied to one who has bled in England's cause, than if I

67

were wedded to the rich and wealthy monster who has betrayed the memory of our father.

Roland. If thou art content, dare I complain? (*Shouts heard outside*) But see, yonder comes the commander of the station, to bid us welcome himself.

Bruce. (*outside*) Here, you brutes, take care of the hosses. Tie 'em up, Tom, and see that the strangers want for nothing.

Enter Colonel Bruce.

Well, captain! Well, young lady! (*Shakes hands*) I'm glad to see you on our border. (*Speaks off*) Here, you brutes, look well to the hosses, for if that Captain Ralph Stackpole gets scent of their halters, there will be no catching the critturs.

Roland. Captain Ralph Stackpole? Pray, sir, who is he?

Bruce. As proper a fellow as ever you saw. Killed two Injuns once, single-handed, on Bear Grass; and has stole more hosses than any other man in the country.

Roland. And such men are commissioned for your officers?

Bruce. Oh, there's no regular commission in the case. He's only a captain of horse thieves, and a capital one he is, too; being all fight, there's no one can equal him. But come to the station, and we'll have a long talk about your uncle, old Major Rowley as we used to call him. I was a corporal under him against the French, but now I'm a colonel. Well, captain, I hope for old acquaintance' sake you'll drive your stakes with us for a month or two.

Roland. I should be pleased to accept your offer, colonel, for my cousin's sake, but we are obliged to proceed. I hope there is not much danger on the road to the falls?

Bruce. Why, as to danger, it's hard telling. The murdering critturs do make sad havoc among us, thar's no denying it. It was but two months ago that old Colonel Crawford's company were beaten.

Roland. Crawford's company beaten!

Bruce. Cut off. There was about forty of them beaten to death by the savages. They roasted the old fellow; and if he wasn't eaten, it was only because he was too old to be tender.

Roland. Horrible! And to this danger must my poor Edith be exposed?

Bruce. Ay, captain; they scalp the women as well as the men. But come, if you're anxious to have the lady in a place of safety, here's the place to stick up your tent poles, and we shall be glad of your company.

Roland. I would gladly accept your offer, but our men are resolved to push forward without delay, and we must e'en accompany them.

Bruce. Well, if you must, you must; so come along, and make the most of your time. There's the old woman and the gals'll make much of you; and as for the boys, they'll all fight for you. (*Noise off*) There they are, busy stowing away the strangers. So come in and get some refreshment; and may you never enter a house where you are less welcome!

Music. Roland *and* Edith *follow* Colonel Bruce *off.*

Scene 2.   *Interior of a log cabin.*

Enter Phoebe *and* Nell, *followed by* Mrs Bruce.

Mrs Bruce. Out on you, you flirting creatures! Hain't you no better idea of what's manners for a kurnel's daughters? I'm ashamed of you, to be romping and tearing there like common folks. Do you remember your father's a kurnel of militia, and behave like genteel creatures.

Phoebe. La, mother, I think we know how to behave as well as any other gals in the settlement.

Mrs Bruce. Well, then, do; for here comes the strange lady. Now do behave yourself. Ain't she a beauty?

Enter Edith.

Well, I declare, I'm uncommon glad to see you! Run, gals, and get something nice for the lady.

Phoebe. What'll you please to take, ma'am? We've got some first-rate hominy.[1]

Nell. Yes, and elegant hog's flesh—no better in the country.

Edith. I thank you, my good friends. All I require is a little water to allay my thirst.

Phoebe *and* Nell *rush to the door.*

Mrs Bruce. Stop there, you wild creatures! Where's your circumference? Do behave yourself, and remember you're a kurnel's daughters. (*Calls*) Telie Doe! Telie Doe, I say! Why don't you make haste?

Music. Telie *enters, her eyes fixed on the stage.*

Telie. I am here. What is your will?

Mrs Bruce. Show this lady to the square room, and give her the best in the house. (*Music.* Telie *crosses slowly, starts on seeing* Edith) Why, what's the matter, Telie girl? Now do make haste and show the lady to her apartment. Don't stand staring there, as if the lady would eat you.

Telie. Sweet lady, tell me your name. Oh, if this be the face that has haunted me in my dreams, by day and by night, better had you sought the lion's den than this western wild.

---

[1] *hominy* coarsely ground maize boiled with milk or water

Edith. My name, fair girl, is Edith. But that we have met before is quite impossible.

Telie. Your pardon, lady. I was deceived. This way—I attend you.

Music. Telie *leads* Edith *off.*

Mrs Bruce. Well, I do declare! I believe that girl is crazy. You can't speak a word to her, but she starts as if the Injuns was scalping her. (*They laugh*) Now do comfort yourselves. Hush! Here comes the kurnel and the brave Captain Roland Forrester—and a right down soldier-looking captain he is, too.

Enter Colonel Bruce *and* Roland.

Bruce. Here's the spot, captain, and there's my old woman. Gals, walk up and show yourselves. (*They curtsey*) You'll find snug quarters here, captain.

Mrs Bruce. What'll you have, captain? Some stuffed shribbles,[1] or pork bissings,[2] or——

Bruce. Stop, stop! Turn the house upside down and provide the best.

Mrs Bruce. (*to girls*) Don't you hear, you deaf Satans? Make haste and don't keep the gentleman waiting. (*They laugh*) Now do distress yourselves, you Phoebe, you Nell.   (*Exit after them*)

Bruce. Ha, ha, ha! Women will be women, and there's an end on't. But I say, captain, where's your sister Miss Edith?

Roland. There, colonel, you are wrong. Edith is not my sister; she is my cousin and, as I hope, will some day be my wife.

Bruce. I honour you, captain, for your choice, and wish you joy. My brave old major's estate has fallen into the right hands, for, if there's any believing the news, you'll be the richest couple in the country.

Roland. You are in error again, colonel. Neither Edith nor myself are heirs to my uncle's estate; a villain named Richard Braxley contrived to destroy the will that made us so.

Bruce. Richard Braxley? He that was a lieutenant under the major at Braddock's?

Roland. The same.

Bruce. Now do I hold that fellow to be a precious rascal, captain; and I think there was lying and villainy at the bottom of that will.

Roland. Yes; this Braxley produced evidences of an early, secret, but solemn marriage and the birth of a girl; and although many believe that girl to be since dead, still Braxley holds the property in her name. So you see, my friend, we are no other than plain adventurers, seeking our fortunes by the sweat of our brow.

[1] *shribbles* ? marrows

[2] *bissings* savoury puddings made from the rich, thick milk a cow gives when newly calved

Noise outside. Enter Big Tom Bruce.

Bruce. What's the matter, Tom Bruce?

Big Tom. Matter enough. The Jibbenainosay is up again!

Bruce. Where? Not on our limits?

Big Tom. No; but near enough to be neighbourly. He has left his mark right in the road.

Bruce. And a clear mark, Tom? No mistake in it?

Big Tom. Right to an iota: a regular cross on the breast and a good dig through the skull—and a long-legged fellow, too; one who looked as though he might have fought old Satan himself.

Bruce. It's the Jibbenainosay sure enough. There's a hurricane coming.

Roland. In the name of wonder, who is the Jibbenainosay?

Bruce. Why, Nick—Nick of the Woods!

Roland. And who is Nick of the Woods?

Bruce. There, captain, you're too hard for me. Some think one thing and some another, but there's many think he's the devil.

Roland. Is it possible anyone can believe so absurd a story?

Bruce. Captain, you don't seem to understand the affair. You must know there's a creature of some sort or other that ranges these woods round about the station, keeping a sort of guard over us like, and killing all the brute Injuns, and placing his mark upon 'em—a regular knife-cut on the breast in the shape of a cross. The Injuns call him Jibbenainosay, which means a spirit that walks; but let him be man, beast or devil, neither knife, bullet or tomahawk can touch or harm him.

Roland. But what do you think of him yourself, colonel?

Bruce. Why, between you and I, captain, I believe it to be the ghost of one Reginald Ashburn, who was murdered five years ago by the savages. I shall never forget the horrible massacre. There was Reginald's father, mother and poor old grandmother and all the rest preparing for his wedding, when the brute Injuns rushed in, burnt the house, murdered them all and took their scalps. The inhuman wretches didn't even spare the bride, the pretty Alice!

Roland. A dreadful story! The thought of Edith makes my blood run cold. Come, let us go and learn all we can from those who brought the news.

Bruce. Who's the bearer, Tom?

Big Tom. Captain Roaring Ralph Stackpole.

Bruce. What! Look to the horses, then; run then, ye brute! (*Exit* Big Tom) Captain, we must keep our eye-winkers gaping, or some of your colts will be missing before sunrise, and especially that full-blooded brown beast of your'n. She would set a better man than Ralph Stackpole's mouth a-watering. Come along, captain.

Music. They exeunt L, *as* Edith *and* Telie *enter* R.

71

Edith. Remain with me, my good girl? Alas, I am even poorer and more friendless than yourself. I have now no home to receive, no parents to welcome, me. Attendance, should I need any, would be such as might ill befit your frame.

Telie. Lady, be not angry with me. I know that you have been used to pomp and servants; here you are in the wild woods among strangers and perhaps enemies. O lady, let me go with you! I can serve you; indeed, indeed I can. Do not spurn me from you.

Edith. Spurn you? Wherefore?

Telie. I am a white Indian's daughter.

Edith. A white Indian's daughter?

Telie. My father was a settler here. A stern and silent man; yet to me he was very kind, till a villain lured him from his peaceful home to join the red man of the boundless forest. Yet ere he went, I know not why, he fired our cottage and left me houseless, friendless. But I am not a partner in his crimes. O, do not cast me from you!   (*Kneels*)

Edith. Rise, my good girl. Believe me, I pity you; but be of good cheer. You shall not lack my friendship; but 'tis not in my power to grant your request to accompany me. Content you, my good girl; it is impossible.   (*Exit*)

Telie. Deny my suit, lady, you may. But to prevent my purpose is beyond your power.   (*Music. She hurries out*)

Scene 3. *The stockade fort, built of logs. Log wall cross stage, and gate* C. *Waterfall in background, and practicable bridge. Male and female* Settlers, Big Tom, Young Tom *and* Ralph Stackpole *discovered.*

Ralph. Silence, you tarnal critturs! My name's Tom Doodle, the rag man, and I'm for any man that insults me—long leg or leather breeches, green shirt or blanket coat, land trotter or river roller. I'm the man for a massacre!

All laugh and shout, as Colonel Bruce *and* Roland *enter.*

Kurnel, I'm glad to see you! Same to you, stranger; my name's Ralph Stackpole, and I'm a ring-tailed squealer.   (*Offers his hand*)

Roland. Then, Mr Ralph Stackpole, I'll trouble you to pursue your business without taking any notice of me, as I'm not in the habit of joining hands with savages and horse thieves.

Ralph. Tarnal death to me! I'm a gentleman, and my name's fight!— foot and hand, tooth and nail, claw and mud scraper, knife, gun and tomahawk, or any way you choose to take me. I'm your man! Cock-a-doodle-doo-o-o.   (*Strikes an attitude; all laugh*)

Bruce. Stop there, Ralph; no insults to strangers. Where did you steal that brown mare from?

Ralph. Steal! I steal any hoss but an Injun's! Where's the man dare insinuate that? Blood and massacreation, where's the man?

Bruce. Come, come, Ralph; you know that old mare belongs to Peter Harper on the north side of the clearings.

Ralph. Kurnel, you're a man in authority and my superior officer, therefore there can be no scalping between us; but you're right, by hokey! There's the beast, and just tell me where's the one you're going to lend me. I must be off afore sunset.

Shriek heard off-stage. A Woman *rushes on, followed by* Telie Doe.

Woman. Save, O save my child!

Telie. Help, help, for the love of heaven! A furious panther has seized the child and is bounding away. Help, if ye be men!

Roland. Follow me to the rescue! (*Rushes out*)

Ralph. Tarnal death to the crittur! I'm the man to make him knock under!   (*Music. Exits over bridge*)

Telie. (*on bridge*) He nears the beast. Gracious heaven! A moment and the child is lost. The panther turns and dashes towards the rapids; Ralph raises his gun; he fires. (*Gun fired*) He is hit; he falls; the child is saved!

The Settlers *all shout. Music.* Ralph *crosses bridge with the child, followed by* Roland.

Ralph. Here's the speechifier that gave him his fixings! Arn't I the ramping tiger of Salt River? There's the baby; not a hair of his head but's as good as new. There, no thanks; you're welcome, you're welcome.

Roland. I ask pardon, Captain Stackpole, for my rude words to you. Give me your hand; you are a bold and worthy man, and I am proud to take it.

Ralph. Who's for a fight? Where's your old coon can claw the bark off a gum tree? Where's your wolf of the rolling prairies? Here's a man for you, Tom Bruce. Same to you, Jimmy Big Nose, and to all of you. Ain't I the old snag to shake off a saddle, can go down old Salt on my back and swim up the Ohio! Hurrah for a fight!

Roland. (*aside*) What a strange medley of the bully and the hero is that man!

Big Tom. If you're ralely ripe for a fight, here comes the very man for you. Look, boys, here comes Bloody Nathan.

Big Tom *and the* Settlers *go out to meet* Nathan.

Ralph. (*capering*) Where's the feller? I've heard tell of the brute, and— tarnal death to me!—I'm his superior. Show me the crittur, and let me fly at him. Cock-a-doodle-doo!

Big Tom. (*outside*) Hurrah for Bloody Nathan!

Roland. Who is it they call by so terrible a name?

Bruce. Why, we call him Bloody because he's the only man in the country who won't fight. Some call him Wandering Nathan, because he's here, there and everywhere. Others say his wits are unsettled; and I do hold that that's the truth of the poor crittur.

Big Tom. (*entering*) Here's the man that calls himself Danger!

Music. Settlers *enter shouting for* Nathan *who follows, dressed in sheep skins, and a staff in his hand. He comes down slowly to the front.*

Bruce. Well, Nathan, any news from the lower settlement? Tell us what's going on, and what the cry is down there.

Nathan. Peace! They cry for peace, and their answer is blood! The grown man, the delicate female and the nursing infant lift up their voices and cry for peace; but it comes not. I passed by the smoking ruins—they had been blazing, but they were quenched in hot blood —and I walked through the trampled fields, and there arose a cry of peace, peace; but there was none. So I wandered on to find it. But peace there is none upon the earth; so I go to seek it elsewhere.

(*Going*)

Ralph. (*stops him*) Here, old Bloody, a fight! They say you're a war horse. I'm the ramping tiger of the rolling fork. If you've said your prayers, now's your time; for I'm your man.

Nathan. Ay, you follow the cry that is heard in the air. You scent the trail that is laid on the earth for blood, blood, blood! I have seen rivers of it flowing, warm and gushing; but that was before this solid earth was builded, and men were men, not ravening tigers. I have seen—but you'll tell nobody?—peace, peace, peace!

Ralph. Tarnal death to me! I'll whip the cowardly devil out of you, you superniferous, no-souled crittur. I'm the gentleman to make a man of you, so off with your lamb skins, you bloody-mouthed cur. I'll give you the lockjaw, fling you head foremost, and you'll find yourself in a twinkling sticking fast in the centre of the airth! Look at me! Who and what am I?

Nathan. They said you were made for a man, but the work was botched in the doing. (*All laugh*)

Ralph. Stranger, I've heard of you. They say you're a man that holds it agin duty and conscience to kill Injuns, the red-skinned screamers; that refuses to defend the women, the splendiferous critturs, and sees them take their scalps, fire their cottages——

Nathan. (*drops staff*) Ha, then you saw it too! Wretch! Did you behold the roof-tree blaze, crackle, crash, topple and fall? Did you see the flashing axe descend? Did you see her warm young blood gushing in living streams, flashing, bubbling, flowing around your feet? And did you stand by without one blow? Eternal curses blast ye for it! Were you as solid as the rooted earth, hard as the massive rock, scorching as flame, or raging as the sea—thus, thus, would I seize you by the throat and dash you down to hell! (*Music.* Nathan *dashes* Ralph *to the ground*) Ha, ha, ha! The cry is up and shouts are loud for vengeance! Strike! Kill! Slay! Blood—blood! No peace—no peace!

Music. All shout. Nathan *rushes out.*

Roland. He has killed the man—but he provoked his fate.
Ralph. (*rising*) Thanks to you, stranger; but not so dead as you reckon! Here's my shoulders, but where's my head?
Big Tom. Hurrah for Bloody Nathan! He has whipped the Salt River roarer! (*All shout*)
Ralph. Well, I reckon he has. I'm a licked man and can't stay here any longer, no way, no how; so lend me a horse, colonel, and trust to my honour.
Bruce. Where are you going?
Ralph. To St Asaph's, colonel. Only say the word and—tarnal death to me—I'm off like an elk of the prairies!
Bruce. Well, Tom will show you the horse. But remember, you are to leave him at Logan's; if you carry him a step farther, you'll never carry another. Judge Lynch is looking at you; so beware!
Ralph. Honour bright, colonel. There's my paw, and that's gospel! 'Help him that needs help'—that's the rule for a Christian. So farewell, colonel; same to you, stranger. Come along, Big Tom Bruce. I'll be off like a streak of lightning through a gooseberry bush!

Exit Ralph, *with* Big Tom Bruce. *Stage gradually grows dark, and the moon is now seen through the trees.*

Bruce. Well, captain, I suppose you and your friends will not object to a little snoozing after your tramp, though I'm afraid we shall find but close quarters for so many. So let the women be snugly stowed and, as the weather's dry, the men won't object to the open air.
Roland. That is no inconvenience to a soldier, my friend. I for one will even seek repose where it seeks me. The grass is soft, and I fatigued enough to sleep soundly on a far worse couch than this. So good night to all! (*Music. All exeunt*) Heaven protect my Edith, and may dreams visit her couch pure as her angel spirit. Sleep has me wholly.

He spreads his cloak on bank, and lies down. Music. He sleeps. Telie *enters, closes gate, listens.*

Telie. He sleeps. All are wrapped in slumbers. Now to warn him of his fate! He little dreams of what he may suffer. Shall I wake him? No; his fatigue demands repose. Yet will I whisper in his ear a warning counsel. (*Goes to* Roland *and whispers*) Cross by the lower ford; the upper one is beset by foes. Beware! Be wise, Roland Forrester!
(*Retires. Music*)

Roland. (waking) Ha! Is there witchcraft in this wild western land? Sure,
I heard a voice direct my course for tomorrow? It was but fancy.
Our path lies by the upper ford; I must not alter it.

Telie. (without) There certain death awaits thee.

Roland. Ha, again! This time I dream not. Who art thou?

Telie. The lower ford, remember!

Roland. Sure, this is but some trick of Bruce's sons to try my temper or
my courage; and yet the voice was as soft as woman's. Be it what it
may, it concerns not me; nor shall they laugh at my credulity.

Music. He lies down and sleeps. Braxley *appears on bridge, crosses and
enters through gate.*

Braxley. Hark ye, Jack Atkins, or Doe, or whatever you choose to call
yourself. Where are you?

Doe *enters.*

Are you mad, or asleep? What are you dreaming about?

Doe. Why, curse it, if you must know, I was thinking about young
Roland. If he must die the dog's death, let the dogs do it. Christian
work for Christian men, say I!

Braxley. Pshaw, Jack! You're growing sentimental. We've got the bird
safely caged, and I'm not going to lose all my trouble for nothing.
Besides, consider: it'll make your fortune.

Doe. So you told me before, when you made me perjure myself, like a
lying white Injun that I am; and that's more despisable than all the
rest.

Braxley. Well, cheer up! Help me to secure the girl; and as you're too
tender-hearted to give the captain his sleeping draught, why, we'll
get one of the red dogs to do it for us. So; now to reconnoitre the
station.

Music. They go out, and over the bridge. Telie *watches them off.*

Telie. Ah, the murderers here! They seek his life. Quick! to alarm the
station.

As she is going out, Braxley, Doe *and* Piankeshaw *enter.*

It is too late—they return. *(Conceals herself)*

Braxley. Hist, hist! The least noise would alarm the station. Now to
discover our prey! *(They search round; see* Roland. *Chord)* Hush, we
have him here! *(To* Piankeshaw) Mark the spot, and let your tomahawk be buried deep in my rival's heart!

As they are about to despatch Roland, Telie *catches* Braxley's *arm, and*
Doe *stays* Piankeshaw. *Chord.*

Telie. Hold, murdering villains! Richard Braxley, forbear!

Braxley. Ha! What meddling intruder's this? Whoe'er thou art, think not to betray us.

Music. They rush upon her; she eludes them and hides behind gate, and as they pass out in pursuit she closes gate upon them and bars it. Music changes. She comes down, kneels, blesses Roland, and exit. Piankeshaw returns, climbs over wall and comes down.

Piankeshaw. White man think. Red man do. Long knife asleep; Piankeshaw take his scalp, and give it to his squaw in his wigwam. Softly, softly as the creeping panther!

Music. As he goes up to despatch Roland, Nathan appears, cloaked. Hurry. He seizes Piankeshaw.

Nathan. Dog of an Indian, red skin, red wolf, die! Murdering coward, die a murderer's death! (*Dashes him down and places cross on his breast*) Blood for blood! Remember the avenger!

Rushes out. Loud thunder. Roland starts up.

Roland. Ha, a storm has risen wildly! (*Sees body*) How! What's here? The lightning flashes on a blood-stained corpse! Ha, within there! Help, if ye be men!

Music. Colonel Bruce and all the Settlers rush on.

Bruce. (*raising body*) What's here? The Jibbenainosay is up again! Here's his mark upon his breast.
Roland. In the name of heaven, who has done this deed?
Nathan. (*appearing suddenly on bridge*) 'Twas I, the Jibbenainosay!

Music. Picture of horror. Lightning, thunder, &c. Tableau.

ACT II

Scene 1. *The station at Brucetown. Time: sunrise.* Emigrants *discovered, preparing to depart.* Mrs Bruce, Phoebe *and* Nell *enter to assist them.*

Emigrants.   CHORUS
> Away, away; 'tis break of day,
> In the east the sun is dawning.
> With speed and care our march prepare,
> In the pleasant morning.

Enter Roland *and* Edith.

Roland. Gaily sung, my friends. I am glad to find that, in spite of last night's storm, you are so early afoot. To horse then, my men, and away for St Asaph's! We must be through the cane-brake ere the sun gives us his sultry greeting.

Edith. How bright and beautiful is all around us! The sweet song of the blackbird and the cry of the whippoorwill seem to invite us to their leafy homes. The fresh green turf spreads a fragrant carpet for our feet, and the breeze, which stirs the forest leaves, whispers on my ear a most enchanting music.

Roland. Bravely said, my beloved Edith. How it delights me to see you thus contented and cheerful! Now to speak to our kind, hospitable host the painful word 'Farewell'; and then wend upon our way.

Bruce. (*without*) The unpronounceable rascal!

Enter Colonel Bruce.

A brave morrow to you, captain.

Roland. Why, what is the matter, worthy sir?

Bruce. Matter enough; and, besides, it consarns you and me more than any other two on airth. There's been a black wolf in the camp, and your blooded brown mare has absquatulated—stolen by that etarnal roaring Ralph Stackpole! And here's the history of the case. I loaned him one of my own critturs, jest to get rid of him. Well, what does the brute do but ride off till he was out of sight, and then down he sot in ambush till all was quiet, when he comes back, turned my hoss among the others, and helped himself to your blooded brown—the etarnal villain!

Roland. I must follow the rascal instantly. Would I had known this earlier!

Bruce. And whar was the use? Thar was not two minutes lost after the hoss was missing afore my son Tom and a dozen others war galloping after, right on the brute's trail.

Roland. Colonel, your promptitude demands my thanks. (*To Emigrants*) Friends, I confess I am unwilling to leave behind my noble charger; yet let me not detain you in your march. You shall proceed. I will overtake you ere the sun sets, if Colonel Bruce will lend us an escort.

Bruce. Sartain, captain; and if a fresh leg can outrun a weary one, you shall find your friends before they reach the cane-brake.

Edith. The delay, then, will be nothing. We shall but exchange the slow pace of the march for a gay and beautiful gallop through the woods, and rejoin our friends before they cross the ford. For a short time then, farewell!

Music. The Emigrants *all exeunt, singing the opening chorus.*

Bruce. There they go; good fortune go with them! And now, my young lady, here's my old woman and the gals will show you round the station, while I and the captain await the horsemen's return.

Mrs Bruce. (*as she goes*) Come, miss; I'm proper glad you're left behind.

(*Exeunt* Edith, Mrs Bruce *and the girl.*)

Bruce. Take my word for it, captain, that etarnal skurmudgeon will see the end of his thievery. I told him Judge Lynch was out, and the boys will take care I was not found lying. If he don't neck a rope's end, why, there's no hemp in Kentuck.

Roland. Surely, colonel, they will not hang a fellow of such intrepidity?

Bruce. I hope not; but it's hard telling. I do like the brute; he's a screamer among the Injuns. But thar's no standing a hoss thief—the unpronounceable scoundrel!   (*Shouts heard without*)

Roland. Colonel, you have prophesied truly; for here they come and with them my charger.

> *More shouts. Enter* Young Tom Bruce.

Young Tom. Thar's your hoss, stranger. I reckon the crittur's a bit warmed, though, with his morning's work; but that's nothing to speak on.

Bruce. But where's that brute Stackpole?

Young Tom. There, dad, you're too hard for me. The lynch boys are arter him, and now we'll feel easier about our hosses.   (*Shouts heard*)

Roland. What mean those sounds of alarm?

Bruce. Something out of kilter, I reckon; for here comes Big Tom Bruce, snorting like a Kentucky war horse.

> *Enter* Big Tom Bruce *and* Little Tom Bruce.

Big Tom. There's a thousand Injuns—Shawnees, Delawares and Miamies —all laying siege to Bryant's Station!

Bruce. Send out men without delay. Some of you off for Logan and his forces. Here, Little Tom Bruce, mount the roan Longlegs and fly to St Asaph's. 'Tis high time you were trying your hand at an Indian's topknot.

Little Tom. Uoh, uoh, uoh!   (*Exit hastily*)

Bruce. (*calling after him*) Ride, you brute, ride! Who brought the news, Tom?

Big Tom. Nathan Slaughter.

Bruce. Tell Colonel Logan before he can draw girth I shall be with every fighting man in my fort on the north side of Kentucky. Sound the horn, Tom. Ride for your life.

> Big Tom *exit; horn sounds, and shouts heard.*

Whar's Bloody Nathan? Here, you Satan's imp, you no-souled crittur! Where in the devil's name are you?

> *Enter* Nathan.

Nathan. You need not call so loud; I hear you. I come for some corn. Shall I have it?

Bruce. Where have you been wandering? Tell us what you have seen.

Nathan. A sight worth seeing, a sight worth living for, a sight worth dying for! I saw the red Indians arming to a man; I saw the feather-tinctured chief brandish his tomahawk; I saw the fire-eyed savage whet his scalping knife for the young and the brave; I saw—but I want the corn, so I came for it.

Bruce. And why?

Nathan. I see the clouds, but ask them not from whence they come; I hear the wind, but demand not whither it goeth. As the green leaves turn crimson and then fall to the earth, so pass all things through my brain—gorgeous of hue, but withering, withering away. Can I have the corn?

(*Crosses to door*)

Bruce. Will you not join our men? Will you not lead the way, and fight agin the Injuns?

Nathan. I lead the way? I came for corn. I dip my hands in blood? Shall I have it? Not I—I am a man of peace. What though your numbers be scattered, your homestead fired, and your very name become extinct? What though this should happen?

Bruce. What then?

Nathan. Why, better men than you have borne it before you.

Bruce. Miscreant of humanity! Tell me whar the Injuns are concealed, or I'll have your cowardly hide flogged off of you!

Nathan. I shall not be the first or last to witness man's injustice.

Bruce. Wretch! I'll send a ball through your skull that shall let out your crazy brains!

Nathan. Today we live; tomorrow we die.

(*Crosses to exit*)

Bruce. Come, come, Nathan. Good, kind Nathan, leave your haunt in the forest and dwell with us.

Nathan. Ha, ha, ha! I dwell with thee? My home is with the invisible spirits of earth and air—the spirits of the departed. They whisper me in the rustling leaves, kiss my hot brain in the foaming breeze, and weep for my wrongs in the falling dew. But there is one with a deep gash across her white breast, who beckons me to a land where sorrow is not and death cannot enter, where all is peace, peace. Will you give me the corn?

Re-enter Edith.

Roland. I think I have observed where the wanderer's heart is vulnerable. Nathan, you are an outcast; and yet the time has been, perhaps, when home and social ties were yours. Memory is deeply steeped in oblivion, yet some sparks may flash across the darkness to tell of mother, wife or child. (*Leads* Edith *across*) Look upon this fair girl; she may recall the memory of former days.

Music. Edith *kneels to* Nathan, *who becomes gradually moved, and kisses her brow in emotion.*

80

Nathan. The blessings of a tearless eye and a blighted heart be upon thee. Go. Tell them to meet their foes at the ford of Kentucky.

(*Exit*)

Bruce. Well, that's a queer crittur. I tried to reason with him, but he's as wild and skeery as Old Nick himself. But I must be off.

Re-enter Big Tom Bruce *and* Young Tom Bruce.

Big Tom. The Injuns are marching towards the district of Kentucky, in greater force than was ever seen in the land before.

Bruce. Let 'em come, the brutes! Call out Ikey Jones the fifer. Tell Ben Sharp to rouse the reg'lators. Them that ain't ready to start, tell 'em to follow on to the ford of Kentucky; and them that can't join me thar, let 'em follow on to Lexington; and if they don't find me thar, let 'em go on to Bryant's, or anywhar thar's Injuns. Hurrah, you brutes!   (*Exit* Big Tom Bruce)

Roland. Come, Edith. We must prepare to follow our friends before the path is rendered impracticable.

Bruce. And we, who war to be your escort, captain—but you are a soldier, and see the case.

Roland. I do, and have no desire to weaken your force. One man is all I ask, as a guide.

Bruce. The guide is chosen, prepared and ready.

Enter Telie.

Telie. Not a man can be spared. I will be your guide!

Roland. You? I cannot expose you to such a danger.

Telie. To me the danger is nothing to what it may be to yonder fair girl. Every moment that you delay, your danger increases.

Roland. But thus to drag you from your home is but a thankless payment for such kindness.

Telie. I'll guide you safe; I know the path, ay, every inch of it. For seven years I've traversed the wild woods, and know the course will lead you free from danger. Fear not, but follow; and when you reach your destined home, you'll think of her who saved you from impending danger.

Bruce. You needn't be alarmed, captain; there's not a mark about the station for twenty miles that she don't know. So farewell, lady; good luck to you, captain. I'm sorry to part so unceremonious-like, but when there's a thousand Injuns ready cut up and dried for killing—why, duty is duty, you know.

Roland. Success attend you, colonel. I trust that we shall meet again; and believe me, I shall not forget your hospitality.

Telie. The day is waning fast; already does the joyous sun smile on the lake, and pour from diamond urns a golden shower which, beautifying, gilds this gorgeous drapery of autumn. Then let us hasten on our way; benighted in these wild woods will expose us to a danger to which our weakness would fall an easy prey.

Roland. Let us proceed, then, at once.

Music. They take leave of Colonel Bruce *and exeunt, preceded by* Telie. *Shouts heard; enter all the* Settlers, *armed.*

Bruce. Now, boys, if you're all ready, let's tote off at once. You must fight like wild cats, for if thar's half as many as they say, thar's Injun meat enough for us all. So strike up 'Yankee Doodle' or 'The Rogue's March', for by the etarnal old scratch all them white men that ain't a-horseback in twenty-five minutes are rogues worse than the red Injuns.

Music. All shout and march off, headed by Colonel Bruce.

Scene 2. *A cut wood.*

Enter Braxley *and* Abel Doe.

Braxley. Come, cheer up, my jolly Jack. You've less brains than I've given you credit for. We had bad luck with the matter at first, I know; but now all's safe, and if you'll only stand by me in this business I'll make you rich; and as to being a rascal, why, it's only being a man of sense provided you are a rascal in a sensible way— that is, a profitable one.

Doe. That is the doctrine you've been preaching up ever since I knowed you, and you've made a fortin by it; but as for me, I've toed the crack after your own leading, and I'm just as poor as ever and ten times more despisable.

Braxley. Pshaw, Jack, don't be impatient. You know I told you, when you took the girl and adopted her as your own, that the instant I secured the estate of the old major you should share the plunder; and as Edith and the youngster are co-heirs, the latter put out of the way—you understand—will make his portion less, which, when the matter's ended, as I promised, shall be yours. In a word, Jack, I design to marry the sole claimant and heir at law, and step into the estate with a clear conscience.

Doe. But there's the will you got up such a cry about! There's them in Virginny that know the affair, and won't let it drop so easy. You take the gal back, and the cry is 'Where's the true gal, the major's daughter?' I reckon you'll find yourself in a trap of your own making.

Braxley. Why, in that case, Jack, all we have to do is to act as it were like honest men, and find—after much hunting, mind you—the major's last will.

Doe. But you told me that you burnt it.

Braxley. I know I told you so, friend Jack, but that was a little bit of a deception to make you easy. Here it is. (*Produces will*) I kept it, you see, to guard against accidents. Will this satisfy you all is safe?

Doe. It's just the thing, to an iota. There's no standing agin that in any court in Virginny. (*Yell without*)

Braxley. Hark! The Indians we placed on the scent have found the track, and their fate is certain. The girl be it my task to secure. As for the guide, dispose of her as you will; but the soldier dies!

Music. A party of Indians *cross from* L *to* R *cautiously, as if examining the footprints on the ground, and exeunt, followed by* Braxley *and* Doe.

Scene 3.   *Forest. On one side is an old log hut, partly destroyed by fire; the whole scene bearing a wild and desolate appearance.*

Enter Roland *supporting* Edith, *followed by* Telie Doe.

Edith. Alas! I can go no farther; my limbs refuse their office. Leave me, Roland, and seek your own safety in flight.

Roland. Leave thee, my Edith? Never! If we must perish, we will die together! (*To* Telie) O generous maiden, thou hast perilled life for us. Is there no hope?

Telie. Yes—in heaven! I warned you to avoid this path, but you would not heed me. But see, here is a place of shelter; let us enter it, and may heaven befriend us!

Music. Telie *leads* Edith *towards the hut; as they are about to enter it,* Nathan *appears at the door. Chord. They recoil.*

Nathan. Who are you, and what do you seek in the refuge of the outcast and the wanderer?

Roland. Strange being, by what unknown power do you traverse the pathless wilderness, and confront us at every turn? What mysterious destiny unites our fates?

Nathan. An evil one to you. Be sure that want and woe, madness and misery, dog my steps; no living thing that sheltered beneath my wings but fell a victim to my baleful fate. Fly me, avoid me! The raging pestilence has less of venom, the murdering savage more pity.

Telie. The gale is freshening, and the elm boughs rustle loudly in the wind. Outcast and wanderer though you be, you will not refuse shelter to the forlorn and fainting stranger?

Nathan. You say truly; I cannot and I will not. Enter, daughter of affliction; enter the abode of misery.

Music. Nathan *leads* Edith *into hut.*

Roland. My brain turns; my senses reel! Edith brought by me to perish in this wilderness! Maiden, give me some hope, some means of freeing her, or look to see me in mad frenzy fall upon my sword and end my most worthless life.

Telie. Be not rash, Roland Forrester, and I will save you from the impending ruin that surrounds you. Beware of one who follows in your path, to meet with whom would be more dangerous than to grapple with the wounded tiger.

Roland. By heaven, you speak of Richard Braxley!

Telie. He seeks your life, to rob you of your Edith and bear her off to revel in the splendour his villainy has deprived you of; but I will thwart him.

Roland. How can I thank this devoted interest for a stranger?

Telie. By recollecting one who has long remembered you. Have you forgotten, when wounded at the Battle of James's River, when, by all deserted, you were left for dead, a stranger came to bathe your wounds, and watch returning life which slowly beamed upon your pallid brow? And oh, the joy, the transport, which filled that stranger's breast, to find herself the happy instrument of saving one so brave, so noble! You returned to the fight; nor saw her more till kind Providence hither bent your steps, to bless the heart which, though all forsake, will still beat true to you.

Roland. Amazement! How shall I repay such kindness and faith?

Telie. It cannot be repaid. How can you look with gratitude upon one who is the offspring of an outcast, or favour with your smile the daughter of a renegade?

Roland. Sweet girl, were you fathered by a fiend, your virtues would redeem him. Speak your request.

Telie. Roland Forrester, I——   (*Yells heard*)

Roland. Ha! They are upon us. Now to conquer or die!

Re-enter Nathan *hastily, from hut.*

Nathan. No; there is no Indian living will approach this fated spot when evening shadows fall. As yet, the danger comes not. Young maid, thou hast dared as women dare for those they love. Be of good cheer; courage and constancy still may save them. They will be saved; but thou, maiden, thou hast the stamp upon thy brow, the fatal signet which these eyes can read, that tells of wasted love, blighted hopes, and early death. Go in, girl! Mine eyes would weep again, did they gaze longer on thee.   (*Leads* Telie *into hut, and returns*)

Roland. Nathan, you are a man of peace. You hold blood-guiltiness a sin. To you the Indians are not hostile. Tell me, is there no hope of safety or escape?

Nathan. Young soldier, 'tis scarcely five years since these eyes witnessed, on this fearful spot, a tragedy so terrible that nothing ever can compare with it in ghastly horror. You who live in peace and plenty know not the fearful deeds done on the western border. I tell you, boy, this clay whereon you tread was saturated with the warm life's blood of the young, the beautiful and beloved. Yon blackened ruins are mingled with their cinders, and these giant oaks, these hoary woods, echoed to their dying shrieks. All died—the aged matron, lifting her withered hands to bless her grandchild's wedding, the manly father, the kindly mother, the nursing infant, and she, the pride of all, the pearl, the lovely flower that twined its gorgeous blossoms around the heart and was to each and all a blessing, the pride of all, the virgin bride—and they slew her on her wedding day, while love's purest vows were on her lips. I saw the blow descend, the blood-smeared tomahawk. I felt the life's blood gushing on my face. I heard her dying shriek, and could not save her! Young man, marvel not that I wander now a thing distraught, a wrecked and wretched outcast. *(Falls prostrate)*

Roland. (raising him) In heaven's name, of whom do you speak?

Nathan. Of the family of Ashburn. Their untombed spirits are here around me. They linger yet for vengeance. See there! look where even **now** she stands, folding her bridal robe around that bleeding wound! See how mournfully she lifts her eyes to mine! Depart not yet, spirit of the beloved! Soon will the work of vengeance be complete, and I rejoin thee in the land where all is peace. See, she beckons me—she passes—she is gone! Shade of the lovely and beloved, I follow you! *(Music. Rushes out)*

Roland. Eternal heaven, in what a situation am I placed! Two helpless women depending on me for protection, surrounded by foes, ignorant of the forest, and unaided by a single friend! Hark! Surely I heard a footstep?

Music. Yells heard. Wenonga *and two* Indians *rush on.*

Wenonga. Ha! The pale-face! I am Wenonga, the Black Vulture of the Shawnees. I am Wenonga, and have no heart!

Roland. Demon! This to prove thy words!

Music. Roland *and* Wenonga *struggle off; and as the two* Indians *are following,* Ralph Stackpole *enters, shoots one and knocks the other down, jumps on him and crows.*

Ralph. Arn't you got it, you tarnal half-imp! You nigger-in-law to old Satan! Thar's a par on you.

Re-enter Roland.

Holloa thar, captain! Ain't I licked 'em handsome? Hurrah for Kentuck and Old Salt! Cock-a-doodle-doo!

Roland. Stackpole, my friend! 'Twas you who saved me, then?

Ralph. Tarnal death to me! Yes, captain, I knew it was you in a squabbification. I heerd the yelling. 'Thar's Injuns' says I, so I jumped into a sugar trough, and if I didn't bring her down over them thar falls faster than a well-greased thunderbolt and slicker than snakes, niggers ain't niggers nor Injuns Injuns.

Roland. Worthy fellow, save but my Edith and all I possess on earth shall be yours.

Ralph. I'm the gentleman to see her out of a fight, tarnal death to me! I'll mount Shawnees, and die for her just like nothing; so bring along the angeliferous crittur, and I'll tote her down the falls in the dugout, like a colt in a cornfield.

Roland. Down that raging flood? Impossible!

Ralph. That's what I'm here arter, sodger; not to talk of cannot, but to show that I'm the man to die dog for them that pats me, for I'm all fight from top to bottom, and thar ain't no more run in me than thar is in a snail with the slow fever.

Roland *brings* Edith *and* Telie *down.*

Roland. Look up, sweet Edith; all is safe.

Ralph. O you angeliferous madam! Just look up, and say the word. Here am I, Ralph Stackpole the screamer, that can whip all Kentuck, white, black, mixed or Injun; and thump me round the airth with a crab-apple if I don't help you out of the bushes and do all your fighting, tarnal death! I'm getting so awful rily, that it'll take all the fish-skin in creation to settle me.

Music. All exeunt.

Scene 4.   *Rocky pass and waterfall.*

Music agitato. Enter Telie Doe, Edith, Roland *and* Ralph.

Telie. Here, sweet lady, for a while I must leave you.

Edith. Leave us? You surely will not forsake me now?

Telie. Forsake you, lady! The mysteries of these forest wilds forbid me further to accompany you; yet when danger lurks unseen, you'll find I'll not desert you.

Edith. I see your motive. 'Tis plain you would ensnare us; for that you led us hither. Go, deceitful girl; this treachery will meet with its reward.

Telie. Lady!—But no; I will not upbraid you. The time will come when you will feel how deadly your suspicion wrongs me; yet ere I go, know that my case is just—is pure. The faggots are prepared, the torch impregnates the air, and the murderers prowl to drink their

victims' blood! Lady, farewell. You may yet learn to love and trust
the daughter of the renegade. (*Exit*)

Ralph. Never mind the gal. She'll make one less to sink the dug-out. Thar
she flops about among the snags! Thar's a boiling pot above and a
boiling gulf below; and if you ever seed etarnity at midnight, you'll
see a sample on it now. Arn't I the crittur to shake old Salt by the
forepaw? Arn't I the leaping trout of the waters? Can take angeliferous madam down any shoot as ever was seed equal to a streak of
lightning. If I can't, may I be tee-to-taciously explunctified! (*Exeunt*)

Scene 5. *View of Salt River, with the cataract in motion. Moonlight. Set
rocks, and two practicable.*

Enter Ralph, Roland *and* Edith.

Ralph. Roll away, old Salt! Ain't I the crittur for you? Don't mind the
old fellow, splendiferous madam, for thar's more in his bark than his
bite. Tarnal death to me, he looks as sweet and as lickerish as a
whole trough full of sugar tree. We'll just take a dip at him to wash
the mud off our shoes, and then say farewell to old Salt and the
aborigines together.

Music. Yells heard. Wenonga *and* Indians *rush on;* Wenonga *seizes*
Edith, *and throws her round to* Braxley *who enters.* Wenonga *disarms*
Roland, *who is seized with* Ralph *by* Indians.

Braxley. Now, Edith Forrester, now thou art wholly mine!

Ralph. Grim death and massacreation! O you perditioned brutes! Let
me loose, you sum totalized red niggers, or tarnal death to me, I'll
haunt you when I'm dead and eat you all, from a smoke-dried
varmint skurmudgeon to a squally babby papoose.

Music. Wenonga *aims a blow at* Edith; Braxley *catches his arm. At the
same time* Abel Doe *rushes on and strikes at* Roland, *but is prevented by*
Telie, *who follows him on.*

Telie. Beware the ambush! Beware the Jibbenainosay!

Braxley. Man or devil, phantom or fiend, thus I claim my prey!

Music. He seizes Edith, *and is bearing her up the rock when the*
Jibbenainosay *is precipitated down the cataract in a canoe of fire; the* Indians
*all utter a yell of horror, and fall on their faces. Tableau of astonishment by
the others.*

ACT III

Scene 1. *Wood and cut wood.*

Roland *discovered, lying wounded. Music.*

Roland. Gone—all gone! Wretch that I am, why should my life be spared? Edith—she who alone did make life blessed and valuable—is lost to me for ever, borne from me by savages. I cannot follow her. My blood flows fast. Thus, then, do I cast away the lingering remnants of a wasted life.

Music. He is about to throw himself upon his sword when Nathan *enters through cut wood, and arrests his arm.*

Nathan. Madman, hold thy frantic arm; nor stain the sacred solitude of nature with thy suicidal blood. Art not ashamed to bear the form and wear the reason of a man, yet shrink away to howl and die like a wounded reptile in its lair? Up, up for shame, and learn that whatever may be thy woe, earth holds those more wretched still.

Roland. Impossible! No combination of all fearful things e'er caused a misery like mine! Man, strange in thy speech and strong in heart, hadst thou e'er loved and like me lost the object of thy passion, like me wouldst thou fall prostrate on the earth and curse thy fate as I do.

(Falls exhausted)

Nathan. Frenzied fool, be still! Thou knowest not what thou sayest. Art thou wretched because thine eyes did not behold the Indian axe cleave through her brain? Dost thou complain because her death cry did not fall on thy startled ear? Impatient and ungrateful fool! When thou hast seen the old grey-haired mother that loved thee, the innocent sister who nursed at the same breast, the bride who was entwined with thy heart's cords—if thou hadst seen these butchered in thy sight, if thou hadst felt their hot blood spout upon thy breast where they had lain in love, if thou hadst heard their appalling cries for help, stricken before thy face by the red, murdering Indians, then, then what hadst thou done?

Roland. Declared eternal war upon them and their accursed race, sworn undying vengeance, and sought it without ceasing!

Nathan. Thou answerest rightly. *(Takes his hand)* By day and by night, in the wood and in the wigwam, through summer and rough winter, thou wouldst hunt their hearts' black blood; to vengeance thou wouldst dedicate thy life and limb, heart and soul, all. All of the accursed and branded thou wouldst kill, kill. Up then, and follow in the track! Neither faint nor flag. Halt not for pity or for fear, and the maiden will again be thine.

Roland. By heaven, you have given me new life and hope! Lead on!
Yet which path shall we pursue? I know not the capturing Indians.

Nathan. But I know full well; ay, to my inmost soul, each nerve and
pulse within me answers to his name, and calls aloud for vengeance
on Wenonga! Wenonga, the Black Vulture of the Shawnees!
Wenonga, the faithless, blood-stained slayer of helpless innocents!
Wenonga—but the foot of the avenger is on his trail. (*War whoop
without*) Ha! Some of the murdering band return. Away! Here
conceal thyself, and let me bind thy wounds. Fail not, and fear not.

Music. Nathan *exits* R *with* Roland, *as* Ralph *enters* L, *disguised as an
Indian.*

Ralph. Whoo, whoo, whoop! Tarnal death to me, here am I, Roaring
Ralph the ring-tailed squealer! I reckon my tracks measure like a
streak of lightning. Here, you tarnal, temporal, long-legged, tater-
headed, pumpkin-eating red niggers! You coon whelps! Get up and
show yourselves; for I'm the man to fight, take a scalp, shake a fist,
show a leg, or anything you please, in reason or out of reason.

Roland *enters and strikes* Ralph *down.*

Roland. Die, dog of an Indian!
Ralph. Tarnal death to you, white man! What are you arter?
Roland. How! Is it possible? Do I see Captain Ralph Stackpole?
Ralph. Why, death and massacreation, captain, is it you?
Roland. Why—how did you escape? I saw you taken prisoner with
mine own eyes.
Ralph. Captain, that's more than I can tell you. But here I am, come to
help angeliferous madam out of the hands of them Injuns, according
to my sworn duty as her natural born slave and redemptioner. I was
hard on the track when you doused me with your flapper.
Roland. I apologize for the blow I gave you. Will you join me in the
pursuit?
Ralph. Sartain, captain. We'll snuff the track together, and while you're
hunting up the angeliferous crittur I'll steal a hoss for her to ride off
upon.
Roland. I like your scheme; but indeed, Ralph, you have such ill luck
following you that I am almost afraid of you.
Ralph. Afeared of me? Ain't I just slicked myself out of the paws of
five mortal aborigines? And ain't that luck enough for any fellow?
Only wait, and I'll show you a sample of hoss stealing that'll make
your hair stand on end; and there's no two ways about it.

Re-enter Nathan.

Nathan. You are welcome, woodsman, in a needful time. We must start
for the village of the Black Vulture on the instant.

Ralph. In that case, I'm your crittur. I say, old Bloody, you're the man that doused my house in a fair tussle, and I'll lick any man that says a word agin you.

Nathan. I will enter the village, disguising myself in these Indian habiliments. Thou, young soldier, and this rough fellow, shall bide at hand till I return from reconnoitring. If I fall, the maiden's fate remains with thee. But be patient and prudent, and all shall be well.

Ralph. But I say, do you think I've come so far arter madam to give up the helping her to any two-legged crittur whatsoever? I'm the crittur that knows this here town, injacent, outjacent and sarcumsurrounding, and that I'll stick to; for cuss me I've stole hosses in it!

Nathan. Content thee, my friend. There is neither stone nor tree, fence nor wigwam, in Wenonga's village but is known to me in darkness as in light. Strip the clothing off the wolf; 'twill serve to free the lamb.

Ralph. Well, if it's your opinion I'll serve madam better by snugging under a log than by sniffen arter her among the cabins, why, I'm just the gentleman to knock under conformable to reason.

(*Gives* Nathan *his blanket and head-dress*)

Nathan. (*lays hand on* Roland's *arm*) Listen, young man, to me, and heed well my words. If, by any foolish desire to strike against your cousin's captors, you leave the ambush I assign to you, deeply will you rue your madness. Trust her deliverance to me, whose arm is strong, whose blood is fire, and whose heart is stone. Farewell; and remember well my saying. (*Takes up blanket and exit*)

Ralph. Well, captain, there'll be scalping enough for all three of us, and the sooner we gets at it the better. So, captain, you stick to the crittur and help madam, and I'll take the back track; and if I don't follow arter with the beautifulest lot of horse-flesh that ever was seen, may I be tee-to-taciously chawed up myself.

Roland. Agreed, then; for this inactivity, when Edith's freedom is the work on hand, fires me to madness.

Music. Exeunt Roland L, Ralph R.

Scene 2. *Interior of* Wenonga's *wigwam. Couch, with skins on it, on which* Edith *is asleep.* Telie *seated on stage near her.*

Telie. She sleeps! Worn out with weariness and woe, at length exhausted, she sinks to slumber. Sleep on, sweet lady, and may thy slumber prove a balm to thy despairing heart. Forlorn and wretched captive, what woeful destiny is fate preparing for thee—exposed to the merciless fangs of inhuman fiends who seek to torture and destroy; and, what is far worse, to dread dishonour from the monster who pursues thee; no kinsman to defend, no friend to rescue! But while my feeble arm can aid, will I protect thee with my last drop of blood!

Braxley *enters.*

Braxley. How now, girl, what dost thou here?

Telie. Rather, what dost *thou* here, Richard Braxley? Ay, well may you start at mention of a name so black with crime and treachery.

Braxley. Hence, idle fool! I came not here to listen to thy prating.

Telie. Thou hast; ay and more, thou shalt hear me brand thee for the wretch thou art, thou vile destroyer of the orphan's right and captive's hope, basest of all that bears the name of man, thou villain traitor!

Braxley. By hell, to be thus braved by a puny girl!

Telie. Stand off! Touch me not, or I'll send thy coward soul to endless flames before thy master calls for thee.

Braxley. Death and hell! Thus, then, do I silence thee.

Music. He makes a pass at her, which she eludes. She seizes him by the neck and hurls him down, and stands over him with gun. Edith *rises and comes down. Picture.*

Edith. Hold! In mercy, hold! Peril not your life to leave me friendless. In pity, do not desert me!

Telie. Fear not, lady; I will not forsake you. For thee, base villain, hear and heed me well: dare but to offer violence to this defenceless maiden, and prepare thy soul for the blasting doom now hovering over thy treacherous head. Beware! Tempt not the vengeance of one who dares defy thee!

Exit with gun. Edith *retires to couch.*

Braxley. Mad, busy, meddling fool! She must be silenced; and then my work of toil is ended, and Edith Forrester becomes wholly mine. (*Calls*) Here, Jack Atkins, Doe, Shawnegenwam! Where are you loitering?

Enter Abel Doe.

Doe. Why, what's the matter, Dick Braxley? You look skeery.

Braxley. Curses on that girl! But for her I should have gained my purpose.

Doe. Come, come, Dick; no words agin the gal. Say what you like agin me, but I'll stand no larking agin Telie Doe.

Braxley. Why, she's a good and a pretty one, but she's likely to prove a dear bargain to both of us. Only let me get a flash at her!

(*Presents pistols, off*)

Doe. Coward! Dare but to point your weapon agin that gal, and I'll denounce you to the judges and show you for what you are.

Braxley. Indeed? Do your worst; I defy and curse you.

Doe. A friend today and an enemy tomorrow, as the saying is. You'll repent this. (*Exit*)

Braxley. Look up, Edith Forrester. I am no savage. Do you know me?

Edith. I know you too well: Richard Braxley, the persecutor of the helpless orphan. Are you not content?

Braxley. Anger has not alienated, contempt has not estranged me; I am still the friend of Edith Forrester. (*Approaching her*)

Edith. Approach me not, or I will call for help.

Braxley. And from whom do you expect it? From wild, besotted Indians who, if roused from their drunken slumbers, would be more likely to dispatch you with their weapons than to pity your sorrows?

Edith. O, man, man! Why do you thus persecute me?

Braxley. Promise to be mine, or you quit not this spot with life.

Edith. Let it be so, then; kill me if you will. Death is more welcome than the title of wife to thee.

Braxley. Hear me, Edith Forrester. You are mine beyond the hope of escape, proud girl! Mine, though I should wade through fire and blood to gain my purpose. Who can or dare deny it?

Music. Nathan *enters, disguised as an Indian, and forces* Braxley *down.*

Nathan. That dare I! Speak, and thou diest! One word or stir, and the knife is at thy throat! Now, maiden, thou art rescued. Now thou art safe. Fear not, and speak not. (*Binds* Braxley; *is going off with* Edith; *shouts heard without*) Hark! The cry is up. Silence is now our only chance of stealing from the cabin. Softly, maiden, softly.

As he leads Edith *to door,* Roland *enters.*

Ha! What dost thou here, madman! Thou hast ruined all. Her fate be upon thy head.

Roland. 'Tis that reckless barbarian, Stackpole; he has let all the horses loose upon the village. Edith, at least we'll die together.

Nathan. Away, away! One blow to save her life! Forward, for the love of heaven, while I keep these at bay.

Music. Hurry. Enter Wenonga *and* Indians. Nathan *springs at* Wenonga, *is secured by* Indians, *and falls on stage. Picture. Closed in.*

Scene 3. *Log hut.*

Enter Indians *conducting* Roland, *bound, followed by* Braxley. Indians *secure* Roland *and exeunt.*

Braxley. So, my gallant rival, you are at length within my power. How like you the galling thongs which bind you to my will? Thy Edith, too, is in my grasp, and waits but for thy death to give a willing consent to our union.

Roland. Liar! Edith consent to become thine? I know her too well. Wert thou to slake at once thy thirst for blood, she never would be thy bride. I defy thy power!

Braxley. Be not too impatient, my valiant hero. My deeds shall speedily test thy courage. Brace thy nerves to bear the fiercest tortures, for when you reach the stake you shall behold Edith Forrester the wedded bride of Richard Braxley. *(Exit)*

Roland. Eternal heaven! Wilt thou not strike with the lightnings of thy anger this fierce destroyer of virgin purity and peace? Wilt thou not send a helping hand to save my Edith?

Enter Telie Doe, *muffled in a cloak.*

Telie. Your prayer is heard! *(Discovers herself)*

Roland. Can it be possible! Do I look upon Telie Doe, the renegade's daughter?

Telie. Not so. My evil star of destiny has passed away, and I am now myself.

Roland. What canst thou mean? Thine eye is flashing and thy step is proud. Are thy fortunes changed?

Telie. (as she unbinds him) Ay, thanks to the great Jehovah! Listen, Roland Forrester. Of my ties and kindred knew I nothing, but now the secret is disclosed. I am the lost child of Major Forrester. That villain Richard Braxley, to make his end secure, tempted and caught the victim of his wishes, and with a bribe he gave the offspring of his patron to Abel Doe, to be consigned to silence and to death. But he relented from his murderous purpose, bore me to these wilds, and reared me as his own. 'Twas but even now he sought and told me all; disclosed to me the villain, his treachery, and his falsehood!

Roland. Sweet girl, I could not wish to claim a nobler kinswoman. May happiness attend thy new-discovered wealth.

Telie. To me that wealth is worthless, unless 'tis shared with thee. Dear Roland, I love thee!

Roland. Now heaven forbid it! To chain the wind, or count the billows of the roaring sea, were less unprofitable than to waste affection upon me. I think that this love is but a vain chimera of a grateful fancy.

Telie. Alas! Then droop my hopes to blight the heart which promised
so much bliss. Roland, though I may not have the form to please the
eye, the face to enchant, yet I have a heart to love as pure and true
as e'er did throb within the breast of earth's most finished daughter!

Roland. Lady, wert thou as far surpassing all created things as heaven
is removed from earth, to me thou couldst be but as a sealed foun-
tain. I love another; have, from infancy to manhood, built my heart's
warmest wishes on my cousin, Edith Forrester. Be, then, as generous
as thou art fair; exert thy power to save her, and I will die content.

Telie. No, you shall not die. Give me that joy which now alone can
speak of comfort to one betrothed to misery and woe; and although
another may possess your heart, yet think with kindness on her who
fondly loves, and loves but to despair. No rival jealousy shall taint
my breast or lead me to an act which heaven spurns. Thou shalt yet
be happy. Thy Edith shall be saved, though my own life purchase
the ransom. *(Exit)*

Roland. Noble-hearted girl! O, woman, woman! In the crowded city or
the silent desert, thou art still the same—faithful in love, fearless in
danger, man's first and last, his surest, truest friend.

(Music. Exit, following Telie)

Scene 4. *Shawnee village. Bridge at back, practicable. Waterfall. Set
rocks.*

Nathan *discovered, bound to stake.* Wenonga *and* Indians *discovered.*

Wenonga. I am Wenonga, the Shawnee chief. I have fought the long
knives and drank their blood. When they hear my voice, they run
howling away like dogs. Their scalps are at my belt. I never feared
the white man. Why should I fear the white man's devil? Where is
the Jibbenainosay, the curse of my tribe? He kills them in the dark.
My brother is a great medicine-man. He knows where to find the
Jibbenainosay, and will show him to me.

Nathan. Wenonga shall see the avenger of the white man's blood.
Wenonga shall see the Jibbenainosay; but he must see him alone.

Wenonga. Let my people and warriors depart. *(Music.* Indians *exeunt)*
I am an old man and a warrior. I had young warriors that would
soon have gone on the war-path. Where are they? The Jibbenainosay
has been in my wigwam. He has killed them all!

Nathan. Ay, all—man, woman, child! There was not one of them
spared, for they were of the blood of Wenonga.

Wenonga. Wenonga is a great chief. He is childless; but childless has
he made the pale-face. My brother shall show me the Jibbenainosay,
or die!

Nathan. The chief lies. He can talk big words to a prisoner, but he fears the Jibbenainosay.

Wenonga. I am a warrior, and will fight the white man's devil.

Nathan. The chief shall see him. Then cut me loose from my bonds, and I will bring him before thee. Wenonga hesitates! Ha, ha, ha! The chief would stand face to face with the Jibbenainosay, yet fears a naked prisoner.

Wenonga. I have heard the voice of the dead, and am not afraid of the living. (*Cuts* Nathan *loose*) Let me see the Jibbenainosay.

Music. Nathan *springs forward, throws off Indian disguise, and appears as* Reginald Ashburn.

Nathan. Behold him here! Look, murdering villain, upon the destroyer of thy race—the avenger of his own! Die, thou human wolf, infuriate tiger, die! Die! (*Hurry. Grapples with* Wenonga, *wrests hatchet from him, and kills him*) And with thy dying glance behold the fearful fiend, the Jibbenainosay, in Reginald Ashburn! Ha, ha, ha! Mother, sister, wife—at last ye are revenged!

> (*Laughs wildly and exit, dragging the body*)

Enter Telie Doe *and* Roland.

Roland. Whither do you lead me, and where is Edith?

Telie. Be patient, and fear not. This way you will elude all search and mock pursuit.

Roland. And Edith?

Telie. Shall follow straight. I'll not deceive you. You shall find me as faithful and as true as when I saved ye as the daughter of the renegade.

Roland. Girl, I dare not trust thee.

Enter Braxley *on bridge.*

Braxley. Ha! What do I see? My rival—and free!

Roland. Yes, villain, to thy confusion! Where is Edith? Give her to me!

Braxley. Never! She is in my power; and thus I secure her mine!

Fires pistol at Roland, *and exit.* Telie *throws herself before him and receives the shot.*

Telie. Thou art saved, dear Roland!

Roland. Generous girl, for me you bleed. My worthless life has cost thee thine. Look up, sweet maid, look up!

Telie. 'Tis happiness to die for one we love. This earth, though full of joys to others, to me has no sacred ties of love. The last glimmer of earthly light is dying from my gaze, the low wind is sighing through the trees, and yonder sunbeam struggling through the clouds of heaven brings a messenger of peace, to bear me to a purer world. Oh, happy flight! I wing my way midst songs of joy! 'Tis transport —ecstasy—'tis sweet oblivion!

Music. She dies; Roland *lays her on bank. Music changes to hurry.* Braxley *appears on bridge, with* Edith *in his arms.*

Braxley. Now, Roland Forrester, I defy thee!

Roland. Monster, hold! By all the feelings in a human breast, by all thy hopes of heaven——

Braxley. Behold thy promised bride! Consent to make her mine, or down yon boiling cataract I'll hurl her to destruction!

Music. Ralph *enters suddenly on bridge; stabs* Braxley.

Ralph. Don't be in a hurry, stranger. (*Throws* Braxley *off bridge*) Give my compliments to old Salt! (*To* Edith) Cheer up, angeliferous crittur! Hurrah for a fight!

Music. Ralph *brings* Edith *down. Screams and yells heard;* Indians *and* Settlers *led by* Colonel Bruce *enter, fighting; the* Indians *are overpowered as* Nathan *enters, dragging body of* Wenonga.

Nathan. Revenge! Revenge!

Bruce. 'Tis Reginald Ashburn!

At the sound of his name, Nathan *pauses, drops the body, relapses from his frenzy, staggers back, and falls into the arms of* Colonel Bruce.

Nathan. Reginald Ashburn! That was indeed my name, ere hell-hounds seared my brain and turned my blood to fire. They murdered all. Have I not been fearfully avenged?

Bruce. You have—fearfully, fatally, avenged!

Nathan. Lift me, lift me! Let me gaze once more upon the sad relics of departed bliss! (*Gazes on scalps*) These flowing ringlets once adorned a form as fair as ever God created or man destroyed—my Alice! Dear remnants of the loveliness for ever lost! My murdered bride, father, mother, child! My work of vengeance is completed. Ye are avenged—terribly avenged! Ha, ha, ha! Hush! Hark! Heard ye not the rustling of leaves, the murmuring of the brook? That is my long-lost home. My Alice awaits me there—my fair, my lovely bride. I come, I come, I come!

Dies. Music. The wigwams are burning. Grand tableau.

The Drunkard

A TEMPERANCE DRAMA IN FOUR ACTS BY 'W. H. SMITH' and 'A GENTLEMAN'

First performed at the Boston Museum, 16 March 1844

CAST

EDWARD MIDDLETON	Mr W. H. Smith
WILLIAM DOWTON, his half-brother	Mr C. W. Hunt
MR CRIBBS, a lawyer	Mr G. H. Wyatt
ARDEN RENCELAW, a philanthropist	Mr G. C. Germon
FARMER GATES	Mr C. H. Saunders
FARMER STEVENS	Mr G. Howard
SAM EVANS } villagers	Mr S. Adams
OLD JOHNSON } villagers	Mr G. E. Locke
BAR-KEEPER of 'The Arbour'	Mr Willard
FIRST LOAFER	Mr J. Adams
SECOND LOAFER	Mr Thompson
LANDLORD	Mr Harris
WATCHMAN	Mr Coad
ERRAND BOY	
BANK MESSENGER	
MRS WILSON	Mrs Woodward
MARY, her daughter	Mrs G. C. Germon
JULIA, her daughter	Miss A. Phillips
AGNES DOWTON, a maniac	Mrs Thoman
PATIENCE BRAYTON, a villager	Mrs C. W. Hunt
MISS SPINDLE, a spinster	

Bridesman, bridesmaid, clergyman, male and female villagers, children, police officers, rowdies, watchmen and mob.

The action takes place over a period of nine years in New York and a village nearby.

Period: 1844

WILLIAM HENRY SEDLEY

Flautist, fencing-master, pugilist, comedian and stage manager. Born
Montgomeryshire, 4 December 1806. Went into the theatre at the age of
fourteen, taking the name of Smith to save the reputation of his family.
Call-boy at Shrewsbury, walking gentleman at Lancaster, and light
comedian at Glasgow. Toured Rochdale as juvenile lead in 1827, then
sailed for Philadelphia to play heroes at the Walnut Street Theatre. In
later years his stately figure, ringing voice and merry laugh made him a
famous Sir Oliver in *The School for Scandal*. Settled in Boston as stage
manager of the Tremont Theatre (1829–36), the National Theatre
(1837–9) and the Boston Museum (1842–55), where he collaborated on
The Drunkard with a local gentleman sometimes identified as the
Temperance poet and preacher, John Pierpoint. Died in San Francisco,
17 January 1872.

THE DRUNKARD

Sedley created the role of Edward Middleton on 16 March 1844 at
Moses Kimball's Boston Museum. There was a rival production at the
Brooklyn City Hotel next month, but *The Drunkard*'s fame did not
really begin until 17 June 1850, when P. T. Barnum, the great show-
man and humbug, added the play to his collection of freaks, Chinese
curios and dioramas at the American Museum in New York. The
Lancashire Bellringers performed between the acts, and afterwards the
audience could sign a gigantic Temperance Pledge in the entrance hall.
With the help of these embellishments, *The Drunkard* became the first
play in New York to run for more than a hundred consecutive performances. By 7 October, it had added another fifty. Barnum's Edward
was the gifted William Goodall, who died of dissipation six years later;
he was succeeded in the role by Moorhouse at Hamblin's Bowery
Theatre (3 July 1850), Harry Watkins at the Academy of Music (20
November 1856), Boniface at the New Bowery (15 February 1866),
C. W. Clarke at Barnum's New Museum, who became so identified with
the role he was known as 'Drunkard Clarke' (18 June 1866), and
William J. Fleming at The City Theatre (16 September 1878).

The first burlesque production I have traced was directed by Miss Mildred Ilse at the Theatre Mart, Los Angeles, on 6 July 1933. It ran continuously for twenty years, then played alternate nights with a mnsical version called *The Wayward Way*, and finally closed on 17 October 1959 after 9,477 performances. This is still a record for the longest run of any show at one theatre anywhere in the world; Agatha Christie's *The Mousetrap* at the Ambassadors Theatre, London, reached 8,839 performances on 1 March 1974, but soon after moved to the St Martin's where it is still going strong. London saw *The Drunkard* at the, Irving Theatre on 9 February 1953, with David Markham as Edward, Sally Cooper as Mary and Frederick Peisley as Lawyer Cribbs; according to *Picture Post* (13 February), the audience 'joined in the proceedings with righteous vigour'. *The Wayward Way* was produced at the Lyric Theatre, Hammersmith, on 16 November 1964, and transferred to the Vaudeville on 28 January 1965; Edward was played by David Holliday and William Dowton by Jim Dale. More recently, a burlesque travesty of *The Drunkard* was presented by five actors at the Howff Theatre Club on 12 February 1974; Mrs Wilson was kept alive for light relief, Cribbs acquired a tool villain, and audiences were promised crates of whisky for the funniest interjection. Finally, a film version of *The Drunkard* was made in 1934 and called *The Old-Fashioned Way*. W. C. Fields appears as an impoverished impresario called The Great McGonigle, now reduced to playing Cribbs in a stock touring company. He is knocked off the stage into the orchestra, the curtain falls painfully upon his foot, and then rises taking his curly black wig with it. The reviews were charitable.

The present text is based upon that published in Lacy, which is virtually a reprint of French's American edition. Internal evidence suggests that this text was prepared for the 1850 revival, which shifted the location of the city scenes from Boston to New York.

ACT I

Scene 1. Interior of a pretty rural cottage—flowers, paintings, &c. Every-thing exhibits taste and simplicity. Table, with Bible and armchair, R. Table and chair, with embroidery frame, L.

Mrs Wilson *discovered in armchair,* Mary *seated by table.*

Mrs Wilson. It was in that corner, Mary, where your poor father breathed his last. This chair is indeed dear to me, for it was in this he sat the very day before he died. Oh, how he loved this calm retreat! and often, in his last illness, he rejoiced that the companion of his youth would close his eyes in these rural shades, and be laid in yon little nook beside him. But now——

Mary. Dear mother, it is true that this sweet cottage is most dear to us, but we are not the proprietors. Old Mr Middleton never troubled us much. But as our worthy landlord is no more, it is generally believed that our dear cottage will be sold.

Mrs Wilson. Ah! It is that I fear; and when I think that you, my beloved child, will be left exposed to the thousand temptations of life—a penniless orphan—— (*Knock heard*) Hark! Who knocks? Dry your tears, my darling. Come in!

Enter Lawyer Cribbs. *He comes down centre.*

Good morning, sir. Mary my child, a chair.

Cribbs. (*sitting*) Good morning, Mrs Wilson. Good morning, my dear young lady. A sad calamity has befallen the neighbourhood, my good Mrs Wilson.

Mrs Wilson. Many a poor person, I fear, will have reason to think so, sir.

Cribbs. Yes, yes—you are right. Ah, he was a good man, that Mr Middleton. I knew him well. He placed great confidence in my advice.

Mary. Was he not very rich once, Mr Cribbs?

Cribbs. Yes, yes, when the times were good. But bad speculations, unlucky investments, false friends—alas, alas, we have all our ups and downs, my dear madam.

Mrs Wilson. Ah, Mr Cribbs, I perceive you are a man who——

Cribbs. Has a heart to feel for the unfortunate. True, madam; it is the

101

character I have attained, though I am not the man to boast. Have you any prospect of—that is, have you provided——

Mary. It is true then, too true! The cottage and garden will be sold!

Cribbs. Why, what can the young man do, my dear? A gay young man like him, fond of the world, given somewhat to excess no doubt, giddy, wild and reckless! As the good man says, 'When I was a child, I thought as a child'. (*A pause.* Cribbs *looks round the room*) Well, madam, business is business. I am a plain man, Mrs Wilson, and sometimes called too blunt, and—and——

Mary. You mean to say that we must leave the cottage, sir?

Cribbs. (*pretending feeling*) No, not *yet*, my dear young lady. I would say it is best to be prepared; and as Edward is sudden in all his movements, and as my entreaties would never change him—why, if you could find a place before he moves in the matter, it might save you from much inconvenience, that's all.

Mrs Wilson. You impose upon us a severe task, my dear sir.

Cribbs. Bear up, my dear madam, bear up. If I may be so officious, I would try Boston. At the Intelligence Offices there, any healthy young woman like your daughter can obtain a profitable situation. Think of it, think of it, my good madam. I will see you again soon; and now, heaven bless you!

(*Exit*)

Mrs Wilson *and* Mary *look for a moment at each other, and then embrace.*

Mrs Wilson. Well, comfort, my daughter, comfort. It is a good thing to have a friend in the hour of trouble. This Mr Cribbs appears to be a very feeling man. But before taking his advice, we would do well to make our proposed trial of this young man, Edward Middleton. You have the money in your purse?

Mary. It is all here, mother. Thirty dollars, the sum we have saved to purchase fuel for the winter.

Mrs Wilson. That will partially pay the rent score. When this young man finds we are disposed to deal fairly with him, he may relent. You turn pale, Mary. What ails my child?

Mary. Dear mother, it is nothing—it will soon be over. It must be done; but I fear this young man. He has been described as so wild, so reckless. I feel a sad foreboding——

Mrs Wilson. Fear not, Mary. Call him to the door, refuse to enter the house, give him the money, and tell him your sad story. He must, from family and association at least, have the manners of a gentleman; and however wild a youth may be when abroad among his associates, no gentleman ever insulted a friendless and unprotected woman.

Mary. You give me courage, dear mother. I should indeed be an unnatural child, if—— (*aside*) yet I am agitated. Oh, why do I tremble thus?

(*Puts on a village bonnet, &c.*)

Mrs Wilson. (kissing her) Go forth, my child. Go as the dove flew from the ark of old, and if thou shouldst fail in finding the olive branch of peace, return and seek comfort where thou shalt surely find it, in the bosom of thy fond and widowed mother! *(Exeunt severally)*

Scene 2. *Front and cut wood in centre.*

Enter Cribbs.

Cribbs. Well, that interview of mock sympathy and charity is over, and I flatter myself pretty well acted too. Ha, ha! Yes, the widow and her child must quit the cottage, I'm resolved. First, for the wrongs I years ago endured from Old Wilson; and secondly, it suits my own interests, and in all cases between myself and others, I consider the last clause a clincher. Ha, here comes Edward. I will meet him.
(Goes off, right)

Enter Mary, *fearful and hesitating*, L.

Mary. I have now nearly reached the old mansion house. In a few moments I shall see the young man, this dissipated collegian. Oh, my poor mother must be deceived! Such a man can have no pity for the children of poverty, misfortune's suppliants for shelter beneath the roof of his cottage. Oh, my poor mother, little do you know the sufferings that——. Ha, a gentleman approaches. My fears tell me this is the man I seek. Shall I ever have courage to speak to him? I will pause till he has reached the house. *(Retires)*

Enter Edward Middleton *and* Cribbs.

Cribbs. I wished to see you with regard to the cottage and lands adjoining. I have an opportunity of selling them. When last we talked upon this subject——

Mary *appears at back, listening.*

Edward. I was then ignorant that a poor widow and her only daughter——
Cribbs. Who are in arrears for rent——
Edward. Had lived there many years, and that my father highly esteemed them. To turn them forth upon the world, in the present condition of the old lady——
Cribbs. Which old lady has a claim upon the Almshouse——

Mary *shudders.*

Edward. In short, Mr Cribbs, I cannot think of depriving them of a home dear to them as the apple of their eye, to send them forth from the flowers which they have reared, the vines which they have trained in their course; a place endeared to them by tender domestic recollections, and past remembrances of happiness.

Cribbs. Oh, all that and more! The fences which they have neglected, the garden gate off the hinges, the limbs of the old birch tree broken down for firewood, the back windows ornamented with an old hat——

Edward. Cease, Mr Cribbs. All this has been explained; my foster-brother William has told me the whole story. The trees were broken down by idle schoolboys; and with regard to an old hat in the window, why, it was the hat of a man—can as much be said of yours, Mr Cribbs?

Cribbs. You are pleased to be pleasant today, sir. Good morning, sir, good morning.   (*Exit, muttering*)

Edward. I'm sorry I offended the old man. After all, he was the friend of the family. Though it is strange, my poor father almost always took his advice, and was invariably unfortunate when he did so.

Re-enter Cribbs.

Cribbs. Good morning again. Beg pardon, sir. I now understand you better. You are right. The daughter—fine girl, eh? Sparkling eyes, eh? Dimples, roguish glances? Ah, when I was young, eh? Ah! Well, never mind. You have seen her, eh?

Edward. Never. Explain yourself, Mr Cribbs.

Cribbs. If you have not seen her, you will, you know, eh? I understand. Traps for wild fowl. Mother and daughter grateful—love—passion—free access to the cottage at all hours.

Edward. Cribbs, do you know this girl has no father?

Cribbs. That's it! A very wild flower growing on the open heath.

Edward. Have you forgotten that this poor girl has not a brother?

Cribbs. A garden without a fence—not a stake standing. You have nothing to do but to step into it.

Edward. Old man, I respect your grey hairs. I knew an old man once—peace to his ashes!—whose hair was as grey as yours; but beneath that aged breast there beat a heart pure as the first throbs of childhood. He was as old as you—he was more aged; his limbs tottered as yours do not. I let you go in peace. But had that old man heard you utter such foul sentences to his son, had he heard you tell me to enter, like a wolf, this fold of innocence and tear from her mother's arms the hope of her old age, he would have forgotten the winters that had dried the pith within his aged limbs, seized you by the throat, and dashed you prostrate to the earth, as too foul a carcass to walk erect and mock the name of man.

Cribbs. But Mr Middleton, sir——

Mary. (*rushes forward and kneels*) The blessings of the widow and the

1. Mazeppa at Astley's, 1831

Within the engraving:

London Published by T.H[...]

Ornament Maker

10 May's Buildings S.t Martins Lane

2. John Cartlitch as Mazeppa, King of Tartary

"Again do I stand erect, again assume the God like attitude of Freedom and of Man"

3. Miss Adah Menken as Mazeppa

4. Backstage at *Mazeppa*

5. The Jibbenainosay precipitated down the cataract in a canoe of fire.
Stock poster for *Nick of the Woods*

6–7. Designs for the two vision scenes in Charles Kean's production of *The Corsican Brothers*, 1852

8. Sarah Bernhardt as Marguerite Gautier

fatherless child be upon thee! May they accompany thy voice to
heaven's tribunal—not to cry for vengeance, but plead for pardon
on this wicked man!

Cribbs. Ha, the widow's daughter! Mr Middleton, you mistake me. I—I
cannot endure a woman's tears. I—poor child! (*Aside*) I'll be
terribly revenged for this! (*Exit*)

Edward. This, then, is the widow's child! Rise, my dear, and be assured of
my sympathy for your mother's sorrows, and of my assistance in your
need.

Mary. Oh, thanks for this cheering kindness! But sir, I have an
errand for you. (*Holding out money*) This is part of the rent which——

Edward. Nay then, you have not overheard my discourse with the old
man who has just left us. I have told him——

Mary. That we should still remain in the cottage. Oh sir, is that a
reason we should withhold from you your due—now paid with
double pleasure, since we recognise a benefactor in our creditor?
Take this, I entreat. 'Tis but a portion of the debt; but be assured
the remainder shall be paid as soon as busy, willing hands can earn it.

Edward. Nay, nay, dear girl. Keep it as a portion of your dowry.

Mary. Sir?

Edward. If you have overheard the dialogue that I just held with that
old man, you must know that I sometimes speak very plain.

Mary. (*apprehensively*) Yes, sir.

Edward. I have spoken plainly to him. Shall I now speak plainly to you?

Mary. Alas, sir! It is not our fault that the fences are broken down.
When my poor father lived, it was not so. But since——

Edward. When that vile old man spoke to me of your charms, I heeded
him not. There are plenty of pretty girls in this section of the country.
But I have since discovered what I had before heard—something
more than the ordinary beauty which he described. A charm of
mental excellence, noble sentiment, filial piety. These are the charms
which bind captive the hearts of men. I speak plainly, for I speak
honestly; and when I ask you to keep that money as a portion of
your dowry, need I say into whose hands I would like to have it fall
at last?

Mary. (*who droops her head during the above*) To affect—to affect not to
understand you, sir, would be an idle return for kindness such as
yours; and yet——

Edward. I sometimes walk down in the vicinity of your cottage, and——

Mary. Should I see you go by without stopping, why, then——

Edward. Then what, dear girl?

Mary. Then I should suppose you had forgotten where we lived.

Edward. Thanks! (*Kissing her hand*) Ah, little did I think, when I thought
of selling that dear old cottage, that it should be regarded as a casket,
invaluable for the jewel it contained. (*Leads her off*)

Scene 3. Interior of Miss Spindle's *dwelling house. Toilet table, looking glass, scent bottles. All denotes vulgar wealth, devoid of elegance or taste.*

Miss Spindle *discovered at toilet table.*

Miss Spindle. The attractions of the fair sex are synonymous. True, old Bonus is the destroyer of female charms. But as my beautiful poet Natty P.[1] says, in his sublime epistle to Lucinda Octavia Pauline, 'Age cannot wither me, nor custom stale my infinite vacuity'. But time is money; then money is time, and we bring back, by the aid of money, the times of youth. I value my beauty at fifty dollars a year, as that is about the sum it costs me for keeping it in repair year by year. Well, say that my beauty is repaired in this way, year by year; well, what then? I have heard a gentleman say that a pair of boots, when repaired and foxed, were better than they were when new. Why should it not be so with our charms? Certainly, they last longer in this way. We can have red cheeks at seventy, and—thanks to the dentist—good teeth at any time of life. Woman was made for love. They suppose that my heart is unsusceptible of the tender passion. But the heart can be regulated by money, too. I buy all the affecting novels and all the terrible romances, and read them till my heart has become soft as maiden wax, to receive the impression of that cherished image I adore. Ah, as true as I live, there goes his foster-brother William by the window. Hem!—William! (*Taps at window*)
William. (*sings without*)
> When I was a young and roving boy,
> Where fancy led me I did wander;
> Sweet Caroline was all my joy,
> But I missed the goose and hit the gander.

Enter William Dowton.

Good day, Miss Spindle.
Miss Spindle. You heard my rap, William?
William. As much as ever, Miss Spindle. Such fingers as yours don't make a noise like the fist of a butcher.
Miss Spindle. My hand *is* small, William, but I did not suppose that you had noticed it.
William. I only noticed it by the lightness of your tap. So I supposed you must be very light-fingered.
Miss Spindle. Pray sit down, William. Take a chair. Don't be bashful— you're too modest.

---

[1] *Natty P.* The Roman poet Ovid. The misquotation comes from *Antony and Cleopatra*, II.ii.240.

William. It's a failing I've got, Miss Spindle. I'm so modest, that I always go to bed without a candle. (*Both sit*)

Miss Spindle. Shall I tell you what I have thought, William?

William. Why, that's just as you agree to with yourself. I don't care much about it, one way or t'other.

Miss Spindle. You were singing as you came in, William. I suppose you know I sometimes invoke the help of Polyhymnia?

William. Why, I don't know as to the help of Polyhym-him-nina, but if you want a good *help* you cannot do better than hire Polly Striker, old Farmer Jones's wife's daughter by her first husband.

Miss Spindle. You don't understand the heathen mythology, William.

William. Why, I hear Parson Roundtext talk sometimes of the poor benighted heathens. But I am free to say that I can't come anything in regard to their conchology, as you call it. Will you have some shell-barks or chestnuts, Miss Spindle?

Miss Spindle. No, William. But this is what I have thought. William, there are two sorts of men.

William. Oh yes, Miss Spindle—long ones and short ones, like cigars. Sometimes the short ones are the best smoking,[1] too.

Miss Spindle. You mistake my meaning, William. Some are warm and susceptible of the charms of women——

William. Warm? Oh yes, Florida boys and Carolina niggers, eh?

Miss Spindle. While others are cold and apparently insensible to our beauties.

William. Oh yes, Newfoundlanders, Canada fellows and Bluenoses.[2]

Miss Spindle. Now William, *dear* William, this is the confession I would confide in your generous secrecy. I have a trembling affection, and then, a warm yet modest flame.

William. (*aside*) Trembling affection—warm flame? Why, the old girl's got the fever and the ague!

Miss Spindle. And how to combat with this dear yet relentless foe——

William. Put your feet into warm water and wood ashes, take two quarts of boiling-hot 'arb tea, cover yourself with four thick blankets and six Canada comforters,[3] take a good perspicacity, and you'll be well in the morning.

Miss Spindle. Sir!

William. That's old ma'am Brown's cure for fever and ague, and I never yet found it fail.

Miss Spindle. Fever and ague? You mistake me, William. I have an ardent passion.

William. Don't be in a passion, Miss Spindle. It's bad for your complaint.

Miss Spindle. You will not understand. I have a passion for one——

[1] *smoking* material for ridicule
[2] *Bluenoses* Nova Scotians
[3] *comforters* long woollen scarves for the throat

William. For one? Well, it's very lucky it's only for one.

Miss Spindle. Can you not fancy who that one is? He lives in your house.

William. Well, I'm darned, Miss Spindle! It's either me or Mr Middleton.

Miss Spindle. I never can bestow my hand without my heart, William.

William. Why, I think myself they ought to be included in the same bill of sale.

Miss Spindle. Ah, William, have you ever read *The Children of the Abbey*?

William. No, Miss Spindle, but I've read *The Babes in the Wood*.

Miss Spindle. I have read all the romantics of the day. I have just finished Mr Cooper's *Trapper*.

William. (*aside*) Oh! I daresay she understands trap, but she don't come the trapper over my foster-brother this year.

Miss Spindle. (*aside*) He understands little of the refinements of the civilized circular. I must try something else. (*Aloud*) How do you like my new green dress? How does it become me?

William. Beautiful! It matches very well indeed, marm.

Miss Spindle. Matches with what, William?

William. With your eyes, marm.

Miss Spindle. It becomes my complexion, William.

William. It's a beautiful match—like a span of grey horses.

Miss Spindle. Does your master fancy green, William?

William. O yes, marm—he loves it fine, I tell you.

Miss Spindle. But in what respect? How did you find it out?

William. In respect of drinking, marm.

Miss Spindle. Drinking?

William. Yes. He always tells the cook to make green tea.

Miss Spindle. Well, William, how about the cottage? When are you going to turn out those Wilsons?

William. The girl will be out of that place soon, depend on that, marm.

Miss Spindle. I'm glad to hear it. I never could endure those Wilsons; and it's a duty, when one knows that respectable people like your master are injured, to speak out. I know they haven't paid their rent; and do you know that girl was seen getting into a chaise with a young man, when she ought to have been at work; and she did not return till nine o'clock at night, William, for I took the pains to put on my hood and cloak and look for myself, though it was raining awful.

William. That was the time you cotched the fever, the fever and ague, marm. Well, goodbye.

Miss Spindle. Are you going, William?

William. Yes, marm; I shall be wanted to hum. You take care of your precious health, marm. Keep your feet warm and your head cool, your mouth shut and your heart open, and you'll soon have good health, good conscience, and stand well on your pins, marm. Good morning, marm.

(*Sings*) To reap, to sow, to plough and mow,
And be a farmer's boy—and be a farmer's boy! (*Exit*)

Miss Spindle. The vulgar creature! But what could I expect? He ought to know that American ladies ought never to have any pins. But I am certain, for all this, Edward—dear Edward!—is dying for me. As the poet Dr Lardner[1] says, 'He lets concealment, like a worm in the bud, feed on the damask curtains of his—cheek'. Damask bud? I'm quite sure it's somewhat about bud. Yes, I am convinced my charms as yet are undecayed; and even when old age comes on, the charm of refined education will still remain. As the immortal Chelsea Beach poet[2] has it,

You may break, you may ruin, the vase if you will,
The scent of the roses will cling round it still.

(*Exit, affectedly*)

Scene 4. *Landscape view.*

Enter Patience Brayton, Sam Evans, Old Johnson, male *and* female Villagers. *Music.*

Patience. Come, there's young men enough—let's have a ring-play.
All. Yes, a ring-play, a ring-play! Fall in here!
Sam. Come, darnation! Who'll go inside?
Patience. Go in yourself, Sam.
Sam. Well, I'm agreed. Go on.

They form a circle and revolve round Sam, *singing.*

All.   I am a rich widow, I live all alone,
I have but one son and he is my own.
Go son, go son, go choose you one,
Go choose a good one, or else choose none.

Sam *chooses one of the girls. She enters the ring. He kisses her, and the ring goes round.*

Now you are married, you must obey
What you have heard your parents say.
Now you are married, you must prove true,
As you see others do, so do you.

The ring goes round. Patience, *who is in the ring, chooses* Old Johnson.

[1] *Dr Lardner* unknown; but the misquotation comes from *Twelth Night,* II.iv.112f. Miss Spindle has another stab at it on p. 114.
[2] *Chelsea Beach poet* apparently an amateur versifier, and Miss Spindle's friend.

Patience.   Mercy on me, what have I done?
               I've married the father instead of the son.
               His legs are crooked and ill put on—
               They're all laughing at my young man.   (*A general laugh*)

Sam. Come girls, you forget 'tis almost time for Mary Wilson's wedding.
Patience. Well now, ain't we forgetting how proud she must be, going to marry a college-bred.
Johnson. She'll be none the better for that. Larning don't buy the child a new frock.
Sam. Well, let's have a dance, and be off at once.
All. Yes! Partners! A dance, a dance!

A village dance, and all exeunt. Enter Cribbs.

Cribbs. Thus end my prudent endeavours to get rid of those Wilsons. But young Middleton—there is yet some hope of him. He is at present annoyed at my well-intended advice, but that shall not part us easily. I will do him some unexpected favour, worm myself into his good graces, incite him to the village bar-room, and if he falls, then— ha, ha! I shall see them begging their bread yet. The wife on her bended knees to me, praying for a morsel of food for her starving children! It will be revenge—revenge! Here comes his foster-brother William. I'll wheedle him; try the ground before I put my foot on it.

Enter William Dowton, *whistling.*

William. Lawyer Cribbs, have you seen my poor half-witted sister Agnes, eh?
Cribbs. No, William, my honest fellow, I have not. I want to speak to you a moment.
William. (*aside*) What does old Razor Chops want with me, I wonder? (*Aloud*) Well, lawyer, what is it?
Cribbs. You seem to be in a hurry. They keep you moving, I see.
William. These are pretty busy times, sir. Mr Edward is going to be married. (*Aside*) That's a dose! Senna and salts!
Cribbs. Yes, yes—ahem! Glad to hear it.
William. Yes, I thought you seemed pleased. (*Aside*) Looks as sour as Sam Jones, when he swallowed vinegar for sweet cider.
Cribbs. I am a friend to early marriages, although I never was married myself. Give my best respects to Mr Edward.
William. Sir?
Cribbs. William, suppose I leave it to your ingenuity to get me an invitation to the wedding, eh? And here's a half dollar to drink my health.
William. No, I thank you, lawyer. I don't want your money.

Cribbs. Oh, very well; no offence meant, you know. Let's step into the tavern, and take a horn to the happiness of the young couple.

William. Lawyer Cribbs—or Squire, as they call you—it's my opinion when your Uncle Belzebub wants to bribe an honest fellow to do a bad action, he'd better hire a pettifogging bad lawyer, to tempt him with a counterfeit dollar in one hand and a bottle of rum in the other. *(Exit)*

Cribbs. Ah, ha! You're a cunning scoundrel, but I'll fix you yet.

Agnes. (sings without)
> Brake and fern and cypress dell,
> Where the slippery adder crawls——

Cribbs. Here comes that crazy sister of his. She knows too much for my happiness. Will the creature never die? Her voice haunts me like the spectre of the youth that was engaged to her. For my own purposes, I ruined, I triumphed over him. He fell, died in a drunken fit, and she went crazy. Why don't the Almshouse keep such brats at home?

Enter Agnes, *deranged.*

Agnes. (sings)
> Brake and fern and cypress dell,
> Where the slippery adder crawls,
> Where the grassy waters well,
> By the old moss-covered walls.

For the old man has his grey locks, and the young girl her fantasies.

(Sings)
> Upon the heather, when the weather
> Is as mild as May,
> So they prance, as they dance,
> And we'll all be gay.

But they poured too much red water in his glass. The lawyer is a fine man, ha, ha! He lives in the brick house yonder. But the will! Ha, ha, ha, the will!

Cribbs. (angrily) Go home, Agnes, go home!

Agnes. Home? I saw a little wren yesterday. I had passed her nest often. I had counted the eggs. They were so pretty—beautiful, so beautiful! Rough Robin of the mill came this morning and stole them. The little bird went to her nest, and looked in—they were gone. She chirruped mournfully, and flew away. She won't go home any more!

Cribbs. Agnes, who let you out? You distress the neighbourhood with your muttering and singing. *(Threatening)* I'll have you taken care of!

Agnes. There's to be a wedding in the village. I saw a coffin carried in, full of bridal cake.

(Sings)
> And the bride was red with weeping,
> Cypress in her hair——

Can you tell why they cry at weddings? Is it for joy? I used to weep when I was joyful. You never weep, old man. I should have been married, but my wedding-dress was mildewed, so we put off the marriage till another day. They'll make a new dress for me. They say he won't come again to me. And then, the will! Ha, ha! old man—the will!

Cribbs. Ha, confusion! Get you gone, or thus——

Seizes her and raises cane. William *enters rapidly and throws him round to corner of the stage.*

William. Why, you tarnation old black varmint! Strike my little, helpless, half-crazed sister! If it was not for your grey hairs, I'd break every bone in your black-beetle body! If all I have heard be true, you'll have to account for——

Cribbs. (*rising*) You'll rue this, young man, if there's any law in the land. A plain case of assault and battery. I'll put you in jail. Predica-ments, praemunires, fifas and fieri facias! [1] I'll put you between stone walls!
                                    (*Exit, blustering*)

William. Put me between stone walls! If you'd have been put between two posts with a cross beam and a hempen rope long ago, you'd had your due, old land-shark! You stay here, darling Agnes, till I come back. —Fiery faces and predicaments? If I get you near enough to a horse-pond, I'll cool your fiery face, I'll warrant.   (*Exit*)

Agnes. (*scattering flowers and singing*)
                    They lived down in the valley,
                        Their house was painted red;
                    And every day the robin came
                        To pick the crumbs of bread.

But the grass does not wither when they die. I will sit down till I hear the bells that are far off, for then I think of his words. Who says he did not love me? It was a good character he wanted of the parson. A girl out of place is like an old man out of his grave. (*Bells chime, piano*) They won't ask me to their merry-makings now.

(*Sings*)   Walk up, young man, there's a lady here
                        With jewels in her hair—

(*Suddenly clasps her hands and screams*) Water—water! Hear him, oh hear him cry for water! Quick! he'll turn cold again! His lips are blue. Water—water!
                                    (*Exit, frantically*)

---

[1] *Predicaments . . . facias* a jumble of gibberish (fifa), legal tags (predicaments) and inappropriate writs (praemunire, fieri facias)

Scene 5. *A village. Exterior of a beautiful cottage; vines, entwined roses, &c. The extreme of rural tranquil beauty. Rustic table with fruit, cake, &c. Rustic chairs and benches.*

Enter procession of Villagers, Edward, Mary *and* Mrs Wilson; William; Clergyman; Children *with baskets of flowers;* Bridesman *and* Bridesmaid, *&c. &c. Bells ringing. They enter, come down to front, cross, and go upstage, singing chorus.*

Chorus.   Hail! hail! happy pair!
          Bells are ringing, sweet birds singing,
        All around now speaks of bliss;
          Bright roses bringing, flowers flinging,
        Peace, purity and happiness!

Edward. Dearest Mary—ah, now indeed my own! Words are too poor, too weak, to express the joy, the happiness that agitates my heart. Ah, dear, dear wife! May each propitious day that dawns upon thy future life but add another flower to the rosy garland that now encircles thee!

Mary. Thanks, Edward, my own loved husband. Thy benison is echoed from my inmost heart. Ah, neighbour Johnson, many thanks for your kind remembrance of your pupils. My dear friends your children, too, are here.

Johnson. Yes, my dear Mary, your happiness sheds its genial rays around old and young. Young man, I was a witness at your father's wedding. May your life be like his, an existence marked by probity and honour, and your death as tranquil! Mrs Wilson, I remember your sweet daughter when but a child of nine years, and that seems only yesterday.

Mary. Dear Patience, I am glad to see you too; and who is this? (*Points to* Sam) Your brother?

Patience. No, an acquaintance that——

Sam. Yes—an acquaintance that——

Mary. Oh yes, I understand.

Mrs Wilson. My dearest children, the blessing of a bereaved heart rest, like the dews of heaven, upon you! Come, neighbours, this is a festival of joy. Be happy, I entreat.

William. Well, if there's anyone here happier than Bill Dowton, I should like to know it, that's all. Come, lads and lasses—sing, dance, and be merry!

Dance. Tableau.

A lapse of six years.

ACT II

Scene 1. *A chamber in* Miss Spindle's *house.*

Lawyer Cribbs *and* Miss Spindle *discovered, seated.*

Cribbs. Be explicit, my dear madam. This is a most serious affair—
breach of promise, marriage promise. How my heart bleeds for you!
Dear young lady, suffering virtue! But tell me the particulars.

Miss Spindle. Oh, sir, why will you cause me to harrow up my feelings,
my bleeding heart, by the recital of my afflictions? I have 'let
concealment, like a caterpillar on a button-wood, feed on my cambric
cheek and——'. (*Aside*) I can't remember the rest of it.

Cribbs. Alas, poor lady! Pray, go on.

Miss Spindle. The first of our acquaintance was down at a corn-husking.
Not that I make a practice of attending such vulgar places, Squire,
but——

Cribbs. Oh, certainly not—certainly not.

Miss Spindle. Well, I was over-persuaded. I set up and stripped the dry
coatings from the yellow corn—only two ears. I husked no more,
Squire.

Cribbs. Indeed, indeed! Two ears—you are certain it was but two ears?
It is best to be particular. We shall make out a *prima facie* case.

Miss Spindle. Well, I got hold of a red ear—it was the last I husked. I
think it was a red ear—so I was obliged to be kissed. Oh, Squire,
think of my mortification, when I was told that such was the
invariable rule, the custom at a husking!

Cribbs. (*with energy*) Your sufferings must have been intolerable.

Miss Spindle. Oh, sir, you know how to feel for delicate timidity. A big,
coarse young man called Bill Bullus rose up to snatch the fragrance
from my unwilling cheek——

Cribbs. (*groans*) Oh!

Miss Spindle. I put up my kerchief—it was a cambric, a fine cambric,
Squire Cribbs—and said I had a choice in those things, looking at
Edward, whom I knew to be a gentleman, you know. He took the
hint immediately. Bullus fell back appalled at my manner, and
Edward—oh, sir, spare my blushes!

Cribbs. I understand, he—yes. I understand.

Miss Spindle. He did it, sir! I felt the pressure of his warm lips on——

Cribbs. Your cheek, of course.

Miss Spindle. Oh, no, no, sir. It was said by my friend the Chelsea
Beach bard, that from my lips he stole ambrosical blisses.

Cribbs. Enormous! But go on.

Miss Spindle. You may judge what was my confusion.

Cribbs. Certainly, Miss Spindle.

Miss Spindle. The ear of corn was not more red than was my burnished cheek.

Cribbs. I do not know, my dear young lady, but you might make out a case of assault and battery.

Miss Spindle. It was very rude for a college-bred. Well, after that, he bowed to me as we were coming out of church.

Cribbs. Aha! The evidence comes in. Have you got proof of that, most injured fair one?

Miss Spindle. Oh, sir, no proof would be required. I trust that a person of my respectability need bring no proof of what they know. Well, after that, I was going down to Mr Simmons', and lo! a cow stood in the road. I must pass within twenty feet of the ferocious animal if I continued my route. Providentially, at the very instant, Edward came down the road that turns up by Wollcott's mill. He saw my strait. He saw that I stood trembling like some fragile flower tossed by the winds of heaven. Like Sir William Wallace flying to the rescue of the Greeks, he came, panting on the wings of love. He rushed like an armed castle to the side of the cow and she wheeled about like the great leviathan of the deep, and trotted down towards the school-house.

Cribbs. I can imagine your feelings, Miss Spindle—a delicate young lady in imminent danger. But he did no more than any man would have done.

Miss Spindle. Well, sir, you may judge what were the feelings of my palpitating heart, tender as it always was——

Cribbs. Have any letters passed between you?

Miss Spindle. Oh, yes, yes! Five or six, sir.

Cribbs. We've got him there, aha! If Miss Spindle would be so condescending as just to show me one of those letters——

Miss Spindle. He's got them all in his possession.

Cribbs. Unfortunate! Horrible! How did he obtain possession of those letters?

Miss Spindle. Oh, I sent them—sometimes by one person, sometimes by another.

Cribbs. How, madam? *His* letters, I mean. How did he get——

Miss Spindle. Oh, sir, mark his ingratitude! I sent him half a dozen——

Cribbs. (*discouraged*) Oh! I understand. The correspondence was all on one side, then?

Miss Spindle. Not one letter did he write to me. Ah, sir, think of it—all my tenderness, all my devotion. Oh, my breaking heart!

Cribbs. (*aside*) Oh humbug! Well, good day, Miss Spindle. I have a pressing engagement, and——

Miss Spindle. Well, but Lawyer Cribbs, what is your advice? How ought I to proceed?

Cribbs. Get your friends to send you to the insane hospital and place you among the incurable, as the most fusty, idiotic old maid that ever knit stockings. (*Exit, hastily*)

Miss Spindle. Spirit of Lucretia Borgia! Polish pattern of purity! Was there ever such a Yankee hedgehog! (*Exit, angrily*)

Scene 2. *Landscape view.*

Enter Cribbs.

Cribbs. So far the scheme works admirably. Day by day, he sinks deeper into the gulf of disgrace and ruin. I left him in a fix the other evening, after having led him into company that suited my purpose; and when I saw he was fairly in for a violent and disreputable broil, I left him. Ha, ha! I know his nature well. He has tasted, and will not stop now short of madness or oblivion. I mostly fear his wife. She will have great influence over him. Here comes Edward. Caution—caution! (*Retires*)

Enter Edward.

Edward. Is this to be the issue of my life? Oh, must I ever yield to the fell tempter, and, bending like a weak bulrush to the blast, still bow my manhood lower than the brute? Why, surely I have eyes to see, hands to work with, feet to walk, and brain to think! Yet the best gifts of heaven I abuse, lay aside her bounties, and with my own hand willingly put out the light of reason. I recollect my mother said—my dear, dying mother—they were the last words I ever heard her utter—'Whoever lifts his fallen brother is greater far than the conqueror of the world'. Oh, how my poor brain burns! My hand trembles! My knees shake beneath me! I cannot—will not—appear before them thus. A little—a very little—will revive and strengthen me. No one sees. William must be there ere this. Now for my hiding place. Oh, the arch cunning of the drunkard! (*Goes to tree, and from the hollow draws forth a bottle; looks round and drinks.* Cribbs *behind, exulting*) So, so. It relieves, it strengthens. Oh, glorious liquor! Why did I rail against thee? Ha, ha! (*Drinks and drains bottle*) All gone! All! (*Throws bottle away*) Of what use the casket when the jewel's gone? Ha, ha! I can face them now. (*Turns, and meets* Cribbs. *Aside*) He here? Confusion!

Cribbs. Why, Middleton! Edward, my dear friend, what means this?

Edward. Tempter, begone! Pretend not ignorance. Were you not there when that vile fray occurred? Did you not desert me?

Cribbs. As I am a living man, I know not what you mean. Business called me out; I left you jovial and merry with your friends.

Edward. Friends? Ha, ha! the drunkard's friends! Well, well, you may speak truth; my brain wanders. I'll go home. Oh, misery! Would I were dead!

Cribbs. Come, come, a young man like you should not think of dying. I am old enough to be your father, and I don't dream of such a thing.

Edward. You are a single man, Cribbs. You don't know what it is to see your little patrimony wasted away, to feel that you are the cause of sufferings you would die to alleviate.

Cribbs. Pooh, pooh! Sufferings? Your cottage is worth full five hundred dollars. It was but yesterday Farmer Anson was enquiring how much it could be bought for.

Edward. Bought for! Cribbs,——

Cribbs. Well, Edward, well.

Edward. You see yon smoke, curling up among the trees?

Cribbs. Yes, Edward. It rises from your own cottage.

Edward. You know who built that cottage, Cribbs?

Cribbs. Your father built it. I recollect the day. It was——

Edward. It was the very day I was born that yon cottage was first inhabited. You know who lives there now?

Cribbs. Yes. You do.

Edward. No one else, Cribbs?

Cribbs. Your family, to be sure.

Edward. And you counsel me to sell it! To take the warm nest from that mourning bird and her young, to strip them of all that remains of hope or comfort, to make them wanderers in the wide world— and for what? To put a little pelf into my leprous hands, and then squander it for rum!

Cribbs. You don't understand me, Edward. I am your sincere friend, believe me. Come——

Edward. Leave me, leave me.

Cribbs. Why, where would you go thus, Edward?

Edward. Home! Home to my sorrowing wife, her dying mother, and my poor, poor child.

Cribbs. But not thus, Edward, not thus. Come to my house; my people are all out. We'll go in the back way; no one will see you. Wash your face, and I'll give you a little—something to refresh you. I'll take care it shall not hurt you. Come now, come.

Edward. Ought I? Dare I? Oh, this deadly sickness! Is it indeed best?

Cribbs. To be sure it is. If the neighbours see you thus! I'll take care of you. Come, come. A little brandy—good, good brandy.

Edward. Well, I—I——

Cribbs. That's right; come. (*Aside*) He's lost. (*Aloud*) Come, my dear friend, come. (*Exeunt*)

Scene 3. Interior of cottage, as in Act First. The furniture very plain. A want of comfort and order. Table and two chairs.

Enter Mary, *from set door. Her dress plain and patched, but put on with neatness and care. She is weeping.*

Mary. Oh heaven, have mercy on me! Aid me! Strengthen me! Weigh not thy poor creature down with woes beyond her strength to bear! Much I fear my suffering mother never can survive the night; and Edward comes not—and when he does arrive, how will it be? Alas, alas! My dear, lost husband! I think I could nerve myself against everything but——. Oh, misery! This agony of suspense! It is too horrible!

Enter Julia, *from room. She is barefooted. Dress clean, but very poor.*

Julia. Mother, dear mother, what makes you cry? I feel so sorry when you cry. Don't cry any more, dear mother!

Mary. I cannot help it, dearest. Do not tell your poor father what has happened in his absence, Julia.

Julia. No, dear mother, if you wish me not. Will it make him cry, mother? When I see you cry, it makes me cry too.

Mary. Hush, dear one, hush! Alas, he is unhappy enough already.

Julia. Yes. Poor father! I cried last night when father came home and was so ill. Oh, he looked so pale; and when I kissed him for 'good night', his face was as hot as fire. This morning he could not eat his breakfast, could he? What makes him ill so often, mother?

Mary. Hush, sweet one!

Julia. Dear grandma so sick, too. Doctor and nurse both looked so sorry. Grandma won't die tonight, will she, mother?

Mary. (aside) Father of mercies, this is too much! *(Weeps)* Be very quiet, Julia. I am going in to see poor grandma. Oh Religion, sweet solace of the wretched heart, support me, aid me, in this dreadful trial!

(Exit into room)

Julia. Poor, dear mother! When grandma dies, she'll go to live in heaven, for she's good. Parson Heartall told me so, and he never tells fibs, for he is good too.

Enter William, *gently.*

William. Julia, where is your mother, darling? (Julia *puts her finger on her lip, and points to door*) Ah, she comes!

Enter Mary.

How is poor Mrs Wilson now, marm?

Mary. Near the end of all earthly trouble, William. She lies in broken slumber. But where is my poor Edward? Have you not found him?

William. Yes, marm, I found him in the ta—in the village. He had
fallen and slightly hurt his forehead; he bade me come before, so as
you should not be frightened. He'll soon be here now.

Mary. Faithful friend! I wish you had not left him. Was he—oh, what
a question for a doting wife!—was he sober, William?

William. I must not lie, dear lady. He had been taking some liquor, but
I think not much. All, I hope, will be well.

Edward. (*sings without*) 'Wine cures the gout' &c. Ha, ha!

Mary. Oh, great heaven!

William *rushes out and re-enters with* Edward *drunk and noisy*, William
trying to soothe him. He staggers as he passes doorway.

Edward. I've had a glorious time, Bill. Old Cribbs——

Mary. Hush, dearest!

Edward. Why should I be silent? I am not a child. I——

Mary. My mother, Edward, my dear mother!

Edward. (*sinks in chair*) Heaven's wrath on my hard heart! I—I forgot.
How is she? Poor woman, how is she?

Mary. (*trying to hide her tears*) Worse, Edward, worse.

Edward. And I in part the cause! Oh, horrid vice! Bill, I remember my
father's death-bed—it was a Christian's: faith in his heart, hope in his
calm blue eye, a smile upon his lips. He had never seen his Edward
drunk. Oh, had he seen it—had he seen it!

Julia. (*crossing to her father*) Father, dear father!   (*Striving to kiss him*)

Edward. Leave me, child, leave me. I am hot enough already. (*She
weeps; he kisses her*) Bless you, Julia dear, bless you! Bill, do you
remember the young elm tree by the arbour in the garden?

William. Yes, sir.

Edward. Well, I slipped and fell against it as I passed the gate. My
father planted it on the very day I saw the light. It has grown with
my growth. I seized the axe and felled it to the earth. Why should it
flourish when I am lost for ever? (*Hysterically*) Why should it lift its
head to smiling heaven while I am prostrate? Ha, ha, ha!

A groan is heard. Exit Mary. *A pause—a shriek. Enter* Mary.

Mary. Edward, my mother——

Edward. Mary!

Mary. She is dead.

Edward. Horror! Death in the house? I cannot bear this; let me fly——

Mary. (*springing forward and clasping his neck*) Edward, dear Edward, do not
leave me. I will work, I will slave—anything. We can live; but do
not abandon me in misery. Do not desert me, Edward! Love!
Husband!

Edward. Call me not husband. Curse me as your destroyer! Loose your
arms—leave me.

Mary. No, no! Do not let him go. William, hold him!
William. (*holding him*) Edward, dear brother!
Julia. (*clinging to him*) Father! Father!
Mary. You will be abused. No one near to aid you. Imprisoned, or something worse, Edward.
Edward. Loose me—leave me! Why fasten me down on fire? Madness is my strength; my brain is liquid flame! (*Breaks from her.* William *is obliged to catch her*) Ha! I am free. Farewell, for ever!   (*Rushes off*)
Mary. Husband! Oh, heaven!   (*Faints*)
William. (*bursting into tears*) Edward! Brother!
Julia. Father, father!   (*Runs to the door, and falls on the threshold*)

   An interval of two years.

ACT III

Scene 1.   *New York. Broadway.*

Enter Lawyer Cribbs.

Cribbs. I wonder where that drunken vagrant can have wandered? Ever since he came to New York, thanks to his ravenous appetite and my industrious agency, he has been going downhill rapidly. Could I but tempt him to some overt act, well managed, I could line my own pockets and ensure his ruin. Ha, here he comes, and two of his bright companions. He looks most wretchedly. Money gone, and no honest way to raise it. He'll be glad to speak to old Cribbs now. I must watch my time.   (*Retiring*)

Enter Edward, *his clothes torn and very shabby, hat the same, with two* Loafers.

First Loafer. Cheer up, Ned. There's more money where the last came from.
Edward. But I tell you my last cent is gone. I feel ill. I want more liquor.
First Loafer. Well, well, you wait round here a spell. Joe and I will take a turn down to Cross Street. We'll make a raise, I warrant you.
Edward. Well, be quick then; this burning thirst consumes me.
                          (*Exeunt* Loafers)
Cribbs. (*advancing*) Why! Is that you, Mr Middleton?
Edward. Yes, Cribbs; what there is left of me.
Cribbs. Why, I don't see that you are much altered, though you might be the better for a stitch or two in your elbows.

Edward. Ah, Cribbs, I have no one to care for me. I am lost—a ruined, broken-hearted man!

Cribbs. You won't be offended, Middleton, will you? Allow me to lend you a dollar. I am not very rich, you know, but you can always have a dollar or two when you want it. Ask me—there, there. (*Offering money. Aside*) Before sundown, he's a few yards nearer his grave!

Edward. (*slowly taking it, struggling with pride and necessity*) Thank you, Mr Cribbs, thank you. You are from the village. I hardly dare ask you if you have seen *them*.

Cribbs. Your wife and child? Oh, they are doing charmingly. Since you left, your wife has found plenty of sewing; the gentlefolks have become interested in her pretty face, and you know she has a good education. She is as merry as a cricket, and your little girl blooming as a rose and brisk as a bee.

Edward. Then Mary is happy?

Cribbs. Happy as a lark.

Edward. (*after a pause*) Well, I ought to be glad of it; and since she thinks no more of me——

Cribbs. Oh yes, she thinks of you occasionally.

Edward. Does she indeed?

Cribbs. Yes, she says she cannot but pity you, but that heaven never sends affliction without the antidote; and that but for your brutal—hem! your strange—conduct and drunkenness—hem! misfortune—she would never have attracted the sympathy of those kind friends, who now regard her as the pride of their circle.

Edward. Did she really say all that?

Cribbs. Yes, and she pities you. I am sure she thinks of you, and would be glad to see you—to see you become a respectable member of society.

Edward. (*musing*) It is very kind of her—very, very kind! Pities me! Respectable! But Cribbs, how can one become respectable without a cent in his pocket or a whole garment on his wretched carcass?

Cribbs. (*pause*) There are more ways than one to remedy these casualties. If the world uses you ill, be revenged upon the world!

Edward. Revenged! But how, Cribbs, how?

Cribbs. (*cautiously*) Do you see this paper? 'Tis a cheque for five thousand dollars. You are a splendid penman. Write but the name of Arden Rencelaw, and you may laugh at poverty.

Edward. What? Forgery? And on whom? The princely merchant, the noble philanthropist, the poor man's friend, the orphan's benefactor! Out and out on you for a villain and coward! I must be sunk indeed, when you dare propose such a baseness to my father's son! Wretch as I am, by the world despised, shunned and neglected by those who should save and succour me, I would sooner perish on the first dunghill than that my dear child should blush for her father's crimes!

Take back your base bribe, miscalled charity; the maddening drink that I should purchase with it would be redolent of sin, and rendered still more poisonous by your foul hypocrisy. (*Throws down the money*)

Cribbs. (*bursting with passion*) Ah, you are warm, I see. You'll think better when—when you find yourself starving. (*Exit*)

Edward. Has it then come to this? An object of pity to my once adored wife; no longer regarded with love—respect—but cold compassion, pity? Other friends have fully made up my loss. She is flourishing, too, while I am literally starving—starving. This cold-blooded fiend, too! What's to become of me? Deserted, miserable—but one resource. I must have liquor. Ha, my handkerchief! 'Twill gain me a drink or two at all events. Brandy, aye, brandy! brandy! (*Rushes off*)

Scene 2. *A street. Stage half dark.*

Enter Cribbs.

Cribbs. Plague take the fellow! Who would have thought he would have been so foolishly conscientious? I will not abandon my scheme on the house of Rencelaw, though; the speculation is too good to be lost. Why, as I live here comes that old fool, Miss Spindle.

Enter Miss Spindle *in full bloomer costume.*

Miss Spindle. Why, this New York is the most awful place to find one's way I ever was in! It's all ups and downs, ins and outs. I've been trying for two hours to find Trinity Church steeple and I can't see it, though they tell me it's six hundred yards high.

Cribbs. Why, angelic Miss Spindle, how *do* you do? How long have you been in the commercial emporium?

Miss Spindle. Oh, Squire Cribbs, how d'ye do? I don't know what you mean by the uproarium, but for certain it is the noisiest place I ever did see. But Squire, what has become of the Middletons, can you tell?

Cribbs. I've had my eye upon them. They're down, Miss Spindle, never to rise again. As for that vagrant, Edward——

Miss Spindle. Ah, Squire! What an escape I had! How fortunate that I was not ruined by the nefarious influence, the malignant coruscations of his illimitable seductions! How lucky that prim Miss Mary Wilson was subjected to his hideous arts, instead of my virgin immaculate innocence!

Cribbs. Do you know why his wife left the village and came to New York?

Miss Spindle. Oh, she is low, degraded! She sank so far as to take in washing, to feed herself and child. She would sooner follow her drunken husband, and endeavour to preserve him—as she said—than remain where she was.

Cribbs. Well, well; they are down low enough now. Which way are you going, towards Broadway? Why, I'm going towards Broadway myself. Allow me the exquisite honour of beau-ing you. This way, perfection of your sex and adoration of ours. Your arm, lovely and immaculate Miss Spindle. (*Exeunt together, arm-in-arm*)

Enter Edward, *and the two* Loafers.

First Loafer. To be sure I did. I swore if he didn't let me have two or three dollars, I'd tell his old man of last night's scrape; and I soon got it, to get rid of me.

Second Loafer. Hurrah for snakes! Who's afraid of fire? Come, Ned. Two or three glasses of brandy will soon drive away the blue devils. Let's have some brandy!

Edward. With all my heart. Brandy be it. Since I am thus abandoned, deserted, the sooner I drown all remembrance of my wretchedness the better. Come! Boys, brandy be it. Hurrah!

All. (*sing*) 'Here's a health to all good lasses!' &c. (*Exeunt*)

Scene 3. *Interior of 'The Arbour' on Broadway. Bar with decanters, &c. Table with backgammon board at back, two men playing at it. Another reading paper and smoking. Others seated around, &c.* Bar-keeper *behind bar.*

Enter Edward *and* Loafers, *singing 'Here's a health' &c.*

Bar-keeper. The same noisy fellows that were here last night. What is it to be, gentlemen?

Edward. Oh, brandy for me—brandy.

First Loafer. Give me a gin-sling. That's what killed Goliath, ha, ha, ha!

Second Loafer. I'll have brandy. Come, old fellows, tread up and whet your whistles. I'll stand Sam. Tread up!

Edward *and others, after drinking, dance and sing 'Dan Tucker', 'Boatman Dance' &c.*

Bar-keeper. I must civilly request, gentlemen, that you will not make so much noise. You disturb others; and we wish to keep the house quiet.

Edward. Steady, boys, steady; don't raise a row in a decent house. More brandy, young man, if you please. Come, Bill, try it again.

First Loafer. With all my heart, hurrah!

Edward *and* Loafers *sing 'Dance, boatman, dance' &c.*

Edward. More brandy, hurrah!

Bar-keeper. I tell you once for all, I'll not have this noise. Stop that singing!

Second Loafer. I shan't; we'll sing as long as we please. Give me some liquor.

Edward. Aye, more brandy—brandy!

Bar-keeper. Well, will you be still then if I give you another drink?

Edward. Oh, certainly, certainly.

First Loafer. In course we will——

Bar-keeper. Well, help yourselves.   (*Hands decanters*)

Second Loafer. What's yours, Ned?

Edward. Oh, brandy. Here goes!   (*Fills and drinks*)

First Loafer. Here goes for the last!

All. (*singing*) 'We won't go home till morning' *&c.*

Man. (*at table, playing checkers*) Look here, that's my king!

Second Man. (*at table*) You're a liar! I have just jumped him.

Man. I tell you, you lie!   (*Regular wrangle*)

Edward and Loafers. Go it, you cripples!   (*Singing and laughing*)

Bar-keeper. Stop that noise, I tell you! Come, get out!

        (*Pushing man from table. The two men fight*)

Edward and Loafers. Go it, Charley! Hurrah! *&c.*

Regular scene of confusion. Bar-room fight, &c, during which stage is cleared. All fight off, and change to

Scene 4. *A wretched garret. Old table and chair, with lamp burning dimly.* Mary, *in miserable apparel, sewing slopwork, a wretched shawl thrown over her shoulders.* Julia *sleeping on a straw bed on the floor, covered in part by a miserable ragged rug. Half a loaf of bread on the table. The ensemble of the scene indicates want and poverty.*

Mary. Alas, alas! It is very cold. Faint with hunger, sick, heart-weary with wretchedness, fatigue—and cold! (*Clock strikes one*) One o'clock, and my work not near finished. I——. They must be done tonight. These shirts I have promised to hand in tomorrow by the hour of eight. A miserable quarter of a dollar will repay my industry; and then, my poor, poor child, thou shalt have food.

Julia. (*awaking*) Oh, dear mother, I am so cold! (Mary *takes shawl from her shoulders and spreads it over the child*) No, mother, keep the shawl. You are cold, too. I will wait till morning, and I can warm myself at Mrs Brien's fire. Little Dennis told me I should, for the gingerbread I gave him.   (*Goes to sleep, murmuring*)

Mary *puts the shawl on herself, waits till the child slumbers, and then places it over* Julia, *and returns to work.*

Mary. Alas, where is he on this bitter night? In vain have I made

every enquiry, and cannot gain any tidings of my poor, wretched
husband. No one knows him by name. Perhaps already the inmate of
a prison! Ah, merciful heaven, restore to me my Edward once again,
and I will endure every ill that can be heaped upon me! (*Looks
towards child*) Poor Julia! She sleeps soundly. She was fortunate today,
sweet lamb! While walking in the street in search of a few shavings,
she became benumbed with cold. She sat down upon some steps,
when a boy, moved with compassion, took from his neck a handkerchief and placed it upon hers. The mother of that boy is blessed!
With the few cents he slipped into her hands, she purchased a loaf of
bread; she ate a part of it—(*Taking bread from table*) and the rest is
here. (*Looks eagerly at it*) I am hungry—horribly hungry! I shall have
money in the morning. (*A pause*) No, no. My child will wake and
find her treasure gone. I will not rob my darling. (*Replaces bread on
table. Sinks into chair, weeping*) That ever I should see his child thus!
For myself, I could bear—could suffer all.

Julia *awakes noiselessly; perceiving shawl, rises and places it over her mother's
shoulders.*

Julia. Dear mother, you are cold. Ah, you tried to cheat your darling.
Mary. (*on her knees*) Now heaven be praised! I did not eat that bread.
Julia. Why, mother, do you sit up so late? You cry so much and look
so white. Mother, do not cry. Is it because father does not come to
bring us bread? We shall find father by and by, shan't we, mother?
Mary. Yes, dearest, yes—with the kind aid of Him. (*Knock at the door*)
Who can that be? (*Going to door*) Ah, should it be Edward!

Enter Cribbs.

Cribbs. Your pardon, Mrs Middleton, for my intrusion at this untimely
hour, but friends are welcome at all times and seasons, eh? So, so;
you persist in remaining in these miserable quarters? When last I saw
you, I advised a change.
Mary. Alas, sir, you know too well my wretched reasons for remaining.
But why are you here at this strange hour? Oh, tell me—know you
aught of him? Have you brought tidings of my poor Edward?
Cribbs. (*avoiding direct answer*) I must say, your accommodations are none
of the best; and must persist in it—you would do well to shift your
quarters.
Mary. Heaven help me! Where would you have me go? Return to the
village I will not. I must remain and find my husband.
Cribbs. This is a strange infatuation, young woman. It is the more
strange, as he has others to console him whose soft attentions he
prefers to yours.
Mary. What mean you, sir?

Cribbs. I mean that there are plenty of women, not of the most respectable class, who are always ready to receive presents from wild young men like him, and are not very particular in the liberties that may be taken in exchange.

Mary. Man, man! Why dost thou degrade the form and sense heaven has bestowed on thee by falsehood? Gaze on the sharp features of that child, where famine has already set her seal; look on the hollow eyes and the careworn form of the hapless being that brought her into life; then, if you have the heart, further insult the helpless mother and the wretched wife!

Cribbs. These things I speak of have been, and will be again, while there are wantons of one sex and drunkards of the other.

Mary. Sir, you slander my husband; I know this cannot be. It is because he is poor, forsaken, reviled, and friendless, that thus I follow him—thus love him still.

Cribbs. He would laugh in his drunken ribaldry to hear you talk thus.

Mary. (*with proud disdain*) Most contemptible of earth-born creatures, it is false! The only fault of my poor husband has been intemperance —terrible, I acknowledge, but still a weakness that has assailed and prostrated the finest intellects of men who would scorn a mean and unworthy action.

Cribbs. Tut, tut! You are very proud, considering (*Looking around*) all circumstances. But come, I forgive you. You are young and beautiful; your husband is a vagabond. I am rich; I have a true affection for you, and with me—— (*Attempts to take her hand*)

Mary. (*throws him off*) Wretch! Have you not now proved yourself a slanderer? and to effect your own vile purposes! But know, despicable wretch, that my poor husband clothed in rags, covered with mire, and lying drunk at my feet, is a being whose shoes you are not worthy to unloose.

Cribbs. Nay then, proud beauty, you shall know my power. 'Tis late— you are unfriended, helpless, and thus—— (*He seizes her. Julia screams*)

Mary. Help! Mercy!

She struggles with Cribbs. William *enters hastily, seizes* Cribbs *and throws him round; he falls.*

William. Well, Squire, what's the lowest you'll take for your rotten carcass? Shall I turn auctioneer and knock you down to the highest bidder? I don't know much of pernology, but I've a great notion of playing 'Yankee Doodle' on your organ of rascality. Be off, you ugly varmint, or I'll come the steam-engine and set your paddles going all-fired quick!

Cribbs. I'll be revenged, if there's law or justice!

William. Oh, get out! You're a bad case of villainy *versus* modesty and chastity, printed in black letters and bound in calf. Off with you!

or I'll serve a writ of ejectment on you *a posteriori*—I learnt that
much from Mr Middleton's law books.

Cribbs. But, I say, sir—I am a man——

William. You, a man? Nature made a blunder. She had a piece of
refuse garbage she intended to form into a hog, made a mistake,
gave it your shape, and sent it into the world to be miscalled man.
Get out! *(Pushes him off. Noise of falling down stairs)*

Re-enter William.

I did not like to hit him before you, but he's gone down these
stairs quicker than he wanted to, I guess.

Mary. Kind, generous friend! How came you here so opportunely?

William. Why, I was just going to bed at a boarding-house close by
Chatham Street, when I happened to mention the landlord—a
worthy man as ever broke bread—about you. He told me where
you were. I thought you might be more comfortable there, and
his good wife has made everything as nice and pleasant for you
as if you were her own sister. So come, Mrs Middleton; come,
Julia dear.

Mary. But William, my poor husband? *(Noise off)*

William. There's another row! Well, if this New York isn't the
awfullest place for noise! Come, Mrs Middleton. I'll find him
if he's in New York—jail or no jail, watch-house or no watch-
house!

Mary. Heaven preserve my poor dear Edward!

Going up stage to put on Julia's *bonnet, closed in by*

Scene 5. *The Five Points. Stage dark. Noise right and left.*

Enter Edward Middleton *in the custody of two* Watchmen; *he is
shouting.* William Dowton *enters hastily, knocks down* Watchmen,
rescues Edward, *and they exeunt. Other* Rowdies *enter. Fight. Stage
clear. Shouts &c. and off. Enter* Cribbs, *with coat torn half off.*

Cribbs. Oh my! Oh good gracious! How can I get out of this scrape?
I came here with the best intentions—oh my!—to see the law put
in force. Oh dear! Somebody has torn my coat-tail. Good
gracious! Lord have mercy! I've lost my hat—no, here it is.

*Picks up dreadfully shabby hat and puts it on. Runs from one side to
another. Enter* Watchmen *and* William *with* Mob, *meeting him.*

William. (*pointing out* Cribbs *to* Watchmen) That's the chap! The worst
among 'em! *(They seize Cribbs)*

Cribbs. I'm a respectable man!

They pick him up bodily and carry him off shouting. He exclaims 'I'm a lawyer! I'm a respectable man!' *&c.* William *follows, laughing. General confusion.*

An interval of one year.[1]

ACT IV

Scene 1.   *A wretched out-house or shed, supposed to be near a tavern. Early morning. Stage dark.*

Edward *discovered lying on the ground, without hat or coat, clothes torn, eyes sunk and haggard, appearance horrible, &c. &c.*

Edward. (*awakening*) Where am I? I wonder if people dream after they are dead? Hideous—hideous! I should like to be dead, if I could not dream. Parched! parched! 'Tis morning, is it, or coming night, which? I wanted daylight, but now it has come, what shall I do in daylight? I was out of sight when it was dark, and seemed to be half hidden from myself. Early morning! the rosy hue of the coming sunshine veiling from mortal sight the twinkling stars. What horrid dreams! Will they return upon me, waking? Oh, for some brandy! Rum! I am not so ashamed—so stricken with despair—when I am drunk. (*Calling*) Landlord, give me some brandy! What horrid place is this? Pain—dreadful pain! Heavens, how I tremble. Brandy, brandy!   (*Sinks down in agony*)

Enter Landlord, *with whip.*

Landlord. Where in nature can my horse be gone? Is there nobody up in this place? Hollo!
Edward. Hollo! Landlord, I say.
Landlord. What's this? Oh, I say, have you seen my horse? What—as I live, that scape-gallows Middleton! How came he here? (*Aside*) I thought he was in Sing-Sing.
Edward. Oh, I know you—you needn't draw back. We have been acquainted before now, eh, Mr——
Landlord. (*aside*) Zounds, he knows me! (*Aloud*) Yes, yes; we were acquainted once, as you say, young man; but that was in other days.
Edward. You are the same being still, though I am changed—miserably changed. But you still sell rum, don't you?

[1] *one year* useful for Edward in IV.i., but forgotten for Cribbs in IV.ii.ff.

Landlord. I am called a respectable inn-keeper. Few words are best, young fellow. Have you seen a horse, saddled and bridled, near here?

Edward. I've seen nothing. You are respectable, you say. You speak as if you were not the common poisoner of the whole village! Am not I, too, respectable?

Landlord. (*laughs rudely*) Not according to present appearances! You were respectable once, and so was Lucifer. Like him, you have fallen past rising. You cut a pretty figure, don't you? Ha ha! What has brought you in this beastly condition, young man?

Edward. (*springing up*) You! Rum! Eternal curses on you! Had it not been for your infernal poison shop in our village, I had been still a man—the foul den where you plunder the pockets of your fellows, where you deal forth death in tumblers, and from whence goes forth the blast of ruin over the land, to mildew the bright hope of youth, to fill the widow's heart with agony, to curse the orphan, to steal the glorious mind of man, to cast them from their high estate of honest pride and make them—such as I! How looked I when first I entered your loathsome den? and how do I look now? Where are the friends of my happy youth? Where is my wife? Where is my child? They have cursed me—cursed me and forsaken me!

Landlord. Well, what brought you to my house? You had your senses then; I did not invite you, did I?

Edward. Doth Hell send forth cards of invitation to its fires of torment? Oh, I am sick and faint. Make me some amends—my brain is on fire. My limbs are trembling. Give me some brandy—brandy!

(*Seizes him*)

Landlord. How can I give you brandy? My house is far from here. Let me go, vagabond.

Edward. Nay, I beseech you—only a glass, a single glass of brandy—rum—anything! Give me liquor, or I'll——

Landlord. Villain! Let go your hold!

Edward. Brandy! I have a claim on you—a deadly claim. Brandy! Brandy! Or I'll throttle you! (*Choking him*)

Landlord. (*struggling*) Help! Murder! I am choking! Help!

Enter William Dowton.

William. Good Lord, what is this? Edward, Edward!

(*Edward releases* Landlord, *and falls*)

Landlord. You shall pay for this, villain! You shall pay for this!

(*Exit, hastily*)

Edward. (*on ground in delirium*) Here, here, friend! Take it off, will you, this snake? How it coils round me! Oh, how strong it is! There, don't kill it. No, no; don't kill it, give it brandy, poison it

129

with rum! That will be a judicious punishment; that would be justice. Ha, ha! Justice! Ha, ha!

William. He does not know me.

Edward. Hush! Gently, gently, while she's asleep. I'll kiss her. She would spurn me, did she know it. Hush! There. Heaven bless my Mary—bless her and her child. Hush! If the globe turns round once more, we shall slide from its surface into eternity. Ha, ha! Great idea! A boiling sea of wine, fired by the torch of fiends! Ha, ha!

William. He's quite helpless. Could I but gain assistance! He cannot move to injure himself. I must venture.   (*Exit, rapidly and noiselessly*)

Edward. So, so; again all's quiet. They think I cannot escape. I cheated them yesterday. 'Tis a sin to steal liquor,

Enter Mr Rencelaw.

but no crime to purloin sleep from a druggist's store. None, none. (*Produces phial*) Now for the universal antidote, the powerful conqueror of all earthly care—death! (*About to drink.* Rencelaw *seizes phial and casts it from him*) Ha! who are you, man? What would you?

Rencelaw. Nay friend; take not your life, but mend it.

Edward. Friend! You know me not. I am a fiend, the ruin of those who loved me. Leave me!

Rencelaw. I came not to upbraid, nor to insult you. I am aware of all your danger, and come to save you. You have been drinking.

Edward. That you may well know. I am dying now for liquor, and—will you give me brandy? Who are you that takes interest in an unhappy vagabond, neither my father nor my brother?

Rencelaw. I am a friend to the unfortunate. You are a man, and if a man, a brother.

Edward. A brother! Yes; but you trouble yourself without hope. I am lost. Of what use can I be to you?

Rencelaw. Perhaps I can be of use to you. Are you indeed a fallen man? (Edward *looks at him, sighs, and hangs his head*) Then you have the greater claim upon my compassion, my attention, my utmost endeavours to raise you once more to the station in society from which you have fallen. 'For he that lifts a fallen fellow-creature from the dust, is greater than the hero who conquers a world.'

Edward. (*starts*) Merciful heaven! My mother's dying words! Who and what are you?

Rencelaw. I am one of those whose life and labours are passed in rescuing their fellow men from the abyss into which you have fallen. I administer the pledge of sobriety to those who would once more become an ornament to society, and a blessing to themselves and to those around them.

Edward. That picture is too bright—it cannot be.

Rencelaw. You see before you one who for twenty years was a prey to this dreadful folly.

Edward. Indeed! No, no; it is too late.

Rencelaw. You mistake; it is not too late. Come with me; we will restore you to society. Reject not my prayers! Strength will be given you; the Father of purity smiles upon honest endeavours. Come, my brother; enroll your name among the free, the disenthralled, and be a man again. (*Takes his hand*)

Edward. Merciful heaven, grant the prayer of a poor wretch be heard!

(*Exeunt*)

Scene 2. *Union Square. Lights up.* Citizens *passing during the scene.* Children *playing ball, hoop, &c.*

Enter Lawyer Cribbs.

Cribbs. Now this is a lucky escape! It's fortunate that old Sykes the miller was in court, who knew me, or I might have found it difficult to get out of the infernal scrape. What a terrible night I have passed, to be sure! What with the horrid noise of the rats, that I expected every moment would commence making a breakfast of my toes—the cold—and horrible language of my miserable and blackguard companions,—I might as well have passed the crawling hours in Purgatory, ugh! I'm glad it's over. Catch me in such company again, that's all! Now for my design on Rencelaw and Company. I think there can be no detection; the signature is perfect. I'll get some well-dressed boy to deliver the cheque, receive the money, and I'm off to the far West or England, soon as possible. Would I were certain of the ruin of this drunken scoundrel, and the infamy of his tiger-like wife, I should be content.

Enter Boy, *crossing the stage.*

Where are you going so quickly, my lad?

Boy. On an errand, sir.

Enter William Dowton.

Cribbs. Do you want to earn half a dollar?

Boy. With pleasure, sir; honestly.

Cribbs. Oh, of course, honestly.

William. (*aside*) I doubt that, if he rows in your boat.

Cribbs. I am obliged to meet a gentleman on business precisely at this hour, by the Pearl Street House. Call at the Mechanics' Bank for me, deliver this cheque, the teller will give you the money, come back quickly, and I'll reward you with a silver dollar.

Boy. I'll be as quick as possible, sir, and thank you too.   (*Exit hastily*)

William. (*aside*) I knew the old skunk had money, but I was not aware that he banked in New York. Hallo! Here's Miss Spindle a-twigging the fashions; here'll be fun with the old rats. I told her half an hour ago, Cribbs was at a large party among the 'stocracy last night.

Cribbs. (*after putting up his wallet, sees* Miss Spindle) Confound it! Here's that foolish old maid—at such a time, too! Ah, there's no avoiding her.

Enter Miss Spindle.

Miss Spindle. Good gracious! Mr Cribbs, how *do* you do? I declare, how well you do look! A little dissipation improves you.

Cribbs. What?

William. (*aside*) She's beginning already. Hurrah! Go it, old gal!

Miss Spindle. I swow, Mr Cribbs, it's quite a pleasure to see you.

Cribbs. You have all the pleasure to yourself.

William. (*aside*) She'll find out that by and by.

Miss Spindle. Now, don't be so snappish, Lawyer Cribbs. Neighbours should be neighbourly, you know. Who was it that had the pleasure to introduce you?

William. (*aside*) I rather guess I went that stick of candy.

(Cribbs *stares at* Miss Spindle)

Miss Spindle. Now don't look so cross about it. I think you ought to feel right slick, as I do. Now do tell, what kind of music had you? Were there any real-live lions there? Did Colonel Johnson scalp a live Indian to amuse the ladies? Did Dr Dodds put everybody into a phospheric state, when they were all dancing and the lights went out? Did Senator D—— dance a hornpipe to please the children and make a bowl of punch at twelve o'clock? Did——

(*Out of breath*)

William. (*aside*) She'll ask him directly if the elephants played at billiards.

Cribbs. Madam, madam! Will you listen? (*Shouts out*) In the name of confusion, what are you talking about?

Miss Spindle. Why, of the grand *sorrie*—the party, to be sure.

Cribbs. I know nothing of any party; you're insane.

Miss Spindle. Oh no, I ain't, neither. I was told of it by one——

Cribbs. Told by one? Who?

William. (*coming forward*) Me, I calculate. I watched you, I guess.

Cribbs. Watched!

William. Guess I did—so, shut up.

Cribbs. Confusion!

William. I say, Squire, where did you buy your new coat?

Cribbs. Go to the devil, both of you!
William. Where's the tail of your old one? Ha, ha!

(*Exit* Cribbs. William *follows, laughing*)

Miss Spindle. Well, I swow, this is like Jedides' addle eggs! I can
neither make ducks nor chickens on 'em. Well, I've got a good
budget of news and scandal anyhow; so I'll be off back to the
village this very day. This vile city is no safe place for romantic
sensibilities and virgin purity.   (*Exit*)

Scene 3.   *Broadway, with a view of Barnum's Museum.*

Enter Mr Rencelaw, *who crosses the stage.* Bank Messenger *enters
after him.*

Messenger. Mr Rencelaw, Mr Rencelaw! I beg pardon for
hurriedly addressing you, but our cashier desires to know if this is
your signature.   (*Produces cheque*)
Rencelaw. My signature? Good heavens, no. Five thousand dollars!
Is it cashed?
Messenger. Not half an hour. The teller cashed it instantly.
Rencelaw. Who presented the cheque?
Messenger. A young boy, sir, whom I saw just now, recognized, and sent
to the bank immediately. But the cashier—Mr Armond—arriving
directly afterwards, doubted it, and I was dispatched to find you.
Rencelaw. Run to the bank directly; call for a police officer as you pass.
I am rather infirm, but will soon follow. Do not be flurried; our
measures must be prompt, and I fear not for the result.

(*Exit* Messenger)

Enter William Dowton.

Ah, honest William! I have been searching for you. Edward
desired to see you.
William. Thank and bless you, sir. How is he? Where?
Rencelaw. Comparatively well and happy, at my house. His wife and
child will be here immediately; I have sent a carriage for them.
Their home—their happy home—is prepared for them in the
village, and I have obtained almost certain information of his
grandfather's will.
William. Thank heaven! But sir, you appear alarmed—excited.
Rencelaw. A forgery has just been committed, in the name of our firm,
upon the Mechanics' Bank.
William. Bless me! The Mechanics' Bank? Who gave the cheque, sir?
Rencelaw. A boy, William.
William. A boy! How long ago?

Rencelaw. Not half an hour. Why this eagerness?

William. I—I'll tell you, sir. Mr Middleton told me that Lawyer
Cribbs, when the poor fellow was in poverty and drunkenness,
urged him to commit a forgery. Not half an hour since, I saw Cribbs
give a boy a cheque, and tell him to take it to the Mechanics' Bank,
receive some money, and bring it to him somewhere near the Pearl
Street House, where he would find him with a gentleman.

Rencelaw. So, so! I see it all. Come with me to the Tombs and secure
an officer. If you should meet Middleton, do not at present mention
this. Come. (*Exit*)

William. I'll follow you, sir, heart and hand. If I once get my grip
on the old fox, he won't get easily loose, I guess. (*Exit, hastily*)

Scene 4. *Village landscape, as in Act I. Mound and clump of trees.*

Enter Farmer Stevens *and* Farmer Gates, *meeting.*

Stevens. Good afternoon, Mr Gates. You've returned from New York
earlier than common today. Any news? Anything strange, eh?

Gates. Why, ye-es, I guess there is. There were dreadful suspicions
that Cribbs had committed a heavy forgery on the firm of Rencelaw
and Company.

Stevens. Well, I hope, for the credit of the village, he is not guilty
of this bad action, though I have long known his heart was
blacker than his coat. Witness his conduct to the sweetheart of
poor Will's sister, Agnes. Did you tell him the glad news that her
senses were restored?

Gates. No; our hurry was so great. But his mind will be prepared for it,
for good Dr Wordworth always told him her malady was but
temporary.

Stevens. Well, the poor girl has got some secret, I'm sure; and she'll
not tell it to anyone but William. (*Exit*)

Gates. Hark! That's his voice. Yes; here's William, sure enough.

Enter William.

Well, William, everything is just as you directed—but no signs of
the old one yet.

William. I guess he's taken the upper road, to lead all pursuit out of
the track. Mr Rencelaw and the police are at the cross-roads, and
I rather guess we can take charge of the lower part of the village;
so there's no fear of our missing him. Mind, you're not to say
anything to Edward Middleton. Mr Rencelaw would not have him
disturbed till all is secure.

Gates. Oh, I understand. How the whole village rejoiced, when they

saw him and his sweet wife return in peace and joy to the happy
dwelling of their parents! Have you seen your sister, William?

William. No, Farmer, I haven't seen the poor girl yet. Nor do I wish it,
till this business is all fixed.

Gates. Ay, but she wants to see you. She has got to tell you some
secret.

William. A secret! Some of her wild fancies, I reckon; poor girl.

Gates. William, you are mistaken. Your dear sister's mind is quite
restored.

William. What? How? Don't trifle with me, Farmer, I could not
stand it.

Gates. I tell you, William, she's sane—quite well, as Dr Wordworth
said she would be.

William. What! Will she know and call me by my name again? Shall I
hear her sweet voice carolling to the sun at early morning?
Will she take her place among the singers at the old meeting-house
again? Shall I once more at evening hear her murmur the prayers
our poor old mother taught her? Thank heaven! Thank heaven!

Gates. Come, William, come; rouse you—she's coming!

Agnes. (*sings without*) They called her blue-eyed Mary,
When friends and fortune smiled.

William. Farmer, just stand back for a moment or two. All will be
right in a few minutes. (*Exit* Farmer Gates)

Enter Agnes, *plainly but neatly dressed. She sees her brother.*

Agnes. William! Brother!

William. My darling sister! (*They embrace*)

Agnes. I know you, William. I can speak to you and hear you, dear,
dear brother.

William. May heaven be praised for this!

Agnes. William, I have much to tell you, and 'tis important that you
should know it instantly. I know Edward Middleton is here, and it
concerns him most. When I recovered my clear senses, William,
when I remembered the meeting-house, and the old homestead,
and the little dun cow I used to milk, and poor old Neptune, and
could call them by their names——

William. Bless you!

Agnes. Strange fancies would still keep forming in my poor brain, and
remembrances flit along my memory like half-forgottne dreams.
But among them was a vague thought that when insane I had
concealed myself and seen something hidden. Searching round
carefully, I saw a little raised artificial hillock close beneath the
hedge. I went and got a hoe from Farmer Williams' barn, and
after digging near a foot below I found—what think you, William?

William. What, girl, what?

135

Agnes. Concealed in an old tin case, the will of Edward's grandfather, confirming to his dear son the full possession of all his property! The other deed under which Cribbs had acted was a forgery——

William. Where is it now?

Agnes. In the house, safe locked up in mother's bureau till you returned.

Enter Rencelaw, Police Officers, *and* Boy, *hastily.*

Rencelaw. Friend William, Cribbs is on the upper road, coming down the hill.

William. Boy, was that the man gave you the paper?   (*Points off*)

Boy. (*looking off*) I'm sure of it, sir.

William. Come along, then. Now, old Cribbs, I calculate you'll find a hornet's nest about your ears pretty almighty quick.   (*Exeunt*)

Enter Cribbs, *cautious and fearful, looking behind him.*

Cribbs. All's safe. I'm certain no one has observed me. Now for the will; from this fatal evidence I shall at least be secure. (*Advances to the mound, and starts*) Powers of mischief! The earth is freshly turned. (*Searches*) The deed is gone!

Enter Agnes, *hastily.*

Agnes. (*in a tone of madness*)
                    The will is gone; the bird has flown;
                    The rightful heir has got his own!
Ha, ha!

Cribbs. (*paralysed, but recovering*) Ha! Betrayed! Ruined! Mad devil, you shall pay for this.   (*Rushes towards her*)

William *enters, catches his arm, and holds up the will, centre.* Police Officer, *who has got to left centre, seizes other arm, and points pistol to his head.* Rencelaw *holds up forged cheque, and points to it, right centre.* Boy, *left, pointing to* Cribbs. Farmers, *right centre. Picture. Pause.*

William. Trapped! All day with you, Squire.

Rencelaw. Hush, William! Do not oppress a poor, down-fallen fellow creature. (*To* Cribbs) Most unfortunate of men, sincerely do I pity you.

Cribbs. (*recovering, bold and obdurate*) Will your pity save me from the punishment of my misdeeds? No! When compassion is required, I'll beg it of the proud philanthropist, Arden Rencelaw.

Rencelaw. Unhappy wretch! What motives could you have? This world's goods were plenty with you. What tempted you into these double deeds of guilt?

Cribbs. Revenge and avarice, the master-passions of my nature! With

my heart's deepest, blackest feelings, I hated the father of
Edward Middleton. In early life he detected me in an act of vile
atrocity that might have cost me my life. He would not betray,
but pardoned, pitied and despised me. From that hour I hated
with a feeling of intensity that has existed even beyond the grave,
descending unimpaired to his beloved son. By cunning means, which
you would call hypocrisy, I wormed myself into the favour of
the grandfather, who in his dying hour delivered into my hands his
papers. I and an accomplice, whom I bribed, forged the false papers;
the villain left the country. Fearful he should denounce me should he
return, I dared not destroy the real will; but yesterday the news
reached me that he was dead. And now one blow of evil fortune has
destroyed me.

Rencelaw. Repentance may yet avail you——

Cribbs. Nothing. I have lived a villain; a villain let me die!

(*Exit* Cribbs, *with* Officers *and* Farmers)

Rencelaw. William, tell Middleton I shall see him in a day or two. I
must follow that poor man to New York.

William. Oh, Mr Rencelaw, what blessings can repay you?

Rencelaw. The blessings of my own approving conscience. 'The heart of
the feeling man is like the noble tree which, wounded itself, yet
pours forth precious balm.' When the just man quits this transitory
world, the dark angel of death enshrouds him with heavenly joy,
and bears his smiling spirit to the bright regions of eternal bliss.

(*Exit* Rencelaw, *leading* Boy)

William. Well, if there's a happier man in all York State than Bill
Dowton, I should like to see him. My brother Edward again a
man; you, my dear sister, restored to me! Come, we'll go tell all the
news. Hurrah! Hurrah!

(*Singing*)   We'll dance all night by the bright moonlight,
And go home with the girls in the morning.

(*Exeunt*)

Scene 5.   *Interior of cottage, as in Act I, Scene 1. Everything denoting
domestic peace and tranquil happiness. The sun is setting over the hills at
back of landscape.*

Mary *discovered, sewing at handsome work-table.* Julia *seated on low
stool on her left. Elegant table with astral lamp, not lighted. Bible and
other books on table. Two beautiful flower-stands, with roses, myrtles &c.
under windows, left and right. Bird cages on wings, right and left. Covers
of tables, chairs, &c. all extremely neat and in keeping.*

Flute symphony to 'Home, sweet home'. Julia *sings first verse; flute solo accompaniment. The burthen is taken up by chorus of* Villagers *behind. Orchestral accompaniments, &c.*

Edward. (without) Where is my dear, my loved, my faithful wife?

Enter Edward, *well dressed.*

Mary. Edward! My dear, dear, husband!   *(They embrace)*
Edward. Mary, my blessed one! *(To* Julia) My child, my darling!
   Bounteous heaven, accept my thanks!
Julia. Father, dear father! You look as you did the bright sunshiny
   morning I first went to school. Your voice sounds as it used when
   I sang the evening hymn, and you kissed and blessed me. You cry,
   father. Do not cry. But your tears are not such tears as mother shed,
   when she had no bread to give me.
Edward. (kisses her) No, my blessed child, they are not. They are tears
   of repentance, Julia, but of joy.
Mary. Oh, my beloved, my redeemed one! All my poor sufferings are
   as nothing, weighed in a balance with my present joy.
Edward. What gratitude do I not owe the generous, noble-hearted
   man, who from the depths of wretchedness and horror has restored
   me to the world, to myself, and to religion! Oh, what joy can
   equal the bright sensations of a thinking being, when redeemed
   from that degrading vice! His prisoned heart bounds with rapture,
   his swelling veins beat with vigour, and with tremulous gratitude
   he calls on the Supreme Being for blessings on his benefactor.

   Enter Rencelaw.

Respected sir, what words can express our gratification?
Rencelaw. Pay it where 'tis justly due—to heaven! I am but the humble
   instrument, and in your happiness I am rewarded.
Julia. (going to Rencelaw) I shall not forget what mother last night
   taught me.
Rencelaw. What was that, sweet girl?
Julia. In my prayers, when I have asked a blessing for my father and
   mother, I pray to Him to bless Arden Rencelaw too.
Rencelaw. Dear child!   *(Kisses her)*
Edward. I will not wrong your generous nature by fulsome outward
   gratitude for your most noble conduct, but humbly hope that He
   will give me strength to continue in the glorious path adorned
   by your bright example. In the words of New England's favoured
   poet,[1]

          There came a change—the cloud rolled off,
            A light fell on my brain,

---

[1] *New England's favoured poet* presumably Henry Wadsworth Longfellow (1807–82),
but the quotation does not appear in his *Works* (1886)

The Drunkard

And, like the passing of a dream
That cometh not again,
The darkness of my spirit fled,
I saw the gulf before,
I shuddered at the waste behind,
And am a man once more.

Flute, 'Home, sweet home'. Julia, *right, kisses* Rencelaw's *hand, right centre.* Mary *embraces* Edward, *left centre. Tableau, and*

Curtain.

The Corsican Brothers

A ROMANTIC DRAMA IN THREE ACTS BY DION BOUCICAULT

First performed at the Princess's Theatre, London, 24 February 1852

CAST

FABIEN DEI FRANCHI } twin brothers		Mr Charles Kean
LOUIS DEI FRANCHI		
ALFRED DE MEYNARD		Mr G. Everett
BARON GIORDANO } friends to Louis		Mr C. Wheatleigh
MARTELLI		
CHÂTEAU-RENAUD		Mr Alfred Wigan
BARON DE MONTGIRON, his friend		Mr James Vining
BEAUCHAMP } fashionable gentlemen		Mr Stacey
VERNER		Mr Rolleston
ORLANDO } heads of two Corsican families		Mr Ryder
COLONNA		Mr Meadows
ANTONIO SANOLA, judge of the district		Mr F. Cooke
GRIFFO, a domestic		Mr Paulo
GUIDO, a guide		Mr Stoakes
BOISSEC, a woodcutter		Mr J. Chester
SURGEON		Mr Daly
SERVANTS		Mr Haines
		Mr Wilson
MADAME SAVILIA DEI FRANCHI		Miss Phillips
MADAME ÉMILIE DE L'ESPARRE		Miss Murray
MARIA, servant to Madame Savilia		Miss Robertson
CORALIE		Miss Carlotta Leclercq
ESTELLE } ladies of the ballet		Miss Vivash
CELESTINA		Miss Daly

Ladies, gentlemen, masks, dominoes, officers, male and female Corsican peasants, servants, &c.

The incidents of the First Act in Corsica, and of the Second Act in Paris, are supposed to occur at the same time. The Third Act takes place five days later, in the Forest of Fontainebleau.

Period: 1841

DIONYSIUS LARDNER BOUCICAULT

Designer, director, manager, impresario, leading actor and for over thirty years the most prolific playwright on the Anglo-Saxon stage. Born 1822 of Irish-French extraction. Packed Covent Garden at the age of twenty with his comedy *London Assurance* (1841). Adapted many cape-and-sword romances from the French, including *Don Caesar* (1844) for Webster at the Adelphi and *The Corsican Brothers* (1852) for Charles Kean. Sailed for America 1853, and identified a public taste for 'the actual, the contemporaneous, the photographic'. Drew on abolition for *The Octoroon* (1859) and the Indian Mutiny for *Jessie Brown, or the Relief of Lucknow* (1858), which opened in New York before the siege was raised. Pioneered 'sensation drama'. Staged an avalanche in *Pauvrette* (1858), Derby Day in *The Flying Scud* (1866) and the Boat Race in *Formosa* (1869). Enjoyed great personal success playing the feckless comic heroes of his Irish melodramas *The Colleen Bawn* (1860), *Arrah-na-Pogue* (1864) and *The Shaughraun* (1874). Died in poverty 1890.

THE CORSICAN BROTHERS

Alexandre Dumas *père*'s romantic novel *Les Frères Corses* (1845) was adapted for the stage by Eugène Grangé and Xavier de Montépin and premièred in Paris at Dumas' own Théâtre Historique on 10 August 1850, with Emmanuel as Château-Renaud and Fechter doubling the title parts. Charles Kean admired it and commissioned Boucicault to write an adaptation. *The Corsican Brothers* opened at the Princess's on 24 February 1852 and won immediate success. Next day *The Times* praised the 'awful calmness' of Kean's Fabien, and George Henry Lewes in *The Leader* (28 February) raved about the first appearance of the ghost:

Nothing can exceed the art with which this is managed; with ghostly terror, heightened by the low tremolos of the violins, and the dim light upon the stage, the audience, breath-suspended, watches the slow apparition, and the vision of the duel which succeeds: a scenic effect more real and terrible than anything I remember.

As for the duel itself, it was nothing short of

a masterpiece on both sides: the Bois de Boulogne itself has scarcely seen a duel more real or more exciting. Kean's dogged, quiet, terrible walk after Wigan, with the fragment of broken sword in his relentless grasp, I shall not forget.

Irving's revival at the Lyceum (18 September 1880) retained Boucicault's text, Kean's gliding ghost and the traditional spectre melody, but spent a fortune on the spectacle. To Clement Scott, the Opera scene was

realism out-realised. Real private boxes, real curtains, hangings, and real people in the loges, real trees and flowers, the floor of the mimic opera literally crammed with dancers and dominoes, merriment and masks, pierrots and pierrettes, polichinelles, clowns and pantaloons, shepherdesses and débardeurs, ballet girls, monks, pilgrims, and comic dogs. Such a sound of revelry goes up as the curtain rises, that dramatic action is made an impossibility,

conversation a farce.   (*From 'The Bells' to 'King Arthur'* (1896), p.187)

Moments later, and the entire stage is transformed into yet another scene

of surpassing merit—the bare, leafless trees of the silent forest, the frozen pond, the slowly descending snow, the deep orange and red bars of the setting [rising?] winter sun—all prepare one for the epitome of fate.   (p. 189)

How was it done? In his *Personal Reminiscences of Henry Irving* (1906), Bram Stoker takes us behind the scenes and into the secret. The great masked ball

came to an end by lowering the 'cut' cloth which formed the background of Montgiron's salon, the door leading into the supper-room being in the centre at back. Whilst the guests were engaged in their more or less rapid banquet, the covered scene was being obliterated and the Forest of Fontainebleau was coming down from the rigging-loft, ascending from the cellar and being pushed on right and left from the wings. Montgiron's salon was concealed by the descent of great tableau curtains. These remained down from thirty-five to forty *seconds* and went up again on a forest as real as anything can be on the stage. Trees stood out separately over a large area so that those entering from side or back could be seen passing behind or amongst them. All over the stage was a deep blanket of snow, white and glistening in the winter sunrise. Snow that lay so thick that when the duellists, stripped and armed, stood face to face, they each secured a firmer foothold by kicking it away. Of many wonderful effects this snow was perhaps the strongest and most impressive of reality. The public could never imagine how it was done. It was *salt*, common coarse salt which was white in the appointed light and glistened like real snow. There were tons of it. A crowd of men stood ready in the wings with little baggage-trucks such as are now used in the corridors of great hotels; silent with rubber wheels. On them were great wide-mouthed sacks full of salt. When the signal came they rushed in on all sides each to his appointed spot and tumbled out his load, spreading it evenly with great wide-bladed wooden shovels.

(I. 160–1)

At one performance, when the Prince of Wales came to peep backstage, the shovellers were finished in thirty seconds flat; such was the debt which Irving's romantic melodramas owed to inspired stage-management.

Boucicault's play was used again by Irving's disciple, Martin-Harvey, who played it at the Adelphi in 1907 and toured it round the provinces between the wars. Most recently, it formed the basis of John Bowen's adaptation for the Greenwich Theatre in March 1970. This time, of course, there were no gliding ghosts, no visions and no snow. 'I wanted', said Mr Bowen in a programme note,

to write a play, *with* songs, *with* fights, which should take an archetypical plot for a melodrama, made out of a rather Somerset Maughamish story by Dumas, and do what Planchon did for *The Three Musketeers*, but without sending it up. I wanted to make something more like a novel by Stendhal in which human beings are the prisoners of events, which they may set in motion but never cause— as a mouse does not set the trap though his own hunger may cause him to spring it.

The result, according to Michael Billington in *Plays and Players* (May 1970), showed 'the difficulties of trying to rework a melodrama without accepting the clear-cut moral attitudes it originally embodied'. It is a warning directors attracted to the play may profit from; Boucicault, when all is said and done, knows best.

The present text is based upon the manuscript submitted to the Lord Chamberlain by Charles Kean's management in September 1851. Obvious errors have been silently amended, and the meagre stage directions amplified from Lacy's acting edition, which is a faithful English version of Boucicault's French source.

ACT I

Scene 1. *Principal saloon in the château of* Madame la Contessa Savilia dei Franchi *at Sullacaro in Corsica; a large chimney-piece, R, surmounted by a trophy of carbines suspended from the horns of a moufflon; at the back, C, the door of entrance; at the two sides, lateral doors.*

Maria *discovered, singing at her spinning wheel.*

Maria.   The sun shines bright across the plain,
      From Aleria to Sartène,
      But at the end there's gloom!
      For there the murm'ring rivulet flows,
      And sadly bends the laurel rose
      O'er poor Peppino's tomb.
           (*A knocking is heard at the door*)
Some one knocks. (*Knocking again*) Yes, I am not deceived!
Griffo! Griffo!

Griffo *enters.*

Griffo. What's the matter? Is the house on fire?
Maria. No, but there's somebody knocking at the gate.
Griffo. Well, go and open it.
Maria. At this late hour, by myself? No thank you.
Griffo. Timid individual.   (*Goes out*)
Maria. (*putting her spinning wheel away*) Go and open it! Yes, to be
 agreeably saluted by a pistol or a stiletto.

Re-*enter* Griffo.

Well, what is it?
Griffo. A French gentleman—a traveller—who requests our hospitality.
Maria. (*joyfully*) A French traveller! I hope you haven't refused him?
Griffo. Refused! Refuse hospitality in Corsica! Go and announce his
 arrival to the Countess.
Maria. I should like to have a peep at him first.
Griffo. Go, I tell you.
Maria. Just one glimpse. Is he young and handsome?
Griffo. That's nothing to you. He stays all night.
Maria. Oh, then I can wait a little. I fly to tell Madame. (*Exit*)

Enter Alfred de Meynard *and* Guido *with a valise.*

Griffo. (*at the door*) This way, your excellency. I have sent to inform the Signora Savilia of your arrival.

Alfred. My good friend, I fear this unseasonable intrusion——

Griffo. (*smiling*) Intrusion! we have no such word in Corsica. Here a stranger honours the house he stops at. (*To* Guido) Ah! honest Guido, is that you?

Alfred. I can dismiss you now. Here are two piastres.

Guido. Thank you sir.   (*Exit*)

Griffo. Is your excellency acquainted with the Countess?

Alfred. I have not yet that honour, but I bring a letter from her son.

Griffo. From Monsieur Louis?

Alfred. Yes; he is my intimate friend.

Enter Madame dei Franchi *and* Maria.

Madame. From my son Louis, did you say, sir?

Alfred. (*bowing*) Madame, I ought to apologise for my intrusion, but the well-known hospitality of your country, and this letter, will, I trust, plead my excuse.

Madame. (*taking the letter*) I thank you, sir. You can understand a mother's joy when she sees the handwriting of an absent son. (*Reads*) Ah, my dear Louis! He recommends you to us, as one of his most valued friends. There needed not this to ensure your welcome. In Corsica, every traveller may throw his bridle on his horse's neck, and stop where he conducts him. His stay is limited by his own pleasure, and the only regret he occasions is when he announces his departure. Maria, tell them to prepare the chamber Louis occupied before he left us. Griffo, carry there the luggage of our guest; while he stays with us, you will devote yourself entirely to him.   (*Servants exeunt*)

Alfred. I know not how to thank you, Madame.

Madame. On my son's part as well as my own, I repeat your hearty welcome.

Alfred. Oh, I recollect—your second son, Monsieur Fabien.

Madame. I have two sons, twins.

Alfred. I have heard of the extraordinary resemblance which exists between them.

Madame. You shall judge for yourself when you have seen Fabien. He went this morning early to the mountains; I expect his return every instant.

Alfred. I long to shake him by the hand.

Griffo *enters.*

Griffo. (*as he enters*) Madame, Monsieur Fabien has arrived.

Madame. Where is he?

Griffo. Just entering the gate; he stopped to speak with the Judge.
(*To* Alfred) Your excellency's apartment is ready.
Alfred. I thank you, my worthy friend, but I am not tired; my reception
here has driven away fatigue.   (*He continues talking in a low voice with*
Griffo, *to whom he gives his hat and cane*)

Enter Fabien, *carrying a carbine, which he lays down on entering.*

Madame. (*going to meet him*) My son, you have been expected home.
Fabien. By you, dear mother?
Madame. Yes, and by some one else; how late you are this evening.
Fabien. Yes, that devil Orlando is a true Corsican; I could hardly
persuade him. At last however I succeeded and all is settled. This
unhappy feud will now be terminated. He and Colonna have
promised to meet here this evening with their kinsmen and friends,
and having once promised they are sure to come.
Madame. And now let me introduce to you Monsieur Alfred de
Meynard, a friend of your brother.
Fabien. (*going towards* Alfred, *and offering him his hand*) A friend of
Louis! Sir, you are most welcome.
Alfred. Good heavens! It is identity! I could swear that I held by the
hand my old friend.
Fabien. Believe it, sir. Louis and myself are one.
Alfred. The voice, too, is tone for tone the same.
Madame. Monsieur is the bearer of a letter.
Fabien. (*in an agitated tone*) A letter from Louis? Dear mother, allow me
to look at it. (*She gives it, and he reads*) By the date you have not
seen Louis for three weeks—then you know nothing.
Madame. What say you, Fabien?
Fabien. Nothing, mother, nothing. How did you leave my brother,
when you last saw him?
Alfred. His health was excellent.
Fabien. So much for the body; but his mind? Did he appear thoughtful,
harassed, in low spirits?
Alfred. Far from it. He seemed wholly occupied in preparing for his
degree, which he felt confident of obtaining.
Fabien. At that time, then, you observed in him no trace of secret
vexation?
Alfred. None whatever. Have you any reason to think otherwise? Have
you received more recently any evil tidings?
Fabien. Received? No—that is, not in the sense in which *you* use the
word.
Madame. My son!
Alfred. I scarcely comprehend you.
Madame. Fabien, I trust nothing of consequence has happened to your
brother.

Fabien. (going towards her) No, mother, I hope not; still——

Madame. The fears you entertained yesterday on account of Louis——

Fabien. I have them still; they never leave me.

Madame. But you have had no further warning?

Fabien. (after a moment's hesitation) No—none.

Madame. But if your brother's life was threatened——

Fabien. Mother!

Madame. If he was dead, you would have known it?

Fabien. Yes, for I should have seen him.

Alfred. (aside, and astonished) He would have seen him!

Madame. And you would have told me?

Fabien. Assuredly, dearest mother.

Madame. Fabien, I thank you. The absent are in the hands of
Providence—you know that Louis lives. Let us endeavour to
dismiss this anxiety for the moment, and think of nothing but to do
honour to our guest.

She salutes Alfred, *who bows to her—*Fabien *accompanies her to the door
on the left, and she goes out.*

Alfred. (looking at them, as she is going) All this is very strange. But
I am in the land of adventures, and this old château appears the
head quarters of romance.

Fabien. (returning towards Alfred*)* You will excuse us, sir, of speaking
before you of family affairs, but we cannot treat you with reserve,
having come from our dear Louis. The last few words exchanged
between me and my mother appear to you a little unintelligible?

Alfred. I confess it. You have received no recent news of your brother.
Why, then, do you suppose him restless, melancholy and in pain?

Fabien. Because for the last three days I have been restless, melancholy
and in pain myself.

Alfred. Excuse me, but I cannot follow the coincidence.

Fabien. You know, probably, that Louis and I are twins?

Alfred. He has often told me so, and the Countess also mentioned it
when I arrived.

Fabien. There is a strange, mysterious sympathy between us—no
matter what space divides us we are still one in body, in feeling, in
soul. Any powerful impression which the one experiences is instantly
conveyed, by some invisible agency, to the senses of the other.

Alfred. This is most singular.

Fabien. Within these last few days, in spite of myself, my temperament
has changed. I have become sad, uneasy, gloomy, with a depression
of the heart I cannot conquer. I am convinced my brother is unhappy.

Alfred. And you attribute this feeling of causeless fear to some danger
impending over your brother?

Fabien. I am sure of it.

Alfred. And the nature of his unhappiness—cannot you divine it?

Fabien. Not I feel the effect but the cause is hid from me.

Alfred. Perhaps some trifling professional annoyance.

Fabien. Not so. It implicates the heart.

Alfred. I thought him too much engaged with his studies to care for the attractions of the sex.

Fabien. For the sex generally, yes; but he is deeply in love with one.

Alfred. And that one—(*Rising*) But I am indiscreet, pray pardon me.

Fabien. You shall know all. From my brother's friend I will have no secrets. About a year since, the daughter of the general commanding in Corsica came on a visit of two months, with her father, to Ajaccio. She was young, amiable, beautiful. Louis and I had frequent opportunities of meeting her, and as all our feelings are in unison, need I tell you we both saw—and loved her. Each of us perceived the passion of the other, and tried to extinguish his own. I know not whether I succeeded, but Louis thought I had, and his increased affection for me proved his gratitude. The general was recalled to France, his daughter accompanied him, and the lovely vision was dissolved. Some time after, my brother asked me whether I intended to go to Paris, to study law or medicine. We had always promised never to leave our mother solitary. I told him I had no desire to travel. His countenance beamed with joy. He left us, and I remained. Most probably I shall never quit my native village.

Alfred. What! at your age, in the springtime of life—bury yourself from the active world!

Fabien. You wonder, naturally, that anyone should choose to live in such a wild and ignorant land. But I am native to the soil, like the green oak, or laurel rose. I love to explore the forest and to rove over chasm and torrent with my rifle for a companion, to sit upon the mountain ledge with the theatre of nature at my feet, and revel in the sense of liberty and boundless space. In the city I should be stifled as in a prison. No; let Louis obey his destiny. He will become great and noble——

Alfred. While you?

Fabien. Am free, and Corsican.

Alfred. (*laughing*) A characteristic reply. And this lady, you think, is the cause of your brother's uneasiness?

Fabien. Yes. Although he never names her in his letters, his love increases— the wound is a deep one.

Alfred. (*gaily*) Such wounds are seldom mortal, and if you have no other subject of inquietude——

Fabien. Something else has happened to my brother.

Alfred. Do you imagine he is in any danger?

Fabien. I do, certainly.

Alfred. Or dead?

Fabien. No—not dead; had it been so, as I told my mother, I should
  have seen him since.

Alfred. (*smiling*) You would have seen him.

Fabien. Look you, sir, you are what is called a man of the world. I saw
  by the incredulous smile with which you listened to me but now——

Alfred. Oh, believe me——

Fabien. No, do not apologise. You dwellers in cities—what you gain in
  art you lose in nature. You are more prone to believe the miracles
  of a science which you have invented, than to believe the wonders
  of that creation which a divinity has made.

Alfred. Nay, do not mistake surprise for misbelief. I accuse nothing of
  being impossible.

Fabien. All this appears to you childish and absurd. As a man of the
  world you scoff at idle tales of superstition. Yet I could relate a
  tale existing in our family three hundred years ago which might
  shake your scepticism. Do you believe in apparitions?

Alfred. Why no, I can't say I believe, but nothing proves their
  non-existence.

Fabien. Give me then your attention, while I recount briefly a story well
  attested in the annals of the Dei Franchi. (*They both sit down near the
  table*) Three hundred years ago, our immediate ancestor, the Count
  Bartolomeo dei Franchi, died, leaving two orphan sons. The
  extraordinary attachment of these children to each other was the
  theme of Corsica. Arrived at the age of manhood, they bound
  themselves by a solemn oath that not even death itself should separate
  them. This vow each registered in his own blood on a parchment
  they exchanged; the conditions prescribed were that he who died
  first should appear to the other, not only at the moment of his death,
  but also as a warning to foretell it.

Alfred. An oath more easily made than kept.

Fabien. In three months after, one of the two brothers was waylaid and
  murdered in an ambuscade. At that very moment, the other, residing
  in this very house, being seized with a vague sense of danger,
  was engaged in writing to him, and as he impressed his seal upon
  the burning wax, he heard a sigh behind him. He turned and saw
  his brother standing by his side, his hand upon his shoulder,
  although he felt no touch or weight. Mechanically he offered the
  letter to the figure, but it shook its head mournfully, and waving its
  arm to the wall, the masonry seemed to obey the gesture—it opened,
  and the living man beheld the murder in all its harrowing identity.

Alfred. It was a dream.

Fabien. The archives of justice at Bastia attest its truth, for on the
  deposition of the surviving brother, the murderers were detected
  and arrested. Terrified by what they thought the intervention

of heaven, they confessed that the crime had been perpetrated
exactly as seen in the vision, and at the very same hour.

Alfred. This is strange indeed, and terrible. Do you fear, then, that
Louis is dead?

Fabien. No, he lives; but I fear he is wounded.

Alfred. How? By whom?

Fabien. This morning, on my way to the mountains—ah, my mother
returns—do not speak of this before her, I entreat you.

Alfred. Rely on my discretion.

Enter Madame Dei Franchi, Griffo, Maria, *and* Servants *carrying the
supper, which they place on the table.*

Madame. Now gentlemen, when you are disposed, supper is ready.
Well, Fabien?

Fabien. Well, mother, my passing gloom has vanished—I am gay and
joyous. Monsieur de Meynard, take your seat. (Alfred *hands* Madame
to table—they seat themselves, Griffo *and* Maria *waiting*) And so you have
come to visit Corsica? You do well not to postpone your visit.
In a few years, our laws, our manners, will exist no longer. All will
be swept away before the modern mania of improvement; we are
degenerating hourly from our ancient habits.

Alfred. But in this house, at least, I find a noble picture of the earlier
times.

Fabien. Yes, in my mother always. But for me, I am at this moment
engaged in an action my ancestors would have deemed disgraceful
to them.

Alfred. You? Impossible.

Fabien. You'll wonder more when I explain it. Our peasantry in this
district have been long divided into two factions, who hate
each other mortally—the Colonnas and the Orlandos; but for the
first time in Corsica, a quarrel has been compromised.
Surrounded by muskets, rapiers, and stilettos, I am selected as
the arbiter of peace; this evening is fixed for the formality of
pacification.

Alfred. And how originated this famous quarrel, which your good
offices have put an end to?

Fabien. Like many others, from a very trifling cause—so insignificant
I cannot name it without smiling. A hen!

Alfred. A hen!

Fabien. Yes, a wretched barn door hen. Ten years ago this hen escaped
from the farm yard of the Orlandos to that of the Colonnas. The
first demanded the hen, the others said it was theirs. During the
dispute, the aged grandmother of the Colonnas, who held the fowl,
wrung its neck and threw it in the face of the mother of the Orlandos.
One of the Orlandos seized the hen and was about to throw it back

when a Colonna, who had a loaded carbine, fired, and shot him on the spot.

Alfred. And how many lives have been sacrificed in this silly altercation?

Fabien. The killed are nine, the wounded five.

Alfred. And all for a poor hen! No doubt both parties are worn out, and entreated you to interfere.

Fabien. Far from it. They would have exterminated each other, rather than have made the slightest overture. Our prefect wrote to Louis, who is gentleness itself, to say that if *I* interfered all might be reconciled. He pledged his word for me, and I was bound in honour to redeem it. This evening, in this hall, the ceremony will take place. (*Bells are rung at a distance*) Hark! the village bell announces the hour when all are summoned to attend.

Griffo *enters* R.

Griffo. Monsieur Fabien, here's one without desires to speak with you.

Fabien. Who is he?

Griffo. Orlando.

Fabien. In right good time. (*Going to* R) Come in, honest Orlando.

Orlando *appears at the door* R, *dragged in by* Griffo.

Orlando. I beg pardon, but——

Fabien. But what?

Orlando. Why this—that is—I don't exactly know—but——

Fabien. Come in, man, come in.

Orlando. Oh, yes—come in, that's easily said, and easily done too—but when I am in——

Fabien. Well, what then?

Orlando. Monsieur Fabien dei Franchi, it chokes a man to be reconciled to an enemy.

Fabien. Remember, Orlando, you have given your word.

Orlando. Yes, yes, I have—Oh, if I hadn't!

Fabien. Recollect, too, your side has had the advantage. Five Colonnas killed, against four Orlandos.

Orlando. That's some consolation—but nevertheless——

Maria *enters* L, *with the dessert.*

Maria. Monsieur Fabien, some one without enquires for you.

Fabien. Where?

Maria. (*pointing to the* L *door*) There!

Fabien. Who is it?

Maria. A Colonna.

Fabien. Good; desire him to walk in. Griffo, go round by that door and lock it on the outside. (*Exit* Griffo R, *locks door on the outside, and re-enters* C) I repeat it, Orlando, you have the advantage.

Orlando. But mind, he must bring a hen with him.

Fabien. Decidedly.

Orlando. A white hen.

Fabien. Oh, white or black, that makes no difference.

Orlando. White, white, nothing but white.

Fabien. Well, it shall be white.

Orlando. And alive.

Fabien. And alive.

Orlando. If it should be dead, remember, the contract fails.

Fabien. Be satisfied—it *shall* be alive.

Orlando. He must offer his hand first.

Fabien. No, you both offer at the same time; you agreed to that.

Orlando. I don't remember that part of the agreement.

Fabien. How! can an Orlando's memory fail, when he has passed his word?

Orlando. (*with a deep sigh*) Ah! If I hadn't! It's very hard, nevertheless. But five dead Colonnas against four Orlandos, that's something.

Maria *appears at the door* L, *pushing in* Colonna.

Maria. Go in, I tell you.

Colonna. Well, if I must, I must.

Orlando *has crept towards the door* R, *and endeavours to get out, but finding it fastened on the outside, he resumes his confidence, and eyes* Colonna *fiercely.*

Fabien. (*to* Colonna) Remember, you have given your word.

Colonna. You see, Monsieur Fabien, here's the point: there has been one killed more on our side than on the other—the terms are not equal.

Fabien. Granted so far; but there are four Orlandos wounded against one Colonna.

Colonna. Wounded don't count.

Fabien. It is too late now to argue. Have you brought the hen?

Colonna. The hen?

Fabien. You remember your promise; come, you must have brought it.

Colonna. Yes, yes.

Fabien. Where is it?

Colonna. Here.

Fabien. Here! Where?

Colonna. In my pocket.

Fabien. Of course a white one?

Colonna. Yes, white, certainly. There's one small black spot——

Fabien. No matter, I'll take that on myself. It is alive?

Colonna. It was when I started, but on the way I sat down once or twice, and perhaps——

Fabien. Produce it. (*To* Griffo) Lock that door on the outside as you did the other. (*Exit* Griffo L, *locks door on the outside, and re-enters* C) Hold your fowl in your hand and be ready.

Colonna. As I bring the fowl, he must be the first to offer his hand.

Fabien. Not so; both together, that's the agreement.

Colonna. Is it positively so written down?

Fabien. Positively. Come, Colonna.

Colonna. (*with a deep sigh*) Oh! If I hadn't promised! But a Colonna must keep his word.

Fabien. (*to* Orlando) Who is your surety?

Orlando. Andrea Mari.

Fabien. (*to* Colonna) And yours?

Colonna. My surety? I forgot that entirely.

Orlando. (*turning round to go out*) A failure on his side! I declare the treaty void.

Fabien. (*holding him*) No, no, he has one here. Monsieur Alfred de Meynard, will you act as surety to Colonna?

Alfred. With all my heart.

Fabien. The preliminaries are complete. Throw open the gate, and admit the company.

Madame Dei Franchi *and* Alfred *rise from table;* Griffo *opens the doors at the back. Enter the* Judge of the Peace, *who carries several olive branches in his hand, and the* Male *and* Female Relations *and* Friends *of the two adversaries.*

Judge. (*after taking his place at the head of the table*) My worthy friends, we are assembled here by Monsieur Fabien dei Franchi, in his ancestral mansion, to witness one of those delightful scenes which are acceptable above, and do honour to the human heart. (Orlando *and* Colonna *growl*) Receive each of you the peaceful olive branch, and vow oblivion for the past and friendship for the future.

Colonna. Oblivion, *perhaps;* friendship, *never.*

Orlando. (*to* Fabien) You hear him!

Colonna. Diavolo! 'Tis I, not thou, must restore the hen.

Fabien. (*presenting an olive branch to* Orlando) Friendship for the future, Orlando.

Orlando. I'll make an effort.

Fabien. (*presenting another branch to* Colonna) Colonna, friendship for the future.

Colonna. Well, I'll try.

Fabien. Good; that point's disposed of. Now shake hands.

They pause. Fabien *goes to fetch* Orlando, *whom he brings forward to the middle of the stage, then goes for* Colonna—*whilst he is bringing* Colonna,

Orlando *regains his place—he makes a sign to* Alfred, *who leads* Orlando
forward on one side, whilst Fabien *leads* Colonna *on the other.*

Your hands, I say.   (*They shake hands unwillingly*)
Judge. (*reads*) 'Before us, Antonio Sanola, Justice of the Peace for the
  district of Sullacaro, it has been solemnly and formally agreed
  between Carbano Orlando, and Marco Colonna, that from this day
  forth, the 22nd of March, 1841, the vendetta declared between
  them since the 11th of February, 1830, shall cease for ever.
  In token of which they have severally signed these presents, before
  the principal inhabitants of the village, their respective sureties,
  friends and relatives; and which are further ratified by Monsieur
  Fabien dei Franchi, elected as arbitrator, and by me, Antonio Sanola,
  judge of the district as aforesaid.'
Fabien. Now then, Colonna, restore the hen.

Colonna *makes a movement as if to strike* Orlando *in the face; but
under the stern look of* Fabien *he restrains himself, and presents it with
tolerable civility.*

Judge. Now, gentlemen, your signatures.
Orlando. I can't sign; I don't know how to write.
Judge. Then you must affix your mark. A cross will do.

Orlando, *after many difficulties, is persuaded to make his cross*—Colonna,
*who contrives to write his name in a vile scrawl, resumes his place in high
triumph at his superiority in penmanship over his rival—After this, the*
Judge *requires the witnesses to sign—During this time,* Fabien *goes up to*
Orlando, *who is examining the hen.*

Fabien. Orlando, I congratulate you. No more quarrels between you
  and Colonna.
Orlando. Excellenza! the hen is miserably thin.
Colonna. (*aside to* Fabien) It isn't a hen; it's a little cock.

All having signed the paper, exeunt Peasants *with the* Judge, Orlando
and Colonna *last.*

Orlando. If I hadn't given my hand—but we shall see.   (*Exit*)
Colonna. If I hadn't restored the hen—but time will show.   (*Exit*)
Fabien. (*to* Alfred) Well, sir, you have seen our social manners in
  Corsica; judge whether we are entitled to rank with civilized nations.
Alfred. At least I have a new incident to add to my adventures.
Madame. You will relate to our dear Louis how his brother has
  redeemed his pledge.
Alfred. I shall not fail to do so.
Madame. It grows late; you are doubtless fatigued. Griffo, conduct our
  guest to his apartment.

Fabien. I have some particular orders for Griffo; select another servant.

Madame. In that case, I will attend on him myself.

Alfred. Impossible, Madame, I cannot suffer it.

Madame. In the old times the lady of the castle always acted as chamberlain, and in Corsica we are still in the sixteenth century.

Alfred. If you are peremptory, I must obey. (*To* Fabien) Good night. Remember, we were interrupted; you owe me the remainder of a story.

Fabien. Yes, tomorrow.

(Exeunt Madame dei Franchi, Alfred and Maria)

Fabien. Griffo.

Griffo. Monsieur?

Fabien. You must instantly set out for Ajaccio; there wait the arrival of a letter from Paris. The moment you receive it, gallop back as if life and death were on your speed.

Griffo. You fear something has happened to your brother?

Fabien. Griffo, he is wounded. I must know whether his wound is slight or dangerous.

Griffo. Have you received a warning?

Fabien. Yes; this morning on my way to the mountains I felt a sudden pain as if a sword had pierced my chest. I looked round and saw no one. I laid my hand upon the place; there was no wound. My heart felt crushed, and the name of my brother leaped unbidden to my lips. I looked at my watch; it was ten minutes after nine. (*He turns involuntarily towards the clock*) Look, look, the clock! It points to the same hour, although it must be close on midnight— the clock has stopped.

Madame dei Franchi *re-enters.*

Madame. (*returning*) Yes, I noticed it before. The clock stopped this morning, and without apparent cause.

Fabien. This morning! They must have forgot to wind it up.

Madame. No, on the contrary, it was wound up the day before yesterday.

Fabien. There's no mistaking this; 'tis a second warning.

Madame. What say you, Fabien?

Fabien. Nothing, nothing. Good night, dearest mother.

Madame. Bless you, my son; good night. If evil hovers o'er us, may Providence avert it. (*Exit*)

Fabien. To horse! To horse! Griffo, lose not a moment. At all hazards, I will write to Louis. Put the letter in the post the moment you arrive; 'twill catch the steamer which leaves tomorrow. Haste, haste. I'll bring the letter before your foot is in the stirrup. (*Exit* Griffo) The sudden pain in my side—the strange coincidence between my watch and the clock—(*throws off his coat and waistcoat*)

156

But perhaps 'tis nothing after all. (*He remains in his shirt sleeves, sits at the table and writes*) 'My brother, my dearest Louis, if this finds you still alive, write instantly—though but two words—to reassure me. I have received a terrible admonition—write—write.'

He folds the letter and seals it; at the same time Louis dei Franchi *appears, without his coat or waistcoat, as his brother is, but with a blood stain upon his breast; he glides across the stage, ascending gradually through the floor at the same time, and lays his hand on* Fabien's *left shoulder.*

Fabien. (*turning round*) My brother!—dead!

Madame dei Franchi *enters.*

Madame. (*at the door*) Who uttered that word?
Louis. Silence—look there!

Louis dei Franchi *waves his arm, passes through the wall, and disappears; at the same moment the scene at the back opens and discloses a glade in the Forest of Fontainebleau. On one side, a young man who is wiping the blood from his sword with a handkerchief; two seconds are near him. On the other side,* Louis dei Franchi, *stretched upon the ground, supported by his two seconds and a surgeon.*

Picture.

ACT II

Scene 1. *The masked ball at the Opera, in Paris.* Masks, Dominoes *and* Officers, *in ball costume, walking about, accosting each other and chatting. During the scene, ball quadrilles are played.*

Enter Coralie, *followed by* Montgiron.

Montgiron. Stay, my angel! One word.
Coralie. Let it be a short one.
Montgiron. Love! Is that short enough?
Coralie. (*going*) Short and sweet, but it has too long a meaning.
Montgiron. Not so fast, my pretty Coralie.
Coralie. (*unmasking*) Oh, you know me. Well, Baron, what now?
Montgiron. I give a supper tonight after the ball; will you join us?

Enter Estelle *and* Verner.

Coralie. (*catching at a domino who is passing*) I say, Estelle, here's the Baron has a supper tonight, and is in want of guests.

Estelle. (*unmasking*) Let him address his invitations to us ladies of the ballet.

Coralie. And we'll undertake to provide a full company.

Estelle. So you may ice your champagne with confidence, my dear Baron.

Montgiron. Then I may depend on you?

Enter Beauchamp.

Coralie. Here is my security. Monsieur Beauchamp, you are to retain me in custody until—oh, by the by, what hour?

Montgiron. Three o'clock precisely.

Coralie. Until three o'clock; at which disgracefully late hour, you are to surrender me at the table of the Baron de Montgiron.

Beauchamp. Accepted!

Estelle. Monsieur Verner, till then I confide myself to your sense of propriety.

Verner. Agreed.

All remask and join the crowd. Enter Louis dei Franchi; *he advances, looking anxiously round, like a man who is seeking somebody.*

Louis. (*stopping and looking at his watch*) It is close on half-past one; that was the time named, and this the place. The anonymous letter I have received assured me she would be here. I have traversed these passages, I have examined every domino that passed me, but I cannot find her. Perhaps I have been deceived—oh, would it were so! Émilie, dear Émilie, for you I have suffered much, and will endure still more.

As Louis *disappears in the crowd,* Montgiron *returns with* Giordano Martelli *and several* Gentlemen.

Montgiron. (*to* Gentlemen) Yes, yes, every one his own master at present, but remember you sup with me at three o'clock.

Gentlemen. At three! We understand.

They shake hands with Montgiron *and* Giordano, *and withdraw to the crowd.* Louis *returns.*

Louis. (*to himself*) I seek in vain; I cannot find her.

Montgiron. Louis.

Giordano. Louis dei Franchi!

Louis. (*much surprised*) Giordano! My friend, my countryman!

Giordano. My dear Louis, I rejoice to meet you.

Louis. I thought you were in Algiers with your regiment.

Giordano. I arrived in Paris this morning, on leave of absence.

Montgiron. And now, like a true Anacreon, he seeks the Opera, to blend the myrtle with his laurels.

Giordano. And you? How chances it I meet you in Paris?

Montgiron. He is studying the law—Dupin, Vattel and Grotius; that accounts for his melancholy and abstracted air. Come, cheer up, man. Tonight you must be one of us, and sup with me; you'll meet all our own set: Beauchamp, Verner, Château-Renaud.

Louis. (*quickly*) Château-Renaud!

Montgiron. You know him?

Louis. I have met him once or twice.

Montgiron. Oh, he's in great request; a most accomplished fellow, acknowledged as the best swordsman in France, and by his own account resistless with the fair. He kills a reputation or an antagonist with equal sang-froid.

Louis. (*aside*) Should it be so? Can I have wronged her?

Montgiron. Well, we may reckon on you?

Louis. You must excuse me, I have an appointment here; besides, I am not in spirits for such a party.

Montgiron. An appointment! Oh, bring the fair lady with you.

Louis. You mistake me. I am not here to seek proofs of love, but to save one who seeks her own destruction.

Montgiron. Louis, are you serious?

Louis. I am indeed. Thank you once again, but I must decline.   (*Exit*)

Giordano. Poor fellow, I hope he hasn't got into a scrape.

Montgiron. Oh no, a love affair; six days will settle it.

Giordano. Who is the lady to whom he refers?

Montgiron. I cannot tell. Louis is reserved, and not a talker like Château-Renaud.

Enter Château-Renaud.

Renaud. (*entering*) I beg pardon, but I heard my name. I fear I interrupt you.

Montgiron. Oh, not in the least. 'Tis of you we were speaking.

Renaud. Then I am one too many here.

Montgiron. No, no, pray stay. (*Introducing them*) Monsieur de Château-Renaud, the Baron Giordano Martelli, Captain in the First Chasseurs of Africa: (*they bow*) both distinguished heroes, one in the field of Mars, the other in that of Venus.

Renaud. Now, Montgiron, positively you give me a reputation I do not deserve. How I have ever earned the character you honour me with, I cannot imagine.

Montgiron. Indeed! That's strange, for they do say you gave it to yourself.

Renaud. Who says so?

Montgiron. It was mentioned here not five minutes ago.

Renaud. Ah! By whom?

Montgiron. First, I believe, by me.

Renaud. You said that I boasted of success!

Montgiron. Yes, and I added, which you did not always achieve.

Renaud. The devil you did! Name a single instance.

Montgiron. Fifty, if you please.

Renaud. For example, name one.

Montgiron. Well, without going very far——

Renaud. Name—name——

Montgiron. Madame de l'Esparre.

Renaud. Émilie de l'Esparre!

Montgiron. Yes. They say you have compromised her name, although she never gave you the least encouragement.

Renaud. That is the general opinion, is it?

Montgiron. It is.

Renaud. Then you take me for a coxcomb, a braggart, a would-be Don Juan?

Giordano. Gentlemen!

Renaud. (*to* Giordano) Fear nothing, my dear sir; this is no quarrel, 'tis a simple wager. (*To* Montgiron) Will you bet?

Montgiron. On what?

Renaud. That I prove to you this very night my influence with the lady you have named.

Montgiron. How will you prove it?

Renaud. You shall see her in a few minutes, leaning on my arm, here at this very ball.

Montgiron. Oh, that proves nothing.

Louis *has entered during this conversation.*

Renaud. Well—but if I brought her to your house to supper?

Montgiron. That's quite another matter—but there I defy you.

Renaud. Do you? Name your wager.

Montgiron. A thousand francs. We'll give you till four o'clock.

Renaud. By which hour I engage to bring Madame de l'Esparre to your bachelor party. If I am one moment late, I lose.

Montgiron. Agreed.

Renaud. Adieu till then. (*Exit*)

Louis. (*coming forward*) My dear Baron, you were kind enough to invite me to your supper, which I declined. Will you permit me now to accept your invitation?

Montgiron. Bravo! Our party then will be complete, if Château-Renaud keeps his word. You will not fail, gentlemen?

Louis *and* Giordano. We shall be there. (*Exeunt*)

A curtain descends—Music—It rises and discovers

Scene 2. *A retired part of the Opera House.*

Enter Château-Renaud *and* Émilie.

Émilie. You requested my presence here; I am come, although at the
  risk of my motives being misinterpreted by you and by the world.
Renaud. What have you to fear? Behind that mask and domino, no one
  can recognize you.
Émilie. Once seen, the tongue of slander would assail me; if known, I
  am ruined. I have obeyed the conditions you insisted on; now
  keep your promise and restore to me those letters.
Renaud. Oh certainly, since you insist upon it.
Émilie. You will then return them? Give them to me and let me go.
Renaud. What! suffer you to leave so quickly, when I have agreed to
  your desire that this should be our last interview? No; you must
  first hear me—you must first tell me——
Émilie. What can I say more?
Renaud. Tell me at least the cause of this sudden change, this rupture
  which drives me to despair. Why did you ever encourage my
  addresses? Why did you ever flatter me with hope, to make me
  feel more bitterly the disappointment? Why write those letters,
  pledges of returned affection, and now so coldly ask their restitution?
Émilie. I have given you a right to speak thus to me, to think me
  wavering—fickle—nay, contemptible. I will not deny that you
  possessed my early love. My first affections, as you know, were
  yours; my father saw and crushed our hopes at once. The fate of
  my poor sister—the ill-assorted marriage of Louise—was ever
  present to his mind. A marriage which cost him a daughter, me
  a sister, for from that hour I have never seen her. Where is she now?
  Perhaps deserted, struggling with misery and want. Ill-founded
  rumours, or some other causes of which I am ignorant, taught
  his distempered mind to see in you a copy of my sister's husband.
  To snatch me from the fate he so much dreaded, he made me the
  companion of his journey into Corsica. On my return, his stern
  resolution—regardless of the feelings of my heart—obliged me to
  accept the hand of a man of rank and wealth. The disparity of our
  years, our total want of sympathy, rendered it impossible for me to
  love, although I might respect and honour him. It is now a sacred
  duty I owe to the Admiral de l'Esparre, as well as to myself, to claim
  from you the evidences of our plighted troth.
Renaud. You demand of me no trifling sacrifice.
Émilie. Be not deluded by a thought so vain, so false, as to suppose I
  can again receive you with the feelings that inspired those letters.
  Cease to claim possession of a heart which, with all its sufferings,

all its anguish, belongs now to another. Such sentiments are
unworthy of you, and their avowal tends to degrade us both.

Renaud. Who has dared to impugn my actions thus?

Émilie. Those letters have been seen by others, and most injurious
comments made upon them. Thus, through the thoughtlessness of
vanity, you assist to wound the honour you are bound to guard.

Renaud. Émilie! This is the mere impulse of caprice——

Émilie. Oh no; what seems to you caprice is in my mind almost
remorse.

Renaud. You act not from your own impulse; you have been urged on
to this.

Émilie. I cannot disregard the warning of a friend.

Renaud. And this friend, this devoted, meddling friend, doubtless is
Louis dei Franchi.

Émilie. It matters not.

Renaud. If I have heard rightly, you knew him before your marriage;
you received his visits constantly. He loved you. Perhaps his passion
was returned.

Émilie. This is insulting. The letters—I implore you—the letters——

Renaud. Well, I have promised to restore them, and I will keep my
word. I have them not about me; they are at my residence.

Émilie. Sir! You have deceived me! In reliance on your promise to
restore them here, where I have consented most reluctantly to
meet you, and for the last time, it may be I have already
compromised my position. This last evasion is too palpable. You
may no longer love, but you shall at least respect me.

Renaud. Émilie, you are ungrateful. Listen to me; you have named your
sister; you know not how eagerly I have sought to find her, to
restore her to your arms. I am at last successful——

Émilie. Oh, heavens!

Renaud. I have promised that you shall see her this very night. She
awaits your coming.

Émilie. You do not deceive me?

Renaud. This is too much! I have a carriage at the door and will
escort you to her lodgings instantly. There I will leave you, while
I hasten to procure those letters you insist on my restoring, and
thus at the same moment give you a double proof of my respect
and my devotion.

Émilie. Haste, haste! I am ready. Forgive me if I doubted you.

Renaud. I do, I do! (*Looks at his watch*) Ten minutes to four. I shall
win my wager, and preserve my reputation.   (*Exeunt*)

A curtain descends—Music—It is raised for

Scene 3. *The house of* Montgiron. *A bachelor's saloon, very elegantly furnished; entrance door at the back; through a doorway placed on the left, another apartment is seen, in which there is a table richly covered; on the right a chimney-piece, with a clock over it.*

Enter Servant *from the back, showing in* Louis *and* Giordano.

Servant. This way, gentlemen.

Giordano. The Baron de Montgiron has not yet returned from the Opera, I presume?

Servant. No, sir. My master ordered supper at four precisely. Do you wish for anything, gentlemen?

Giordano. No thank you; you can leave us.

Servant *bows and retires. In the meantime,* Louis *has seated himself and appears absorbed in his own reflections.* Giordano *regards him for some minutes in silence; at length he approaches him and takes his hand.*

Louis, pardon me, but I see you are unhappy. Before others I said nothing; now that we are alone, tell me your secret. The grief that is confided to another loses half its bitterness. I am your friend, your countryman; you do not doubt me?

Louis. No, Giordano. I will trust you with the frankness of a brother. I love, and I am wretched.

Giordano. (sitting down near Louis) Ah, I guessed as much.

Louis. This love first dawned in Corsica. A breeze as soft and balmy as the odour of our orange groves wafted it towards my heart; a rude tempest has torn it from me. When the object of my affection left Ajaccio, knowing she had gone to Paris I resolved to follow her. I left my home, my country, my parent, and my noble generous brother, who loved her also, but who sacrificed his own feelings from regard to mine. I came here full of hope, rejoicing to be near her. I came too late; she was already married to another.

Giordano. Married!

Louis. Yes, married without affection; married at the very moment when I thought to offer her my hand.

Giordano. And have you seen her since?

Louis. Chance threw me into the society of her husband. He sought my company and invited me to his house.

Giordano. A dangerous guest.

Louis. Oh, no, you know me not. The sainted shrine is not more safe from desecration by the kneeling pilgrim, than is the wife of him whose proffered friendship I accepted. I resolved to stifle my unhappy passion, and become worthy of his confidence. But I mistook my strength, and ceased my visits. *(He rises)*

Giordano. What cause did you assign for your absence?

Louis. I needed none; he was ordered on a foreign service. During her husband's absence she lived almost in seclusion, when there appeared a man who seemed to assume a fatal influence over her, and whom I at once recognized as an enemy. That man was Monsieur de Château-Renaud.

Giordano. Château-Renaud! I thought so.

Louis. I see that like myself you are a believer in first impressions. At first sight of this man I started involuntarily, and when introduced we scarcely spoke to each other.

Giordano. You have given me a clue to the sequel; the lady of your love is Madame de l'Esparre?

Louis. You have guessed truly. 'Tis she—'tis Émilie! This Château-Renaud, unrestrained by heart or conscience in the pursuit of pleasure, saw no obstacles, felt no compunction; nay more—he has boasted publicly that having once been an accepted lover he still retains that character, though she is married to another. The idle gossip of the world reached me in my lone retreat. I wrote to Émilie, claiming the freedom of a friend, and pointed out the selfish vanity by which she was compromised. From her I received no answer, but from an unknown quarter was informed that I should meet her at this ball. Impelled by the fatality that governs me, I came, and was a witness of the shameful wager in which her name and honour are involved. (*He lifts his hand to his eyes*)

Giordano. (*after a moment's silence*) Louis, be advised; let us leave this place before the party meets.

Louis. I feel, Giordano, that you are right. It were better that I should avoid this scene; but do we always act as reason dictates? I cannot go. I *must* remain.

Giordano. Summon your pride; reflect. If this woman dares to present herself here tonight, and in this company, she is unworthy the attentions of an honourable man.

Louis. Yes, I am resolved. If she comes, she will find me here. If she raises her eyes, she will meet mine, and she will blush.

(*Boisterous laughter without*)

Giordano. Hark! They are coming.

Enter Montgiron, Beauchamp *with* Coralie, Verner *with* Estelle, Celestina, *and other gentlemen and ladies; the ladies still in character dresses and masks.*

Montgiron. This way, ladies; you are welcome to my poor habitation.

Coralie. Why, Baron, you are lodged like an eastern sultan.

Estelle. (*flopping into a spring chair*) What a delicious chair.

Celestina. What beautiful furniture! I hope it is all paid for.

Beauchamp. Montgiron has an old aunt with heavy dividends.

Verner. What a lucky fellow! I have an old aunt with nothing but ill temper.

Montgiron. Off with your masks, ladies; disguise is useless here.

They take off their masks, place their bouquets, and arrange their toilets.

Coralie. Where is the supper?

All. Ay, where is the supper?

Montgiron. You must excuse me, ladies; we are not quite ready. We cannot sup until the clock strikes four. A circumstance——

Coralie. Nothing happened to the champagne, I hope?

Estelle. Oh, I should expire!

Servants *enter with wine and biscuits, which they hand round.*

Montgiron. Our number is not complete. I have promised to wait for Château-Renaud.

All. Château-Renaud!

Coralie. (*dipping biscuit in wine*) Here's to his speedy arrival.

Montgiron. Until four o'clock. A wager depends on it.

All. A wager!

Montgiron. He has laid me a thousand francs that he will bring here to join our party, a certain lady of our acquaintance.

Louis. (*aside*) This is torture.

Montgiron. If he is one minute late, he loses.

Estelle. How preciously proper she must be!

Coralie. I wish somebody would ask me to supper, and bet me a thousand francs I wouldn't come.

Celestina. Who is the heroine?

Beauchamp. A vestal of the lamp.

Verner. A Joan of Arc at least.

Montgiron. There is no breach of confidence in telling you. 'Tis Madame——

Louis. (*rises, and places his hand upon the arm of* Montgiron) Montgiron, will you accord me one favour?

Montgiron. A favour, my dear Louis?

Louis. Do not name the lady you expect.

Coralie. Why not?

Louis. Because, Mademoiselle, that lady is married to a friend of mine.

Beauchamp. A married woman! The wager improves.

Montgiron. The husband is at this moment cruising off the coast of Mexico.

Louis. In a few weeks he will return to Paris, and I would have him spared all knowledge of his wife's imprudence.

Estelle. Poor fellow! I pity him.

Coralie. Serve him right.

Celestina. Certainly.

Coralie. 'Twill teach him not to go cruising on the coast of Jericho again.

Estelle. Mexico, you dunce.

Coralie. Well, I suppose it makes no difference to his wife. A husband six thousand miles off is the same thing as none at all.

Montgiron. I respect your scruples, Louis. Since you desire it, we will treat the lady in question with the most profound discretion. Ladies—gentlemen—whether Château-Renaud comes alone or not, whether he win or lose his wager, I pledge you all to silence on this adventure.

Gentlemen. Oh, certainly—we promise it.

Montgiron. (*to the* Ladies) And you?

Ladies. We swear!

Louis. I thank you.

Beauchamp. I would advise Château-Renaud to make haste; it wants but three minutes of his time.

Verner. (*looking at the clock*) Is your clock right?

Montgiron. To a minute. I sent word to set it by his watch; the rest is his affair.

Giordano. (*aside to* Louis) Courage, Louis; she will not come.

Louis. (*constantly looking at the clock*) It wants one minute yet. How slowly move those fatal hands—and yet my life hangs upon their speed. Will they never achieve the goal? Will the hour never strike to release me from this agony?

A moment of silence. The first chime of the clock, striking four, is heard.

Giordano. Louis, you wronged her.

Louis *takes a glass, and is about to lift it to his mouth; the clock continues to strike. At the third chime, a loud ringing is heard from the bell in the ante-chamber.*

Louis. (*putting down his glass, and starting*) 'Tis he!

Giordano. Perhaps she's not with him.

Montgiron. (*springing towards the door at the back*) Is he alone?

He disappears for a moment, and all eyes are turned with great curiosity towards the back.

Louis. (*seizing the arm of* Giordano) No, she's there. Her footfall strikes upon my heart.

Giordano. Courage.

Montgiron *returns.*

Montgiron. Enter, Madame, I entreat you.

Château-Renaud *enters with* Émilie, *masked.*

Renaud. Come in, dear Émilie. You needn't unveil unless you like. Bear witness, all of you, it was striking four when we arrived.

Montgiron. You have fairly won. Gentlemen, I have lost my wager.

Émilie. Won! He has won. What? Ah, I am betrayed; my fears were well founded. My presence here, then, was the subject of a wager.

Renaud. Émilie—I——

Émilie. (*to* Montgiron) Speak, sir. You seem to be the master here; I turn to you for a reply.

Montgiron. I confess, Madame, that Monsieur de Château-Renaud induced me to hope that you would honour us with your company.

Émilie. To win this infamous wager, he has stooped to falsehood and to treachery. It was to visit a suffering relative he feigned to conduct me; I came on an errand of charity and affection. (*All express disbelief*) Oh, I fear not to face you now. If there be any here whose brows should wear a blush, I know 'tis not the wife of the Admiral de l'Esparre. (*She unmasks*)

Renaud. Madame, you treat the jest too seriously. Since you are here, you will surely stay?

Émilie. I recognise at least one friend, and in his hands I place myself. Monsieur Louis dei Franchi, will you afford me your protection to conduct me home?

Louis. (*springing towards her*) My life is yours.

Renaud. One moment. Allow me to observe, sir, that *I* brought this lady here, and *I* alone will escort her hence.

Émilie. Gentlemen, I place myself beneath the shelter of your honour; you will shield me from further insult.

Louis. (*placing himself between her and* Château-Renaud) Fear nothing, Madame, I am by your side.

Renaud. (*after having repressed a movement of violence, very calm*) 'Tis well. I know now to whom I may look for explanation.

Louis. (*coolly*) If you allude to me, sir, I shall be at home in half an hour.

Renaud. In less than that you will find a friend to represent me.

Émilie. A duel!

Louis. (*with disdain*) A challenge in the presence of a lady! Oh, sir, it lacked but this to give a finish to your character. (*Offering his arm to* Émilie) Come, Madame, my blood to the last drop is yours; my life is nothing to the honour, the happiness, you have now conferred upon me.

Émilie *takes his arm, they go up, bow to the company, and exeunt.*

Renaud. (*with an air of forced gaiety*) Well, gentlemen, I suppose I have lost after all. But I shall sup with none the worse appetite.

Servant *enters.*

Servant. Supper is ready.

All. Come.

Giordano. (aside, going to procure his hat) Not I. This is no place for me; I will seek Louis, and see this matter terminated.

The rest all move towards the room where the supper is prepared, and Giordano *goes off at the back.*

Curtain descends—Music—Curtain rises, and discovers

Scene 4. *A glade in the Forest of Fontainebleau.* Louis dei Franchi *discovered, lying on the ground wounded, attended by his seconds* Montgiron *and* Giordano; *a surgeon is near him and examines his wound; on the other side,* Château-Renaud *wiping his sword; two other seconds,* Beauchamp *and* Verner, *are near him. It is an exact reproduction of the tableau that terminated the first act.*

Giordano. (to Surgeon) Well, sir, what hope?
Surgeon. None; the lungs are pierced. (*Looking at his watch*) Ten minutes past nine! He has not five minutes more to live.
Giordano. (with great emotion) My poor friend!
Louis. (coming to himself) Giordano, where are you?
Giordano. Here, Louis, by your side. Speak; what would you? Have you no wish to be conveyed to your mother—to your brother Fabien?
Louis. No, no; they will know all.
Giordano. When?
Louis. Tonight.
Giordano. Tonight! And by what means?
Louis. By me. Your hand, Giordano; yours, sir—Émilie, farewell.

He sinks back exhausted and dies. During the utterance of these last words, the back of the scene opens slowly and discovers the chamber of the first act, the clock marking the hour, ten minutes after nine; Madame dei Franchi *and* Fabien, *looking exactly as they did before.*

Fabien. Pray for Louis, dearest mother. I go to avenge him.

ACT III

Scene 1. *The glade in the Forest of Fontainebleau where* Louis *was killed.*

Boissec *discovered, making faggots and singing. The noise of a carriage on the road is heard at a distance.* Boissec *pauses in his work and looks through the trees.*

Boissec. Click, clack! What a cloud of dust! And how they do scamper along yonder—a post chaise tearing away at full gallop. It's a fine thing to be rich. But what is the postillion about? He's taking them right against a heap of stones. If that man isn't drunk, I'm not sober. He'll upset them, ten to one. (*Loud crash without, as of the chaise being overturned*) A hollow bet, won already. There's an end of your journey, whoever you are. (*Still looking, whilst he is filling his pipe*) Ah! Two gentlemen get out and shake themselves. They are looking about for assistance. These gentry often give a great deal of trouble, and pay nothing for it. I'll pretend not to see them; but they see me, and are making signs. (*Shouts of 'Hullo' without*) Now they call. I'm blind and deaf. (*He resumes his work, and sings*)

Enter Château-Renaud *and* Montgiron.

Renaud. I say, my good fellow. (Boissec *continues, without noticing him*) My good friend—. (*Slapping him on the back*) Are you deaf?
Boissec. (*turning half round*) Did you speak to me, sir?
Renaud. Yes, I did.
Boissec. Beg pardon, but I was so busy with my work.
(*He resumes chopping and humming*)
Montgiron. Listen to me. If we take you from your work, we will gladly repay you for your lost time.
Boissec. (*taking his pipe out of his mouth, and bowing*) The case is altered. Gentlemen, I am at your service.
Montgiron. The axletree of our carriage is broke. Do you know any wheelwright in Fontainebleau who could mend it?
Boissec. A first rate one—my cousin. He should have been a coachmaker in Paris, but there's no such thing as justice in this world.
Montgiron. Fly, then, and bring him here with his tools instantly.
Boissec. 'Tis a good mile to his shop.
Montgiron. Ten francs are yours if you dispatch.
Boissec. (*eagerly*) Ten francs! I'm off like a flash of lightning. (*He goes a few steps and returns*) I beg pardon, have you broke any bones in your tumble?
Montgiron. No, no.
Boissec. Because, you see, my cousin is a famous veterinary surgeon also, and can set an arm or a leg with any man in Paris.
Montgiron. We have no need of his skill in that line.
Boissec. Ah, I'm sorry for that. (*Pretends to go, then returns*) I beg pardon again, but an upset in the dust makes people thirsty. My cousin sells capital wine, almost as good as (*aside*) vinegar.
Montgiron. Begone, I tell you, or the ten francs will dwindle to five.
Boissec. (*going*) Au revoir. (*Exit*)

Montgiron *goes up to* Château-Renaud, *who during this dialogue has seated himself upon a fallen tree, and supports his head with his hand.*

Montgiron. Château-Renaud, what ails you, man?

Renaud. If I were superstitious, I should give up this journey.

Montgiron. It has commenced badly enough, that must be admitted.

Renaud. We should have done far better to have remained in Paris.

Montgiron. I think differently, and have determined to be missing for the present. Your duel with Louis, in spite of our precautions, has taken wind. The Attorney General and the Minister of Police are making tender enquiries after us.

Renaud. (*walking about uneasily*) I care little for their enquiries.

Montgiron. But I tell you they are serious this time, and resolved to make an example. Unfortunately, this is not your first affair——

Renaud. And for a trifling mishap or two like this——

Montgiron. You would wish to figure in a court of justice? I have no such ambition. We should be acquitted perhaps; but in the mean time, three months in prison, on spare diet, is anything but amusing. Besides, you have forgot another trifling inconvenience.

Renaud. Indeed! Of what nature?

Montgiron. Louis dei Franchi is dead—but he has left a brother.

Renaud. Well, what of him?

Montgiron. Only this: he is a true Corsican. As soon as he hears of what has happened, he will traverse the world to obtain revenge.

Renaud. I see no reason, because I have fought with one brother, why I should run the gauntlet through the whole family.

Montgiron. In France, no; in Corsica, yes. Take my advice and keep out of the way for a few weeks, until this unhappy affair has blown over.

Renaud. Well, as you wish it, and our plans are formed, let us proceed. I cannot conceal the sensations which oppress me. I am pursued by some fatality. For the first time I feel as if urged on by some controlling influence to something fatal.

Montgiron. (*laughing*) You, Château-Renaud, grown superstitious?

Renaud. 'Tis weak, I own; but the strongest minds are sometimes moved by trifles—the breaking of a mirror, or the howling of a dog. I have laughed at all this a hundred times, and now I am shaken by the overturn of our post chaise. And in what locality? In the Forest of Fontainebleau, in the very glade where five days since— (*looking round him and with terror*). Say—do you not recognise the spot —this path—that tree——

Montgiron. (*looking round*) Yes, 'tis the very place. The accident is strange.

Renaud. Montgiron, there's more than *accident* in this; 'tis destiny— perhaps the hand of Providence.

Montgiron. Our man returns.

Enter Boissec.

Well, friend, you have lost no time. Is the blacksmith at work?

Boissec. Look yonder, and you can see him. In a few minutes all will be right again.

Montgiron. Here's the money I promised you.

Boissec. Thank you, sir. With ten francs in my pocket, I am a gentleman for the rest of the day. (*The sound of a carriage is heard*) Ah, another carriage! If it would only break down like the first, I might double the ten francs. Good day, Messieurs, and a pleasant journey.

He takes up his hatchet, lifts his faggots on his shoulder, and goes off, singing.

Renaud. (*agitated*) Let us leave this spot. Let us get beyond the forest —it feels like a grave. In the whisper of the wind I hear the dying sigh of Louis, and at every turn I dread to meet his ghost.

Montgiron. What folly!

Renaud. It may be folly, but I cannot conquer it. Let us be gone.

As they are going up, enter Fabien *in a cloak.*

Fabien. Stay!

Montgiron. What do I see?

Renaud. (*with terror, to* Fabien) What would you?

Fabien. Can you not guess?

Renaud. Louis dei Franchi!

Fabien. No. Not Louis—but his brother.

Renaud. His brother!

Montgiron. (*aside*) My fears are realised.

Fabien. (*with calm but terrible sternness, advancing towards* Château-Renaud *who retreats from him*) You take me for the spectre of your victim. No; I am one more terrible, more implacable. I am Fabien dei Franchi, come from the wilds of Corsica to demand of you: where is my brother?

Renaud. (*with a sort of arrogance*) Of me? What have I to do with him?

Fabien. You answer as the first murderer. What have you done with him? I'll tell you that. Five days since, at the remotest end of Corsica, I learned how I had lost a loved—an only brother; how you drew your serpent slime across his path, blighted the bright vision of his days, tried to bring dishonour on a woman it was the devoted object of his life to guard. By a base lie you decoyed that woman into a snare from which he rescued her. Then, taking advantage of a mere bravo's skill, you murdered him. (Montgiron *and* Château-Renaud *appear indignant*) Yes! I repeat my words—you are the assassin of my brother.

Renaud. Assassin!

Fabien. Aye; for when a man is deadly with his weapon and goads another man he knows to be less practised than himself to quarrel, he fights him not, he murders him.

Montgiron. Hold, gentlemen, I entreat you. Monsieur Fabien dei Franchi, I cannot comprehend you. Five days ago, you say, you were in

Corsica. How is it possible these sad details could reach you in so short a space of time?

Fabien. The dead travel quickly.

Montgiron. We are not children, sir, to be terrified with nursery tales.

Fabien. (*coldly*) On the same evening of my brother's death I was informed of all; nay more—I *saw* it all. In five days I have traversed two hundred and eighty leagues. When I reached your house, they told me you had just left Paris. I ascertained the route you had taken. I saw your carriage overturned and I exclaimed 'The hand of the avenger is upon him'.

Renaud. (*with resolution*) Well, sir, I am found. What would you with me?

Fabien. A mortal combat. Know you not that a Corsican race is like the fabled Hydra? Kill one—another supplies his place. You have shed my brother's blood; I am here to demand yours, or yield my own.

Renaud. You wish to take my life! And how?

Fabien. Not after the usual practice of my country, from behind a wall or across a hedge, but in the manner sanctioned here, according to rule—according to fashion. (*Throwing open his cloak*) You see I am in proper costume.

Renaud. I would have avoided this most earnestly; I was flying from it. But if I accept the challenge, it is on one condition.

Fabien. Name it.

Renaud. That the quarrel ceases here, and that I am not again to be called upon by another brother or some distant cousin. Let this be the last encounter.

Fabien. The last it *shall* be. I am the only living relative of Louis, and after me, Monsieur de Château-Renaud, be assured none will trouble you.

Renaud. Name your hour, place, and weapons.

Fabien. The hour? I have sworn it should be at the moment when I met you. The weapons? With a sword you killed my brother; with a sword you shall encounter me. The place? The spot where we now stand.

Renaud. This spot?

Fabien. Yes, this spot. You chose it five days since. At the foot of that tree my brother fell; the traces of his blood remain there still.

Renaud. (*with resolution*) Since you are determined, be it so. (*Throws off his coat*) The sooner all this ends, the better.

Montgiron. (*passing between them*) Gentlemen, this cannot be. The duel is impossible; at least at present. Here is but one witness, and you are both unarmed.

Fabien. You are mistaken, sir; I come prepared. (*Calling at the back*) Meynard, approach.

Enter Alfred de Meynard *in a cloak, carrying two swords.*

Here is my second—here are arms for both.

Montgiron. (going up to Alfred) Meynard! Perhaps we may yet find
means——

Fabien. (taking off his coat and waistcoat) Monsieur de Meynard, sir,
knows his duty.

Renaud. (who has removed his waistcoat) I am ready.

Fabien. Meynard, request Monsieur de Château-Renaud to take his
choice.

Alfred *presents the swords to* Château-Renaud, *who selects one.*

Renaud. Now sir.   (*A clock at a distance strikes nine*)

Fabien. (coldly) If you have any last instructions for your friend, you
have still an opportunity.

Renaud. Why shall I use it?

Fabien. Because, as surely as yon sky is over us, in ten minutes you
take your place there, where my brother fell.

Renaud. This is no time for empty boasting, sir.

Fabien. (very calm) Gentlemen, bear witness for me. Do I look like an
empty boaster? Now sir—on guard!

They fight for several minutes, in which Château-Renaud *exerts himself
to kill or wound* Fabien, *but is foiled by his coolness and skill.*

Pause for a moment, you are out of breath.

Renaud. (to Montgiron) His wrist is made of iron. (*After a moment or
two*) When you are ready.

Fabien. I am always ready.

They fight. The sword of Château-Renaud *is broken.*

Montgiron. (springing forward) Gentlemen, the sword of Château-Renaud is
broken. The duel is over, the arms are no longer equal.

Fabien. You are mistaken again, sir. (*Breaking his sword beneath his heel*)
I have made them equal. (*To* Château-Renaud, *pointing to the broken
blade*) Take up that fragment, and let us try once more.

Montgiron. Are you still implacable?

Fabien. As destiny itself.

Alfred *assists* Fabien *to tie the end of his sword round his wrist with a
handkerchief.* Montgiron *fastens* Château-Renaud's *sword in the same
manner.*

Renaud. (aside to Montgiron) He will kill me, Montgiron; I feel
convinced of it. You will continue your journey alone. In eight days
write to my mother, and say I had a fall from my horse. In a
fortnight tell her I am dead. If she learned the fatal news abruptly,
she would die herself.

Montgiron. Château-Renaud, you are mad.

Renaud. No. I am not mad, but in two minutes I am a dead man.

> *During this* Montgiron *has tied the sword round* Château-Renaud's *wrist.*

Alfred. Gentlemen, are you ready?

> Château-Renaud *and* Fabien *close in mortal combat.* Château-Renaud *overthrows him, but just as he is going to strike,* Fabien *plunges his weapon into his heart.*

Renaud. (*falling back close to the tree near which* Louis *fell*) Montgiron, I was a true prophet. Farewell.   (*Dies*)

Fabien. (*rising*) My mother, I have kept my word. Louis! Louis! I can weep for him now.

> *He passes behind a tree up stage; then advances, with face covered by his hands, and sinks weeping upon the fallen tree. A pause.* Louis dei Franchi *appears, rising gradually through the earth and placing his hand on the shoulder of his brother.*

Louis. Mourn not, my brother. We shall meet again.

> *The curtain falls.*

The Lady of the Camellias

A DRAMA IN FOUR ACTS, adapted from *La Dame aux Camélias*
by ALEXANDRE DUMAS *fils*

La Dame aux Camélias was first performed at the Vaudeville Theatre,
Paris, 2 February 1852

CAST

ARMAND DUVAL	M Charles Fechter
GEORGES DUVAL, his father	M Delannoy
GASTON RIEUX, a beau	M René Luguet
SAINT-GAUDENS, an old beau	M Gil-Pérès
GUSTAVE, a law student, betrothed to Nichette	M Lagrange
ARTHUR DE VARVILLE, Marguerite's admirer	M Dupuis
DOCTOR	M Hippolyte Worms
MESSENGER	M Roger
SERVANTS	{ M Guérin { M Léon
MARGUERITE GAUTIER	Mme Eugénie Doche
NICHETTE, a seamstress	Mme Worms
PRUDENCE DUVERNOY, a milliner	Mme Astruc
NANINE, maid to Marguerite	Mme Irma Granier
OLYMPE } ARTHUR } ladies of the demi-monde ANAIS }	{ Mme Clary { Mme Clorinde { Mme Caroline

Guests, gamblers, dancers, servants, &c.

The Vaudeville cast-list also includes

COUNT DE GIRAY	M Allié
ESTHER	Mme Marie
ADÈLE	Mme Baron

who are omitted in this adaptation

The Second Act is set in a country house near Auteuil. The other
acts are set in Paris.

Period: 1848

ALEXANDRE DUMAS *fils*

Poet, dandy, dramatist, reformer, novelist and natural son of a father famous for his bohemian life and prolific writings. Born 1824, educated occasionally, and introduced into Paris society at the age of seventeen. Freed from his debts by the phenomenal success of *La Dame aux Camélias* as novel (1847) and play (1852), Dumas *fils* settled down to reform the morals of the Second Empire in a series of thesis dramas attacking the evils of money, marriage, adultery, bastardy and prostitution. After *The Demi-monde* (1855) came *The Money Question* (*La Question d'Argent*, 1857), *The Bastard Son* (*Le Fils Naturel*, 1858) and *A Prodigal Father* (*Un Père Prodigue*, 1859). Later plays include *Claude's Wife* (*La Femme de Claude*, 1873) and *Denise* (1881). Married an actress in 1861, after the birth of a daughter. Elected to the Académie Française, 1874. Married again in 1895, this time choosing a former mistress. Died the same year, aged seventy-one. Buried with some pomp in the Cemetery of Montmartre, near the grave of his first love, the lady of the camellias.

THE LADY OF THE CAMELLIAS

Rose-Alphonsine Plessis was a peasant girl from Normandy who came to Paris without a sou in 1839 and three years later was installed in a luxurious apartment as mistress of the dashing Duc de Guiche. She took the name Marie Duplessis and a string of wealthy, titled lovers. Dumas met her at the Opera one autumn night in 1844. They retired to Saint-Germain next spring, passed the summer in idyllic happiness and quarrelled late in August. He withdrew to Rouen and a law-suit, she returned to Paris and Franz Liszt. On 30 August 1845 he wrote to her:

> I am not rich enough to love you as I would wish, nor poor enough to be loved as you wish. So let us both forget—you a name which must be almost indifferent to you, I a happiness that has become impossible for me. I need not tell you how sad I am, for you know how much I love you. Adieu, then. You have too much heart not to understand why I am writing this letter, and too much intelligence not to forgive me for writing it. *Milles souvenirs*, A.D.

Marie died of consumption two years later; she was barely twenty-three. Dumas poured his heart out in an elegy, and then worked up their brief affair as a romantic novel which disguised Marie as Marguerite, gave her lover his own initials and threw over their relationship the aura of a pure and tragic passion. *La Dame aux Camélias* was published in 1847 and quickly went through two editions. An adaptation for the stage which Dumas wrote in eight days flat was turned down by several timid managers, banned by the censor, defended by an influential ginger group, and first performed at the Vaudeville in 1852. Fechter played Armand with dangerous abandon, the delicate Eugénie Doche won every heart as Marguerite, and at the end of the performance Dumas was brought on stage to acknowledge an ovation. The play at once became the triumph of the season. Marie's grave was strewn each day with fresh bouquets of white camellias, and every night the theatre disgorged a throng of fashionable ladies dabbing at their eyes with damp lace handkerchiefs. The Count de Gervilliers, a polished libertine who served as Dumas' model for Saint-Gaudens, came every night to admire his portrait and fell in love with Madame Doche, who ruined him, they say, just as Marie had ruined many others. Verdi came, was overcome, and promptly cribbed the plot for *La Traviata*. Season after season the success continued. Eugénie Doche played Marguerite more than 600 times, and was succeeded by every Continental actress who aspired to tragic honours. First came Rose Chéri, Desclée and Talandiera. Then Duse lent the role her own translucent purity, and at one moment in the second act each night would blush on cue. Sarah Bernhardt toured Marguerite to Lyons, Naples, Warsaw and St Petersburg, and then went overseas to conquer Cairo and America. In Vienna the Archduke Frederick gave her an emerald pendant set in gold, in Bucharest Queen Natalie burst into tears, and in London Queen Victoria observed: 'You play the part with modesty, and no one can complain'. On 26 January 1884, Sarah played Marguerite in Paris, and Dumas was so moved he sent her as a souvenir the farewell note which he had written to Marie and bought back later at an auction sale. In 1912 she made a silent film of her performance, and four years later, when she had one leg and was well over seventy, she played the last act to French soldiers in the trenches.

The English-speaking stage for many years refused to admit the immorality of Dumas' play. The first London performances were given in French, or sung to Verdi's music in Italian; the first translations were absurdly bowdlerized. James Mortimer's at the Princess's (5 June 1875) glossed over Marguerite's profession as some obscure 'engagement', while the second act of Lacy's text brought Armand from Paris every morning to visit Marguerite and wrote in some pointed references to their marriage the next day. America was just as prudish. During the 1850s, Laura Keene played in a version which interpreted the whole play as a dream, Jean Davenport appeared in a travesty coyly subtitled *The Fate of a Coquette*, and Matilda Heron in another crudity which emphasized the harrowing humiliations of a 'poor, friendless, sickly girl' whose 'heart was pure' because '*she sinned no more*'. By a curious translator's error, all three called their eponymous heroines Camille. More recent versions are much less mealy-mouthed. And there are many of them, for actresses are drawn to Marguerite as helplessly as actors are to Cyrano or Hamlet. In New York alone, there have been over forty stage productions of *Camille* this century, dominated by Eve le Gallienne in 1931 and Colleen Dewhurst in 1956. The silver screen showed Theda Bara in 1917, Nazimova partnered by Rudolph Valentino four years later, Norma Talmadge in 1927 and Greta Garbo in 1936. London saw Tallulah Bankhead in Playfair's version at the Lyric Theatre in 1930, and Edwige Feuillère's French company at the Duke of York's in 1955—a performance of exquisite sensibility, which I remember still as deeply moving. Since then, the London stage has seen Marguerite in several new disguises, sung by Maria Callas and Joan Sutherland as Verdi's Violetta, acted by Diana Wynyard in Tennessee Williams' play *Camino Real* (1957), and danced by Dame Margot Fonteyn in Ashton's ballet *Marguerite and Armand* (1963). Marguerite Gautier is today the theatre's most famous Magdalen, and Dumas' play has outlived its century to become a classic of its kind.

The present text is based on Lacy's four-act version and Matilda Heron's *Camille*; bowdlerized passages have been restored by direct translation from Dumas' text in the first volume of his *Théâtre Complet* (Paris, 1896).

ACT I

Marguerite's boudoir. A handsome light chamber, elegantly furnished with large mirrors and valuable pictures on the walls, and objects of virtu unobtrusively visible. A fireplace with a fire burning in it; pieces of wood in fire-box by the side of the fire; fender, poker, tongs. Candelabras by mantel-piece, and over it a large glass. A large window with handsome curtains. A piano and stool, with sheets of music on it. Open door, through which is seen table laid for supper with a dish of birds, china plates, castors, salt-cellar, wine in decanters, wine glasses, champagne glasses, wine-cooler with bottles of champagne wired down, knives, forks and napkins folded on plates. Carpet.

De Varville seated in an easy chair at the fire; Nanine *discovered arranging the furniture. As the curtain rises, the door-bell is heard.*

Varville. Someone rang, Nanine.
Nanine. Valentine will open the door.
Varville. 'Tis Marguerite, no doubt.
Nanine. Not yet. 'Tis but ten o'clock, and she said she should not return until half-past ten. (Nichette *speaks without*) Oh, it is Ma'amselle Nichette.

Enter Nichette.

Nichette. (*looking in the door*) Ma'amselle Marguerite not here?
Nanine. No, ma'amselle. You wish to see her?
Nichette. Merely to say good evening on my way home.
Nanine. She will not be long.
Nichette. Oh, no matter. I shall not stay; Gustave is at the door. Another time, thank you; good evening.   (*Exit*)
Varville. Who is that young woman?
Nanine. Ma'amselle Nichette.
Varville. Nichette? That's the name of a cat, not a woman.
Nanine. It is a pet name my mistress gave her. They formerly worked together in the same warehouse.
Varville. Worked?
Nanine. Yes, sir; didn't you know? Oh yes, Ma'amselle Marguerite was an embroideress.

Varville. Indeed?

Nanine. And you really did not know? and yet she makes no secret of
the fact.

Varville. This Nichette is rather pretty.

Nanine. And wise!

Varville. But this Monsieur Gustave?

Nanine. What Monsieur Gustave?

Varville. Who was waiting for her below.

Nanine. He is her husband. That is, he is not her husband yet, but he
will be, and that is the same thing.

Varville. I understand. She is wise as the world goes, but she has a
lover.

Nanine. A very worthy young man who loves her devotedly, and who
will marry her and make her a good husband.

Varville. Oh, then Monsieur Gustave is more fortunate than I. (*Rising
and coming to* Nanine) Nanine, do you think Marguerite cares any
more for me than she used to?

Nanine. Not the least bit in the world!

Varville. But it must be said that she has strange taste, or she never
could endure the tedious visits of that old Monsieur de Mauriac;
they must be very annoying.

Nanine. Poor old man! It is the only happiness he has, and he regards
her as his own child.

Varville. Oh yes, I heard of that very affecting history. Unhappily . . .

Nanine. Unhappily?

Varville. I cannot believe it.

Nanine. Then listen to me, and I will endeavour to convince you. There
are many evil things said of Madame, and with truth; but that is the
very reason why things that are *not* true should not be said. About
two years ago Ma'amselle Marguerite, after a long illness, determined
to visit the celebrated waters of Bagnères, to recover, if possible, her
health. I accompanied her. Among the invalids at the hotel there was
a lovely young girl, the same age as Ma'amselle Marguerite, suffering
from the same complaint, and bearing such strong resemblance to her
that wherever they went they were called the twin sisters. This
young girl was Ma'amselle de Mauriac, daughter of the Duke.

Varville. Ma'amselle de Mauriac died.

Nanine. Yes.

Varville. And the Duke adopted Marguerite as his child, made her his
heiress, and introduced her into society, where she was loved and
honoured. This was not two years since; and tonight she is at
the Opera, the queen of the camellias, fifty thousand francs in
debt.

Nanine. Which you have kindly offered to pay. Yes, you are right,
Monsieur de Varville. Ma'amselle Marguerite acknowledged to the

Duke her true position. He was called away. In his absence her story reached the circle in which she moved. From that moment it was closed against her. She was shunned; and in their cruel sneers they told her to go back to Paris and wear camellias. She did return to Paris, and is gayer now than she ever was before; but no one knows her heart. (*Doorbell rings*) Hush! she is here.

Enter Marguerite. *She is dressed as for a theatre.* Nanine *assists her off with her shawl or mantle.*

Marguerite. (*to* Nanine) Order supper! Olympe and Saint-Gaudens will be here; I met them at the Opera. (*Exit* Nanine, *with mantle. Seeing* Varville, *who rises and bows*) So, you are here again. (*Sits near fire*)
Varville. It is my destiny ever to hover near you.
Marguerite. And it is my destiny to find you ever here on my return. What would you with me now?
Varville. You know the only subject of my heart.
Marguerite. Always the same story—how very tedious!
Varville. Is it my fault that I love you?
Marguerite. There it is again! My good friend, if I were to listen to every man who tells me he loves me, I would not have time to breakfast. I repeat to you, my good sir, for the hundredth time, I don't like you. Be grateful that as a friend I suffer you to visit here; but speak again of love, and henceforth my doors are closed to you.
Varville. And yet, Marguerite, last year at Bagnères you gave me cause to hope.
Marguerite. Yes; but that was a year ago. At Bagnères, a very dull place. I was ill. Things have changed. This is Paris. I am better now.
Varville. Especially since the Duke de Mauriac has fallen in love with you.
Marguerite. You are a fool! Will you go?
Varville. (*walking about*) No!
Marguerite. Then seat yourself at the piano; 'tis all you are fit for.
Varville. What shall I play?
Marguerite. What you will, so that it drowns your voice.

Nanine *re-enters, while he plays a prelude.*

Nanine. (*taking up a bouquet of roses and white lilac from table*) I had forgot, Ma'amselle; this bouquet——
Varville. Which I hope you will accept.
Marguerite. No! You may keep it, Nanine.
Varville. (*not playing piano*) You will not——
Marguerite. Why am I called the Lady of the Camellias?
Varville. Because you never wear any but those flowers.

Marguerite. Which means, it is those only that I love. What folly, then, to bring me these. Take them away, their perfume makes me ill.

(Nanine *goes off*)

Varville. I am unfortunate. Adieu, Marguerite.

(*Going*)

Marguerite. A moment, Varville. Put some coals on the fire—do something useful before you leave. Ugh, the evening is very chilly. (*Coughs slightly*) Quick, the coals!

Re-enter Nanine.

Nanine. Madame, here is Ma'amselle Olympe and Monsieur Saint-Gaudens.

Enter Saint-Gaudens *and* Olympe.

Marguerite. (*to* Olympe) I thought you would never come.
Olympe. 'Tis all the fault of this troublesome Saint-Gaudens.
Gaudens. Oh, of course! How are you, Varville? You sup with us?
Marguerite. No! (*To* Varville) Why are you not gone, sir?
Varville. I am going.
Olympe. Prudence is not here.
Marguerite. She will arrive presently.
Olympe. Of course—if only to borrow a trifle, for she lives by borrowing money, which she never repays.
Marguerite. (*laughing*) Oh, wicked! For you know she makes excellent bonnets, which I purchase of her.
Olympe. But never wear.
Marguerite. Heaven forbid! It is enough that I pay for them. But she is a good creature.
Olympe. No doubt—but 'tis a pity she's always so short of money.
Marguerite. Do you not think it very cold this evening? (*Coughs slightly*) Varville, stir the fire.

(Varville *obeys*)

Enter Prudence.

Prudence. Good evening, everybody! (*Aside to* Marguerite) Armand is coming.
Marguerite. Oh, you have seen him?
Prudence. Yes. He does nothing but rave about you.
Marguerite. Psha! He has known me scarce a week.
Prudence. Ah, but he has long loved you. You were told how, every day during your late illness, a young gentleman came to make the most anxious enquiries after you?
Marguerite. Well?
Prudence. Well—'twas he.
Marguerite. Indeed! 'Twas very kind of him.
Prudence. I am certain that you already love him—a little; and there can be no doubt that he would make you a good husband.

Marguerite. Silence, Prudence! What folly.

Prudence. Well, I shall say no more—only, you see, I am somewhat pressed for a little cash, and if it were just now quite convenient to you——

Marguerite. Certainly.

Prudence. Thank you.

Enter Gaston Rieux.

Gaston. (*to* Marguerite, *ceremoniously*) I most sincerely hope, madame, that you are in perfect health?

Prudence. Yes, yes, we are very well—don't bother. Here is Monsieur Armand Duval.

Enter Armand Duval.

Armand. (*bowing to* Marguerite) Good evening, madame.

Prudence. (*aside to* Marguerite) Take my word for it, he adores you.

Marguerite. Prudence!

Armand. (*aside to* Prudence) Thanks!

        (*Marguerite gives her hand to* Armand, *who, bowing, kisses it*)

Gaston. (*to* Saint-Gaudens, *who has come up to him*) Still young, my old boy.

Gaudens. Of course.

Gaston. Still flirting with the fair?

Gaudens. Yes. There (*pointing to* Olympe) is the object that I at present adore. And poor Varville is not to be permitted to sup with us! Poor fellow, how I pity him!

Gaston. (*approaching* Marguerite) Is not Saint-Gaudens superb? He cannot be more than eighteen.

Marguerite. It is only the aged who never grow old. He really is delightful.

Gaudens. (*to* Armand, *whom* Olympe *has introduced to him*) Any relation, sir, may I ask, to Monsieur Duval the Receiver General?

Armand. I am his son, sir. Do you know my father?

Gaudens. Formerly met him at the Baroness de Nersay's; your mother also, a charming and beautiful woman.

Armand. Alas, sir, she died three years since.

Gaudens. Really—I beg pardon for——

Armand. Oh, sir, I am ever proud to hear my mother named. The brightest joy, after having experienced a great and pure affection, is that of being permitted to remember it.

Gaudens. You were an only child, I think?

Armand. No, sir. I have a sister.

Marguerite. (*calling*) Monsieur Duval!

Armand. Madame?   (Varville *hammers at the piano*)

Marguerite. Be quiet, Monsieur Varville.

Varville. You desired me to play.

Marguerite. When I was alone with you; but I need no pastime now.
Monsieur Duval, I have been told how, two years since, during my
long illness, you came each day to my house and——
Armand. Oh, madame!
Marguerite. You, Varville, did not as much.
Varville. I have known you but a year.
Marguerite. And this gentleman but a week! What stupid things you
always say.

Nanine *and* Servants *bring in the supper table, and place it front; set chairs.*

Prudence. The table! I am perfectly famished.
Varville. Adieu, Marguerite.
Marguerite. Adieu. When shall we again see you?
Varville. When it shall please you, madame.
Marguerite. Then, in that case, goodbye for a long time.
                     (*Varville bows and goes off, annoyed*)
Olympe. Goodbye, Varville. Poor fellow!
Prudence. You use that poor man very cruelly.
Marguerite. Oh, you have no idea how his pertinacity annoys me.
Olympe. You are greatly to be pitied! He is very rich, and I only wish
he would pertinaciously annoy me.
Gaudens. (*to* Olympe) What? Could you have the cruelty to nip my
tender affection in the bud? I, who adore you?   (*All sit*)
Marguerite. Now eat, drink, and have no quarrels that cannot be made
up again.
Olympe. (*to* Marguerite) You complain of Varville's love, and he is
young and rich. What would you say if pestered like me by this
antiquated youth—as poor as a mouse?   (*All laugh*)
Gaudens. You hear how she lacerates my poor heart!—I'll trouble you
for a slice of that fowl.   (*All laugh*)
Prudence. (*pointing to dish*) What are those white animals?
Gaston. Partridges.
Prudence. (*handing plate*) Send me a few.
Olympe. A few partridges! (*All laugh*) I'm sorry, Prudence, that you
have no appetite.
Gaston. Marguerite, take wine with Monsieur Duval; he is as
melancholy as a drinking song.
Marguerite. Come then, Monsieur Armand. To my health!
All. (*raising glasses*) To the health of Marguerite!   (*They drink*)
Prudence. Oh, were I but rich, what parties I would give! But, alas,
poverty—. I am just now very much pressed, Saint-Gaudens, and if it
were in your power to lend me——   (*All laugh*)
Gaudens. Me? I have been myself all the morning trying to borrow.
But never mind; I have an uncle, am his heir, and when he dies——
Olympe. An uncle at his time of life! Is it likely?

Gaudens. Nevertheless, it is a fact; I have an uncle——
Olympe. Then he must be the Wandering Jew.   (*All laugh*)
Prudence. These partridges are delicious.
Gaston. Prudence must have a cast-iron digestion.
Prudence. Why, surely there is no law forbidding one to eat.
Gaston. If there were, you would not survive an hour.   (*All laugh*)
Prudence. Marguerite, will you suffer me to be insulted?
Marguerite. For shame, Gaston! You must be treated like a naughty
    child, and put in a corner till you know how to behave yourself.
Olympe. (*to* Gaston) Yes, go and stand over there. (Gaston *leaves the table*)
Gaudens. I shouldn't object to that, if you would only kiss me when I
    promised to be good.
Gaston. (*at the piano*) This instrument is out of tune.
Olympe. Let us have a dance.
Gaston. I can only play one polka.
Prudence. Well, don't play it yet—I have two more partridges to finish.
                                                            (*They laugh*)
Gaudens. (*rising*) Yes, yes—away with the table! A polka!

    They rise. Servants *enter, clear the table and carry it out.*

Olympe. But surely I shall not be expected to dance with this young old
    gentleman?
Marguerite. (*taking* Saint-Gaudens' *arm*) Oh no, he must be my partner.
Gaudens. Ah, you know how to appreciate merit.
Olympe. And you, Monsieur Duval, must dance with me.

    Gaston *plays a polka. They dance.* Marguerite *stops suddenly.*

Gaudens. What is the matter?
Marguerite. Nothing. A shortness of breath, that——
Armand. (*approaching her*) You are ill, madame.
Marguerite. I assure you it is nothing; let us proceed.

    Gaston *plays like a madman.* Marguerite *again tries, and stops.*

Armand. Be quiet, Gaston.
Prudence. Marguerite is ill.
Marguerite. (*fighting for breath*) Give me a glass of water.
Prudence. But what is it?
Marguerite. Oh, 'tis nothing new to me, and will presently pass away.
    Step into the other room, and before you have your cigars lit, I will
    be with you.
Prudence. Yes, come along; she prefers to be left alone when these
    attacks arrive. (*Aside*) I must finish those partridges presently.
Armand. (*aside*) Poor girl!   (*He goes out with the others*)
Marguerite. (*alone, trying to recover her breath*) Oh! (*Looks in the glass*)

185

How pale I am, oh!
    (*Places her hands to her head, and leans her elbows upon the chimney-piece*)

Re-*enter* Armand.

Armand. (*tenderly*) Well, how do you feel now, madame?

Marguerite. Ah, is it you, Monsieur Armand? Better, thank you.
    Besides, I am accustomed to——

Armand. You are destroying yourself. I would I had the right to save
    you.

Marguerite. It is too late. Why, what's the matter?

Armand. You have made me ill.

Marguerite. Don't be foolish. Pray, go into the next room and enjoy
    yourself with the others. See, they do not heed me.

Armand. The others do not love you as I love you. It is true that I
    am nothing to you, but if you would allow me, Marguerite, I
    would guard you like a brother—shield you from this feverish
    existence, which is bringing you to your grave—surround you
    with a thousand little cares that will make you in love with life—then,
    when you are strong and well, I will be as your guiding star, and
    lead your thoughts to find content in a home more worthy of you.

Marguerite. Monsieur Duval, if you would not offend me, let us change
    this subject.

Armand. You have no heart then, Marguerite?

Marguerite. A heart? Are you really serious?

Armand. Very serious.

Marguerite. Prudence did not deceive me, then, when she told me you
    were sentimental. So, you would take good care of me?

Armand. Trust me.

Marguerite. For how long?

Armand. For ever.

Marguerite. How long has this lasted?

Armand. For two years.

Marguerite. How came it you never told me of this before?

Armand. I never knew you until now.

Marguerite. You could very easily have made my acquaintance. When I
    was ill, and you came each day to enquire after me, why did you
    not ask to see me?

Armand. By what right could I have asked?

Marguerite. Does one have scruples with a woman like myself?

Armand. Yes, too many take a liberty I would not allow another to
    take in the house of a woman I respected.

Marguerite. So you really think you love me?

Armand. (*seeing her laugh*) When you shall give me the right to say so,
    you will one day learn how well.

Marguerite. It were better never told.

Armand. And why?

Marguerite. Because it can result in but one of two things: first, that I will not believe it; or, believing it, cause you to wish I never had. I am but a sorrowful companion at the best. Always ill, nervous, fretful, sad—or if gay, a gaiety more terrible than tears. Expensive, too; a woman who spends a hundred thousand francs a year—this may do for the dear old Duke, who has plenty of money, but it would not do for you. Now we'll talk sense. Give me your hand. Let us join the others, and I'll light your cigar.

Armand. Go, if you will; but allow me to remain.

Marguerite. What's the matter?

Armand. Your gaiety makes me ill.

Marguerite. Shall I prescribe for you?

Armand. Speak.

Marguerite. Go home and go to bed, if what you say is true. Or love me as a friend; come and see me, we will laugh and chat. But do not overestimate what I am worth, for I am not worth much. You are too young and too sensitive to live in our society. You love too well to be unloved; but love wisely. Find another girl to love, or get married. You see I speak quite frankly.

Armand. Marguerite, have you ever been in love?

Marguerite. Never, thank God.

Armand. Oh, thank you, thank you!

Marguerite. What for?

Armand. For what you have just told me; nothing could make me happier. If I were to tell you, Marguerite, that I have passed whole nights beneath your windows, that I have cherished for six months a little button which fell from your glove——

Marguerite. I would not believe you. I have heard these tales before.

Armand. You are right. I know not what I say. I am a fool. Yes, laugh! I deserve it all. Good night!

Marguerite. Armand!

Armand. Did you call?

Marguerite. Let us not part in anger.

Armand. Anger! Oh, Marguerite, if you could read my heart!

Marguerite. Then let us make it up. Come and see me sometimes— often. We will speak of this again.

Armand. Ah, still you laugh.

Marguerite. Speak, Armand; I am not laughing now.

Armand. Will you be loved?

Marguerite. For how long?

Armand. For eternity! Oh, dearest Marguerite, consent then to be mine. We will live quietly, away from this wild Paris, and the friends who now are killing you. We will seek amidst the woods and fields, health and strength for you, and we shall find them. Be my

187

wife! and if the devotion of a heart as true as ever throbbed within the breast of man can effect it, you shall live! live in happiness and joy!

Marguerite. Madness! Everything forbids my loving you. You have position, honour, friends—be wise. I have neither. I am young, gay, reckless, desperate—my name the sport of every tongue in Paris. I have admirers, lovers, all you will—the first in their vanity, the last in their esteem. Friends too, like Prudence, whose friendship mounts to servitude but never to unselfishness. All around destruction, shame, and falsehood. I should bring ruin on you! Your father——

Armand. Oh, trust me, we have naught to fear from him. Let us not hesitate—we are young—we love each other—who then can have a right to control our happiness?

Marguerite. You would not trifle with me, Armand? Forget not that a violent emotion would surely kill me. Remember well both who I am and what I am.

Armand. I remember only that you are an angel, and that I adore you.

Marguerite. Armand! You are moved; you really do believe in what you say. Such sincerity merits a reward. Here, take this flower. (*She gives him a camellia*) And in the morning, when it has faded, bring it back to me again.

Armand. Yes, dear Marguerite, yes. Oh, how happy you have made me!

Marguerite. Armand, tell me once again you love me.

Armand. It's true. I love you.

Marguerite. Now, go.

Armand. Adieu.

He kisses her hand, and goes off, gazing on her as he goes. Laughter and music heard off.

Marguerite. (*gazing at the closed door*) He loves me. There is a new-found meaning in those words that never fell upon my ears before. Oh, what's the use of it?—But why not? Who could have supposed that a man whom a week since I knew not would today so occupy my heart and every thought? Can this be love I feel, I who have never felt love? What am I? A creature of fortune! Then let fortune do with me what it will! All the same, there's something tells me I am happier than I have been before. Perhaps 'tis an ill-omen. Oh, we women of the world! We always foresee that we shall be loved, never that we ourselves shall love. Oh, how happy do I now feel! Joy is the best physician, for I am well again, and strong, and——

Laughter heard off. Prudence, Olympe, Saint-Gaudens *and* Gaston Rieux *enter tumultuously.*

Gaudens. Long live Monsieur and Madame Duval!

Olympe. Invite us to the wedding ball.
Gaudens. Let's practise for it now.
Gaston. Oh, yes; a dance, a dance! Marguerite, play for us.

> Marguerite *plays on piano. Fantastic dance.* Gaston *has a woman's bonnet on his head.* Saint-Gaudens *claps a man's hat on* Prudence. *Loud laughter.* Gaston *dances with* Prudence, *who finally faints in his arms. They all run to her.*

ACT II

A neat drawing-room in a country house near Auteuil. At the back, a fireplace with a plate-glass mirror over the chimney-piece. Doors R and L. French windows opening into the garden. Tables with writing materials and vases of flowers. Chairs, sofas, &c.

> Nanine, *entering with breakfast things, is met by* Prudence.

Prudence. Where is Marguerite?
Nanine. In the garden with Ma'amselle Nichette and Monsieur Gustave, who have come to spend the day with her.
Prudence. I will join them.

> Armand *enters, meeting* Prudence *while* Nanine *goes out.*

Armand. Ah! you here, Prudence! 'Tis well—I wished to speak with you. Two weeks since, you left here in Marguerite's carriage.
Prudence. Exactly.
Armand. Since then, neither carriage nor horses have returned. A week since, on leaving, you complained of cold, and Marguerite lent you a cashmere shawl, which I do not think you have returned. Yesterday I saw her place in your hands bracelets and diamonds— to be reset, she said. Where are the horses, the carriage, the shawl and the diamonds?
Prudence. Must I tell you?
Armand. I entreat you.
Prudence. The horses have taken themselves and the carriage back to the man from whom they came, for they were not paid for.
Armand. The cashmere shawl?
Prudence. Sold.
Armand. The diamonds?
Prudence. Pledged this morning. Perhaps you would like to see the receipts?
Armand. Why did you not tell me?

Prudence. Marguerite forbade me.

Armand. And why these sales?

Prudence. To obtain money, to be sure. Oh, I suppose you imagine it is
quite enough to be in love and live a pastoral and ethereal life
away from Paris. Marguerite has studied the reality and, like a
good girl, resolved that as she could bring you no fortune, neither
would she bring you any debts.

Armand. Good Marguerite!

Prudence. Yes, too good Marguerite; for she has not yet done selling.
I have now in my pocket a bill of sale on everything she possesses,
which was entrusted to me to deliver to her by her man of business.

Armand. What sum would be necessary for——

Prudence. Fifty thousand francs, at least.

Armand. Obtain a fortnight's grace from the creditors, and I will
pay all.

Prudence. You will embroil yourself with your father, and infringe on
your future fortune.

Armand. I had prepared for this. I knew that Marguerite had creditors,
and had written to my lawyer that I wished to dispose of a small
estate left me by my mother, and have just received his answer.
The deed is quite prepared, and presently I shall return to Paris in
order to sign it. In the meantime, pray be careful that Marguerite
knows nothing of——

Prudence. But the papers that I bring?

Armand. When I am gone, give them to her as if nothing had occurred,
for she must be ignorant of our conversation.

Prudence. You may depend on me—and, by the by, Monsieur Armand, I
am dreadfully pressed for money just now, and if you could——

Armand. Hush! she is here. Silence!

Marguerite, *entering, puts a finger to her lips as a sign to* Prudence
to be silent.

Armand. (*to* Marguerite) Dear Marguerite! Scold Prudence.

Marguerite. Why?

Armand. Yesterday I begged her to call at my rooms and bring me any
letters that were there, for it is a fortnight since I went to Paris.
The first thing she does, is to forget them. So I must leave you for
an hour or two. Nichette and Gustave are here to keep you
company—so that you will not miss me much.

Marguerite. Have you yet written to your father?

Armand. No—but I shall this very day do so.

Marguerite. Go, then, and hasten your return.

Armand. I shall not be absent above an hour.

    (*Exit* Armand, *accompanied to the door by* Marguerite)

Marguerite. (*returning*) All is arranged?

Prudence. Yes.

Marguerite. The papers?

Prudence. Here they are. Your lawyer will come today and settle matters with you; but I must go and breakfast now, for I am dying of hunger. You have, I hope, something substantial in the house?

Marguerite. Nanine will attend to you. (*Exit* Prudence)

Enter Nichette *and* Gustave.

Marguerite. You see? This is how we have been living for the last three months.

Nichette. And you are happy?

Marguerite. You are right—I am.

Nichette. And you are right, Marguerite, when you say that happiness is in the heart. How many times Gustave and I have wished that you would fall in love with someone, and lead a calmer life.

Marguerite. Well, you have your wish. I love—and I am happy; but it is your love and happiness I envy.

Gustave. The fact is, we are happy too—are we not, Nichette?

Nichette. I believe we are. After all, happiness doesn't cost much. You think you live simply here; what would you say if you could but see where I live—two little rooms on the fifth storey in the Rue Blanche, with windows that overlook some gardens in which nobody ever walks! How can there be people who have gardens that they never walk in?

Marguerite. (*giving a hand to each*) Ah, you are worthy creatures, and will be happy—as happy as I am now.

Nichette. Marguerite, you cannot guess what Gustave wants me to do— to give up embroidering, and not work any more! He'll be wanting to buy me a carriage one of these days.

Gustave. That may come, perhaps. Then, you will drive out with us, will you not?

Marguerite. Yes, Gustave, that I will.

Nichette. Oh, we will have such a time! You must know that Gustave has a rich old uncle, who is going to make him heir . . . But I forgot to tell you—Gustave is a lawyer now, if you please.

Marguerite. Indeed! You shall plead my first case.

Nichette. Oh, he has pleaded already.

Marguerite. Did he win?

Gustave. No. My client was condemned to ten years' hard labour.

Nichette. Yes! And I was so glad.

Marguerite. Glad? Why so?

Nichette. Because the man deserved it.

Marguerite. And now that Gustave is a lawyer, Nichette will soon be a bride. Is it not so?

Nichette. If he behaves himself.

Gustave. You hear the conditions! Then, Marguerite, may we not hope that you too will be a bride some day?

Marguerite. The bride of whom?

Nichette. Armand.

Marguerite. Armand? That can never be. Armand would marry me tomorrow if I would have it so; but I love him too well to ask of him such a sacrifice. Am I not right, Monsieur Gustave?

Gustave. You are very generous, Marguerite.

Marguerite. Not generous, Gustave, but just. There are some things a woman cannot blot out from her past, things for which her husband would have every right to reproach her. I am unworthy to be Armand Duval's wife. Besides, I have a happiness I never dared to hope for; why should I tempt Providence and ask for more?

Nichette. Gustave would marry you, if he were in Armand's place. Wouldn't you, Gustave?

Gustave. Perhaps. A woman's maidenhood belongs to her first love, and not to her first lover.

Nichette. Unless her first lover is at the same time her first love. There may be examples of this——

Gustave. (*clasping her hand*) And not far away, either.

Nichette. (*to* Marguerite) Well, provided you're happy, the rest doesn't matter.

Marguerite. And how happy I am! To be near the man I love, to hear his voice, to read to him, or hear him read to me! From time to time I can forget the woman I once was, as if she had never been. In a simple white dress, with a great straw hat on my head and a cape over my arm against the freshness of the evening, I take a boat upon the lake with Armand; and as we drift to a halt under the weeping willows on the island, no one, not even I myself, supposes that this pale shadow is Marguerite Gautier. I have spent more money on bouquets than a poor family would need to live on for a year; well, this simple flower which Armand gave me this morning now seems to me enough to scent the air all day. Yes, I am happy. But you do not know all.

Nichette. What's the secret?

Marguerite. You said just now that I should see your home; perhaps I will.

Nichette. But how?

Marguerite. Unknown to Armand, I am about to sell all I possess to liquidate my debts. I shall rent a small apartment near to yours, furnish it very simply, and there we will live together, forgetting and forgot. In the summer we will come back to the country, but not in so fine a house as this. Have I not taken the right path towards happiness?

Gustave. And you will reach the goal.

Enter Nanine.

Nanine. Madame, a gentleman would speak with you.

Marguerite. (*to* Gustave *and* Nichette) Doubtless the lawyer whom I
was expecting; he has the arrangement of the sale. If you will
walk for a while in the garden, I will rejoin you. (*Exeunt* Gustave
and Nichette) Bid him enter.   (*Exit* Nanine)

Monsieur Duval *enters, and remains in doorway.*

Duval. Mademoiselle Marguerite Gautier?

Marguerite. Yes, monsieur. To whom have I the honour of speaking?

Duval. To Monsieur Duval.

Marguerite. Monsieur Duval!

Duval. Yes, mademoiselle, the father of Armand.

Marguerite. (*disturbed*) Armand is not here, sir.

Duval. I know it. But it is with you I wish to come to terms. Pray
hear me. My son, mademoiselle, is compromised and ruined on your
account.

Marguerite. You are deceived, sir. Thanks be to God, I am now beyond
the reach of scandal, and I accept nothing from your son.

Duval. Which means my son is wretch enough to waste with you what
you accept from others.

Marguerite. Pardon me, sir; but I am a woman and in my own house
—two reasons that should plead in my favour for your courtesy.
Your tone is not what I should expect from a gentleman I have the
honour to see for the first time. I pray you will allow me to retire.

Duval. In truth, to hear you speak, it is difficult to believe that such
assurance must be assumed. Oh, I was told that you were a dangerous
woman!

Marguerite. Yes, sir; dangerous to myself, but not to others.

Duval. But it is none the less true that you are ruining my son.

Marguerite. Sir, I repeat, with all the respect I owe to Armand's father,
that you are wrong.

Duval. Then what is the meaning of this letter from my lawyer, which
apprises me that Armand wishes to resign to you a small estate?
                                            (*Gives her a letter*)

Marguerite. I assure you, sir, Armand has done this without my
knowledge; for he knows well that if he offered such a gift I would
refuse it.

Duval. Indeed? You have not always spoken thus.

Marguerite. True, sir; but I have not always loved.

Duval. And now?

Marguerite. I am no longer what I was.

Duval. These are very fine words.

Marguerite. What can I say to convince you? I know the oaths of
women like myself command no faith, but I swear to you by the
love I bear your son—the holiest thing that ever filled my heart—I
swear that I was ignorant of this transaction.

Duval. Yet you must live by some means?

Marguerite. You force me, sir, to be explicit. So far from resembling
the other associations of my life, my liaison with your son has made
me penniless. (*She gives the paper which Prudence had brought her*) I pray
you read that paper. It contains a list of all that I possess on earth.
When you were announced just now, I thought you were the person
to whom I had sold them.

Duval. (*reading paper*) A bill of sale of all your furniture, pictures,
plate, &c., with which to pay your creditors, the surplus to be
returned to you. (*Hands back the paper and regards her with astonishment*)
Have I been deceived?

Marguerite. You have, sir. I know my past life has been clouded; I
have been foolish; but I would give the last drop of my blood
to purge away the stain. Oh, despite what others may have told
you, I have a heart; believe me, there is some goodness in me.
It is Armand's love which has transformed me and saved me from
myself. You are his father, you must be good like him. Let me
entreat you, do not speak badly of me to him; he would believe
you, for he loves you; and I also love and honour you because
you are his father.

Duval. Pardon me for the manner in which I introduced myself just
now. I was angry with my son for his silence and ingratitude,
which I laid at your door. I pray you to excuse me.

Marguerite. I can only bless you, sir, for those kind words.

Duval. Well, it is in the name of your noblest feelings that I am
going to ask of you to give Armand the greatest proof of your
love that you could ever give him.

Marguerite. Oh, sir, I entreat you, say no more. You are going to
ask me something terrible, more terrible than I have ever imagined.
My heart forsees it—I was too happy.

Duval. It is as a father that I speak to you, Marguerite, a father who
comes to ask of you the happiness of both his children.

Marguerite. Of both your children?

Duval. Yes, Marguerite, of both. I have a daughter, young, beautiful,
and pure as an angel. She loves a young man and, like you, has
made that love the dream of her life. Marguerite, although your
soul is cleansed in Armand's eyes, and mine, the world will always
judge you by your past and pitilessly shut its doors against you. The
family of my future son-in-law has learned of your relationship with
Armand, and refuses to consent to Blanche's marriage unless he
gives you up. The future of a young girl who has never done you

wrong could be shattered by your touch. Marguerite, in the name of your love, I ask of you the happiness of my child.

Marguerite. You are very good, sir, to speak to me so frankly. I understand you, and you are right. I will leave Paris and remain apart from Armand for some time. It will be a sacrifice, I confess, but I will make it for your sake so that you may have nothing with which to reproach me. Besides, the joy of my return will obliterate the misery of separation. You will allow him to write to me sometimes, and when his sister is married——

Duval. Thank you, Marguerite; but I am asking something more of you.

Marguerite. More? What could I do more?

Duval. My child, a temporary absence will not suffice.

Marguerite. Ah, you would not have me leave Armand for ever?

Duval. You must.

Marguerite. Never! Do you not know what it is to love as we do? Do you not know that I have neither parents, friends, nor family? When Armand forgave my faults, he swore to be all these, and I have grafted life and hope on him till they and he are one. Do you not know that I have caught a mortal illness, that I have but few years to live? Renounce Armand! Better that at once you kill me.

Duval. Come, come, be calm. You are young and beautiful, and take for a disease the weariness of a disordered life; you will surely live until you reach the age at which 'tis happiness to die. I ask of you an enormous sacrifice, I know, but it is one you are inevitably forced to yield. Listen. You have known Armand for three months, and you love him. But are you certain that this love will last for éver? Have you not perhaps deceived yourself already? And if—too late— you were suddenly to realise you did not love my son, if you were to fall in love with someone else? Forgive me, Marguerite, but your past decides in favour of such doubts.

Marguerite. Never, sir; I have never loved and never will as I do now.

Duval. So be it! But if you are not deceived, my son may be. At his age, can the heart accept a never-changing contract? Does it not change perpetually in its affections? Nature is very hard to please, because she is so prodigal. It may be that you are both deceived. Do you hear me?

Marguerite. Yes, I hear you. Oh, heaven!

Duval. You are willing to sacrifice all for my son; but if he should accept this, what sacrifice could he make you in return? He will take the best years of your life, and what will happen later on, when cloying surfeit comes, as come it will? If he is an average man he will leave you, flinging your past in your face and saying he has only done what all the others did. If he is honourable he will marry you or keep you with him; what kind of union would that be which has neither chastity nor religion to commend it to the world's esteem? What career would then be open to him? What honourable ambition could he then pursue? Your union is not the fruit of two innocent affections; it is an earthy, human passion, born of caprice on one side and imagination on the other. What will remain of it when you are old? The first wrinkles on your brow will tear the veil from his eyes, and his fond illusions vanish with your youth.

Marguerite. Oh, my dream is shattered!

Duval. For three months you have been happy; keep the memory of that time unspotted in your heart, and it will make you strong. One day you will be proud of having saved Armand from a fate which he would all his life regret; and all your life you will have your self-respect. I speak to you as a man who knows the world; I implore you as a father, save my child. Come, Marguerite, prove to me you truly love my son. Have courage.

Marguerite. (*to herself*) Thus, no matter what she does, a fallen woman may never rise again. God, perhaps, will pardon her, but the world remains inflexible! What man would wish to call her 'wife', what child would wish to call her 'mother'? (*To* Duval) You are right, sir. Everything you tell me I have told myself a thousand times. I must obey. One day will you tell your daughter—for 'tis to her I sacrifice my happiness—will you tell her that there was somewhere a woman who in this world had but one hope, one thought, one dream of joy, and that at the invocation of her name this woman renounced it all, and broke her heart, and died—for I shall die of this, sir, and perhaps then God will forgive me.

Duval. (*overcome despite himself*) Poor creature!

Marguerite. You pity me, sir, and I think you weep. May heaven thank you for those tears, for they have made me as brave as you could wish. You ask that I should part company with your son, for his good, his honour and his future. What must I do? Command me, I am ready.

Duval. Say to my son that you no longer love him.

Marguerite. (*smiling sadly*) He would not believe me.

Duval. You must leave Paris.

Marguerite. He would follow me.

Duval. Then——

Marguerite. Then trust me, sir; the sacrifice shall be complete. I swear to be victorious over my love, and ere a week be ended your son shall return to you, for a while perhaps to be unhappy, but for ever cured of his love for me; and I swear too that he shall never know what has transpired between us.

Duval. Marguerite, you are a noble girl—but I fear——

Marguerite. Fear nothing, sir. He will hate me.   (*She rings*)

196

Enter Nanine.

Beg Madame Duvernoy to come to me.

Nanine. Yes, madame.   (*Exit* Nanine)

Marguerite. A last favour, sir.

Duval. Oh, pray speak, madame.

Marguerite. In a few hours Armand will be stricken with the heaviest
grief he has yet known, that he perhaps will ever know. He will
have need of a heart that loves him; be you then near him. And
now, sir, let us part. He may return at any moment; should he see
you, all would be lost.

Duval. What then are you about to do?

Marguerite. Were I to tell you, sir, 'twould be your duty to forbid me.

Duval. What can I do, Marguerite, to reward you for your generous
devotion to my wishes?

Marguerite. You could, when I am dead and Armand heaps curses on my
memory, you could swear to him I loved him well and proved
it fatally. I hear a noise; adieu, sir. We shall never meet again.
May you be happy! (Monsieur Duval *goes out*) Oh, heaven! Give
me strength.   (*She sits at the table and writes a letter*)

Enter Prudence.

Prudence. You wish to see me, dear Marguerite?

Marguerite. Yes; I have something to entrust to you.

Prudence. What?

Marguerite. This letter.

Prudence. To whom?

Marguerite. Look! (Prudence *reads the envelope and starts*) Silence!
Prepare to leave at once. (*Exit* Prudence; Marguerite *goes on writing*)
Now a letter to Armand. But what can I say? Oh, I shall go mad—
I cannot do it! Impossible! I shall never have the courage. It is too
much to ask of poor, weak, human nature.

Armand *has entered, unobserved.*

Armand. What are you doing there, Marguerite?

Marguerite. Armand! Nothing.

Armand. Writing?

Marguerite. No—yes.

Armand. How pale you are! To whom were you writing? Marguerite,
let me see that letter.

Marguerite. This letter is for you, Armand, but in the name of heaven
ask me not to give it to you now.

Armand. A mystery? —But no matter for it now; my father is coming!

Marguerite. You have seen him?

Armand. No; he left a letter at my rooms, and will be here this evening.

Someone informed him of my retreat here and my life with you;
God knows what rumours he has heard. But let him come! He
will see you, and when he sees you he will love you. If not, what
does it matter? I am dependent on him, I admit; but if need be,
I will work and free myself from his bondage.

Marguerite. (*aside*) How he loves me! (*To* Armand) But you must not
incense your father, Armand. He is coming, you say? Then I will
retire and let him see you first. But I will come back; I will be there,
by your side. I will fling myself at his feet and implore him not to
part us.

Armand. How strangely you said that, Marguerite! Something is wrong.
It is not my news which agitates you so. You can scarcely stand.
This letter—— (*He holds out his hand*)

Marguerite. (*stopping him*) This letter says something which I cannot
say to you; you know, there are such things? It is a proof of the love
I bear you, Armand; I swear it. Ask me no more.

Armand. Keep the letter, Marguerite; I know all. Prudence told me
this morning, and it was that which took me to Paris. I know the
sacrifice that you wish to make for me; and while you were
considering my happiness, I was not unmindful of yours. Dear
Marguerite! How can I ever recompense so much devotion?

Marguerite. And now, now that you know all, let me depart.

Armand. Depart!

Marguerite. Withdraw, I would say. Your father may arrive at any
moment. I will be in the garden with Gustave and Nichette; you
have only to call, and I will rejoin you. How could I ever leave
you? You will calm your father, if he is enraged, and win him to
forgive us, will you not? Then we will live together, and love each
other as before, and be as happy as we have been for these last
three months! And you are happy, are you not? And have nothing
to reproach me with? If I have ever caused you any sorrow, forgive
me; it was not my fault, for I love you more than all the world.
And you—you love me—do you not? When you recall one day
the tokens of my love, you would not despise or curse me if——

Armand. But why these tears?

Marguerite. Sometimes I need to weep a little; now, you see, I am
calm. I am going to join Nichette and Gustave. I will be there,
always by your side, always ready to rejoin you, always loving you.
Look, I am smiling. Adieu—for ever! (*She goes out, blowing him kisses*)

Armand. Dear Marguerite! How she fears the idea of a separation!
How she loves me! (*Rings the bell*)

Enter Nanine.

Nanine, if a gentleman—my father—asks to see me, show him in
here at once.

198

Nanine. Very well, sir. (*Exit* Nanine)

Armand. I am taking fright at nothing. My father will understand.
The past is dead. Besides, what a difference between Marguerite
and those other women! I met Olympe today, still occupied with
empty pleasures. (*Takes letters from his pocket*) Here is an invitation to
her ball next week—as if Marguerite and I ever could return to
that society! Ah, how time drags when she is not here. Seven
o'clock! (*Rings the bell*) My father will not come tonight.

Enter Nanine.

Ask madame to come in.

Nanine. Madame is not here, sir.

Armand. How? Where is she, then?

Nanine. I saw her go down the road. She told me to tell you, sir,
that she would return presently.

Armand. Did Madame Duvernoy go with her?

Nanine. Madame Duvernoy and the others left a little before madame.

Armand. Very well. (*Exit* Nanine) She could have gone to Paris to
see about the sale; happily, Prudence will find the means to prevent
her. (*He looks out of the window*) Is that a shadow I can see in the
garden? It must be her. (*He calls*) Marguerite! (*He goes out and calls
again*) Marguerite! Marguerite! (*He returns*) No, there is no one there.
(*He rings the bell*) Nanine! Nanine! Nanine, I say! No answer.
What can this mean? This silence chills me. Why did I let
Marguerite go out? She was hiding something from me. She was
weeping! Has she deceived me? How could I think it, when she
thought to sacrifice all for my sake! Perhaps something has happened
to her! Perhaps she is injured! dead! I must find out.

He goes towards the garden. A Messenger *confronts him at the door.*

Messenger. Monsieur Armand Duval?

Armand. Yes.

Messenger. Here is a letter for you.

Armand. Where from?

Messenger. Paris.

Armand. Who gave it you?

Messenger. A lady.

Armand. Why do you come here?

Messenger. The garden gate was open. There was no one about. I saw
a light, and thought——

Armand. Very well. Leave me. (*The* Messenger *withdraws*) A letter
from Marguerite. Why am I so agitated? Doubtless she is waiting
for me somewhere, and writes to me to go and meet her. (*He goes to
open the letter*) I'm trembling. Nonsense! This is childish.

Monsieur Duval *enters unperceived, and stands behind his son.*

Armand. (reading) 'Armand, by the time that you receive this letter . . .'
(*He utters a cry of fury, turns and sees his father, and flings himself into his arms, sobbing*) Ah! Father! Father!

ACT III

A splendid reception room in the house of Olympe*; gaming table with lighted candles on it, cards, and plenty of loose money. Chairs round. Large chandeliers. Arch,* C*, opening onto a brilliantly lighted saloon.*

Gaston, Doctor, Prudence, Mademoiselle Arthur *and* Mademoiselle Anais *discovered at the gaming table; two* Players *seated with their backs to the audience.* Servants *handing refreshments; music;* Guests *dance and promenade in the saloon.*

Gaston. (dealing the cards for baccarat) Put down your stakes, gentlemen!
Arthur. How much is there in the bank?
Gaston. A hundred louis.
Arthur. In that case, I shall stake five francs.
Gaston. With the enormous sum of five francs to hazard, no wonder you were anxious to know the amount of the bank!
Arthur. I can go in with five francs ready money, or, if you prefer, I can stake ten louis on credit.
Gaston. You are very good but, thank you, no. (*To* Doctor) You are not playing, doctor?
Doctor. No.
Gaston. (dealing cards) Then why are you here?
Doctor. (laughing) To increase my practice, of course; I'm introducing myself to all the charming ladies.
                    (*Laughter and gossip from all round the table*)
Gaston. If this is how you play, I'm passing the bank.
Prudence. Stop! I stake ten francs.
Gaston. Where are they?
Prudence. In my pocket.
Gaston. (laughing) I would give fifteen francs to see them.
Prudence. (putting her hand in her pocket) Bless me! I have forgotten my purse.
Gaston. Well, here's a purser who knows his job. Take these ten francs.
Prudence. Thanks. I shall be certain to return them.   (*Stakes money*)
Gaston. You are certain to do nothing of the kind; and I beg you won't, for the surprise would be too much for me. (*Giving cards*)
    I am nine.   (*He collects in the money*)

Prudence. He always wins. My ten francs gone already!

Gaston. Mine, you mean—returned to their rightful owner.

Arthur. That makes fifty louis that I have lost.

Anais. A thousand francs! Oh, and she had but two louis in her pocket when she arrived.

Arthur. Exactly—I owe the rest.

Anais. I pity your creditors. Doctor, cure Arthur of that serious complaint—losing money which she has not got.

Doctor. Time is the only remedy for that.

Gaston. Put down your stakes, gentlemen; we are not here to amuse ourselves.

Enter Olympe *and* Saint-Gaudens.

Olympe. Still gambling?

Arthur. Still—and for ever.

Olympe. Give me ten louis, Saint-Gaudens, to play with.

Gaudens. There. Ah, there you are, doctor. I must consult you. Cure me of too much good nature. Sometimes I have fits of giddiness.

Doctor. Indeed!

Olympe. What did he want?

Doctor. He thinks there's something wrong with his head.

Olympe. The conceited ass—I have lost. Saint-Gaudens, play for me and try to win.

Prudence. Saint-Gaudens, lend me three louis. (*He gives them*)

Anais. Saint-Gaudens, go and find me a water-ice.

Gaudens. Presently.

Anais. Then tell us the story about your uncle and the heiress.

Gaudens. I'm going, I'm going. (*He goes out*)

Prudence. (*to* Gaston) Do you remember that story?

Gaston. I should say I do. How Marguerite laughed! How Marguerite laughed! By the by, is she here?

Olympe. She has yet to arrive.

Gaston. And Armand?

Olympe. Armand is not in Paris.—Then you know not what has happened?

Gaston. What?

Prudence. They have separated.

Anais. Fiddlesticks!

Prudence. It is true. Marguerite has left him.

Gaston. But when?

Prudence. A month ago.

Anais. She has done well.

Gaston. Why so?

Anais. You should always leave a man before he leaves you.

Arthur. Come, gentlemen; is there a game in progress, or is there not?

Re-enter Saint-Gaudens.

Gaudens. Anais, here is the water-ice you asked for.

Anais. You have been a very long time, my poor old fellow; after all, at your age . . .

Gaston. (*rising*) The bank is broken, gentlemen, and the banker has resigned. Had I been offered five hundred francs to deal the cards for an entire evening I would have refused; and yet here I have been banker for only two hours, and have lost two thousand. Ah! 'tis a delightful occupation.   (*Another guest takes over the bank*)

Enter Armand.

Prudence. Hullo! Here's Armand.

Gaston. (*to* Armand) We were but now speaking of you.

Armand. And what were you saying?

Prudence. That you were at Tours, and would not be here tonight.

Armand. You were mistaken, then.

Gaston. When did you arrive?

Armand. An hour since.

Prudence. Have you seen Marguerite?

Armand. No.

Prudence. She will be here tonight.

Armand. (*coolly*) Indeed? Then perhaps I may see her.

Prudence. Perhaps you may see her! How strangely you talk!

Armand. How would you have me talk?

Prudence. Your heart then is cured?

Armand. Perfectly.

Prudence. So you no longer think of her?

Armand. To say that I no longer think of her at all would be untrue; but Marguerite dismissed me in so sharp a manner that I found myself a pretty fool to have loved her as I did—for in truth I loved her very dearly.

Prudence. Oh, I really think she loved you then, and even loves you still—that is a little. But it was time for her to leave you. Everything she had was being sold to pay her debts.

Armand. And now they are all paid?

Prudence. Entirely.

Armand. And Monsieur de Varville supplied the funds?

Prudence. Yes.

Armand. So much the better.

Prudence. And so I tell her. In short, he has provided her with all her former luxuries—horses, carriage, jewels——

Armand. And she has returned to Paris?

Prudence. Naturally; she had no wish to go back to Auteuil when you

had left, so I returned to wind up her affairs there. And that
reminds me, I have some things of yours at home you must collect.
There was only a small card-case with your monogram that
Marguerite desired to keep; but I will ask her for it, if you would
like it back.

Armand. (with emotion) Let her keep it!

Prudence. As for the rest, I have never seen her as she is now. She
never sleeps, but chases after suppers, parties, balls, and dances
the long night away. Not long ago, she was three days confined
to bed, and when the doctor allowed her to get up she flung
herself at once into a round of feverish excitements, risking her health
and life with desperate abandon. If she continues thus, it cannot
last long. Do you propose to go and see her?

Armand. No; the past is dead—forgotten.

Prudence. Ah, I am delighted to find you take the matter so sensibly.

Enter Gustave.

Armand. (seeing him) My dear Prudence, here is a friend that I must
speak with; will you have the goodness to excuse me?

Prudence. By all means! *(She goes to the gaming table)* I stake ten francs!

Armand. So you received my letter?

Gustave. I did—and here I am.

Armand. You wonder why I should request your presence at such a
gathering?

Gustave. I confess it.

Armand. You have not seen Marguerite of late?

Gustave. No; not since I saw her in your company.

Armand. So you know nothing?

Gustave. Nothing; instruct me.

Armand. And you believed that Marguerite loved me, did you not?

Gustave. I believe so still.

Armand. (giving him Marguerite's *letter)* Read.

Gustave. (after reading it) And Marguerite wrote this?

Armand. She did.

Gustave. When?

Armand. A month since.

Gustave. And what was your reply?

Armand. What could it be? The blow was so unexpected that I thought
I should go mad. Marguerite! To deceive me! When I loved her
so dearly! Oh, such women surely have no souls. Stunned by the
shock, I accompanied my father as far as Tours. At first I thought
to live there, but it proved impossible. I could not sleep; I stifled.
I had loved Marguerite too greatly to become indifferent all at once.
I had to love her or else hate her. At last, I could no longer stand the
strain. I felt that I should die unless I saw her once again, heard

from her own lips the words that she had written. I am here this evening because they tell me she is coming. What will occur, I know not; but I may need a friend.

Gustave. My dear Armand, I am entirely at your service. But for heaven's sake reflect—your affair is with a woman. Be discreet.

Armand. So be it! She has a lover who will call on me for satisfaction. If I commit an indiscretion, I have blood enough to pay for it.

Enter Servant.

Servant. (*announcing*) Mademoiselle Marguerite Gautier! Monsieur the Baron de Varville!

Armand. She is here.

Enter Marguerite *and* De Varville.

Olympe. (*going to meet* Marguerite) How late you are!

Varville. We have just come from the Opera.

(Shakes hands with the gentlemen)

Prudence. (*to* Marguerite) All is well?

Marguerite. Very well!

Prudence. (*in an undertone*) Armand is here.

Marguerite. (*disturbed*) Armand?

Prudence. Yes.

At this moment, Marguerite *meets the eye of* Armand, *who has gone to the gaming table; she smiles timidly; he bows coldly.*

Marguerite. Oh, I was wrong to come to this ball tonight.

Prudence. Not at all; you would have to meet some day; and it may as well be soon as late.

Marguerite. He has spoken to you?

Prudence. Yes.

Marguerite. Of me?

Prudence. Naturally.

Marguerite. What said he?

Prudence. That he bore you no ill will; you were quite justified.

Marguerite. So much the better if he thinks so; but no—it is impossible. He bowed too coldly, and he is too pale.

Varville. (*to* Marguerite, *aside*) Monsieur Duval is over there, Marguerite.

Marguerite. I know it.

Varville. Will you swear to me that you were ignorant of his presence here when you arrived?

Marguerite. I swear it.

Varville. And you will promise me not to speak to him?

Marguerite. I promise; but should he speak, I cannot promise that I will not reply. Prudence, stay near me.

Doctor. (*to* Marguerite) Good evening, madame.

Marguerite. Ah, it is you, doctor! How you scrutinise me!

Doctor. What better could I do when in your presence?

Marguerite. You find me, do you not, much changed?

Doctor. Take care of yourself, take care, I entreat you. I shall call on you tomorrow, to scold you at my ease.

Marguerite. Ah, doctor, how good and kind you are! But you are not leaving already?

Doctor. Presently.   (*He shakes her hand and retires*)

Gustave. (*approaching* Marguerite) Good evening, Marguerite.

Marguerite. Ah, my dear Gustave, how glad I am to see you. And Nichette—is she here?

Gustave. No.

Marguerite. Forgive me; she would have no desire to come. Love her well, Gustave—she must be happy, to be so truly loved.

         (*She wipes her eyes*)

Gustave. What is the matter?

Marguerite. Oh, Gustave, I am so unhappy.

Gustave. There, there, do not weep. Why are you here?

Marguerite. How else can I allay my grief?

Gustave. If you will be advised by me, you will leave this ball before it is too late.

Marguerite. Why?

Gustave. Who knows what may happen? Armand——

Marguerite. But surely Armand hates and despises me?

Gustave. No; he loves you still. See how feverish he is—not master of himself. I know not what may yet transpire between him and Monsieur de Varville. Plead indisposition and depart.

Marguerite. A duel between Varville and Armand! Yes, yes, you are right, Gustave. I must leave.   (*She rises*)

Varville. (*approaching her*) Where are you going?

Marguerite. My love, I'm suffocating and wish to withdraw.

Varville. No, you are not suffocating, Marguerite. You want to withdraw because Monsieur Duval is over there and seems to pay no heed to you. But understand I have no wish to quit whatever place he honours with his presence. We are at this ball, and here will we remain.

Olympe. (*loudly*) What were they playing at the Opera tonight?

Varville. La Favorite.

Armand. The story of a woman who deceives her lover.

Prudence. Pooh! How commonplace!

Anais. Which means it isn't true; there's no such thing as a woman who would deceive her lover.

Armand. I say there is.

Anais. Where are they then?

Armand. All around you.

Olympe. Yes, but there are lovers and lovers.

Armand. As there are women and women.

Gaston. Now then! My dear Armand, you are playing like a madman.

Armand. To see if the proverb holds true: 'Unlucky in love, lucky at play'.

Gaston. Ah! You must be terribly unlucky in love, for you are terribly lucky at play.

Armand. My dear fellow, I reckon on making my fortune tonight; and when I have won it I will go and live in the country.

Olympe. Alone?

Armand. No; with someone who once accompanied me there before, and left me. Perhaps when I am rich——. (*Aside*) She will say nothing then!

Gustave. (*to* Armand, *aside*) Be quiet, Armand, for heaven's sake! You are killing Marguerite.

Armand. It's a good story; I must tell it you. There is a gentleman in it who comes on at the end, a sort of *deus ex machina*, a charming type.

Varville. Sir!

Marguerite. (*to* Varville, *aside*) If you challenge Monsieur Duval, you shall never see me more.

Armand. (*to* Varville) Are you addressing me, sir?

Varville. Yes indeed, sir; you are so lucky at play that your good fortune tempts me, and I understand so well the use to which you would apply your gains that I am eager to see you win still more, and so propose a match.

Armand. (*looking him full in the face*) Which I accept gladly, sir.

Varville. A hundred louis, sir.

Armand. (*astonished and contemptuous*) Agreed; a hundred louis. On which side will you——

Varville. That which you do not take.

Armand. A hundred louis on the left.

Varville. A hundred louis on the right.

Gaston. (*dealing cards*) On the right, four; on the left, nine. Armand wins.

Varville. In that case, two hundred louis.

Armand. Agreed; two hundred louis. But take care, sir; if the proverb says 'Unlucky in love, lucky at play', it also says 'Lucky in love, unlucky at play'.

Gaston. Six! Eight! Armand wins again.

Marguerite. (*to* Olympe) My God, where will this end?

Olympe. (*to create a diversion*) Come along, gentlemen; supper is served.

Armand. Shall we continue the game, sir?

Varville. No—not for the present.

Armand. I owe you your revenge, and promise you shall have it at any game you choose.

Varville. Rest easy, sir; I will take advantage of your goodwill!

Olympe. (*taking* Armand *by the arm*) You are out of luck, my dear
Armand.

Armand. Ah, you only call me 'dear' when I've been winning.

Varville. Are you coming, Marguerite?

Marguerite. Not yet; I would speak a word with Prudence.

Varville. I warn you, Marguerite; if within ten minutes you
do not rejoin us, I shall return and seek you here.

Marguerite. Very well, sir; go.

Olympe *and* Guests *move into the saloon;* Servants *close folding doors
behind them.* Prudence *is left with* Marguerite.

Go to Armand, and in the name of all he holds most sacred
implore him to come to me. I must speak with him.

Prudence. Should he refuse——

Marguerite. He will not. He hates me too much not to seize the
opportunity to tell me so. Go. (*Exit* Prudence) Let me be calm.
He must continue to think of me as he does. Shall I have strength
enough to keep the promise that I made his father? Oh heaven,
make him despise and hate me! for only so may this duel be averted.
Ah, he is here.

Enter Armand.

Armand. You would speak with me, madame?

Marguerite. Yes, Armand, I——

Armand. Proceed, madame; you would exonerate yourself?

Marguerite. No, Armand, that is not the point at issue now; do not,
I implore you, dwell upon the past.

Armand. You are right, madame; it covers you with too much shame.

Marguerite. You overwhelm me with reproaches, Armand. Hear me, I
beg you, without hatred, without anger, without contempt. Come,
Armand, give me your hand.

Armand. Never madame! If this is all you have to say to me . . .
(He offers to withdraw)

Marguerite. Who could believe you one day would refuse the hand I
tendered? But no matter for that now. Armand, you must leave Paris.

Armand. Leave Paris?

Marguerite. Yes—rejoin your father—and at once!

Armand. And why, madame?

Marguerite. Because Monsieur de Varville seeks to challenge you, and
I would not be the cause of such misfortune; I am alone to blame,
and I alone should suffer.

Armand. And so you counsel me to flee a challenge and prove myself a
coward! In truth, what other counsel could be expected from
a woman such as you?

Marguerite. Armand, I swear to you, I have scarce strength enough to tell how much I have this last month suffered; my malady increases hourly; it destroys me. In the name of our past love, Armand, in the name of your mother and your sister, shun me, rejoin your father, and—if you can—forget my very name.

Armand. I understand you, madame; you tremble for your lover and the wealth he represents. I could bring ruin on you with a pistol-shot or sword-thrust. That, indeed, would be a great misfortune.

Marguerite. You could be killed, Armand—there is the true misfortune!

Armand. What matters it to you whether I live or die? Were you so concerned about my life when you wrote to me 'Armand, forget me, I am the mistress of another man'? This letter might have killed me, but I live to be avenged. Ah, did you believe that I would tamely suffer you and your accomplice there to break my heart? No, madame, no. I am again in Paris; between Monsieur de Varville and myself it is now a question of blood. Madame, were you also to die for it, I swear to you that I will kill him!

Marguerite. Monsieur de Varville is innocent of all that has occurred.

Armand. You love him, madame! That is enough to make me hate him.

Marguerite. You know well I do not—could not—love this man.

Armand. Then why did you give yourself to him?

Marguerite. Do not ask me, Armand! I cannot tell you. I dare not answer.

Armand. Then I will answer for you. You gave yourself to him because you are a woman without integrity or soul, because your love belongs to him who pays for it and you have made an auction of your heart, because when you had to make a sacrifice on my account your courage failed you and your instincts got the upper hand, because in short the man who consecrated yours his life and honour was worth less to you than the horses of your carriage and the diamonds about your neck.

Marguerite. Very well. Yes, all you say is true; yes, I am an infamous and wretched creature who did not love you; yes, I deceived you! But if I am so despicable, why should you remember me, why risk your life for my sake—and the lives of those who love you? Armand, on my knees I beg of you—go, leave Paris and never look behind you.

Armand. Then I will go—but on one condition.

Marguerite. Whatever it is, I agree.

Armand. That you go with me.

Marguerite. (*recoiling*) Never!

Armand. Never!

Marguerite. Oh heaven, give me courage!

Armand. (*running to the door, and then returning*) Listen, Marguerite. I am mad—feverish—my brain seethes, my blood is on fire—

there is nothing—no infamy—of which I am not capable. A moment since, I thought that it was hatred which impelled me to you; it was love, unconquerable and infuriating love, love full of hatred, love urged on by remorse, contempt and shame—for after what has passed between us I despise myself for loving you again. No matter. Speak but one word of penitence, blame your fault on chance, on fate, on your own weakness, and it is all forgot! What is this man to me? I hate him only if you love him. Tell me only that you love me still, and I will forgive you, Marguerite; we will take flight from Paris and the past, travel to the ends of the earth if need be, until no human face remains to greet us and all the world comprises but our love.

Marguerite. (exhausted) I would give my life for one hour of that happiness which you propose, but such happiness is impossible.

Armand. Again!

Marguerite. An abyss divides us; we may no longer love each other. Go, forget me!—it must be so; I have sworn it.

Armand. To whom?

Marguerite. To one who had the right to ask of me this solemn oath.

Armand. (his anger rising) Monsieur de Varville, I presume?

Marguerite. Yes.

Armand. (seizing Marguerite *by the arm)* Monsieur de Varville, whom you love! Tell me you love him; say but that and I depart.

Marguerite. Very well, then. Yes, I love Monsieur de Varville.

Armand *hurls* Marguerite *to the ground and offers to strike her. Then he dashes to the saloon and flings open the folding doors.*

Armand. (to Guests *in the saloon)* Everybody! Come in here.

Enter De Varville *and all the other* Guests.

Marguerite. What are you doing?

Armand. (to Guests) Do you see this woman?

All. Marguerite Gautier?

Armand. Yes! Marguerite Gautier. Do you know what she has done? She sold all she possessed to live with me—so much she loved me. This was generous, was it not? But do you know what I have done? I have behaved like a scoundrel. I accepted the sacrifice without giving anything in exchange. But it is not too late; I am penitent and have come to make amends for all. You will all bear witness that now I owe this woman nothing!

He showers *Marguerite* with bank-notes. *She utters a cry and falls back senseless.* Varville *advances on* Armand, *and hurls his gloves in* Armand's *face.*

Varville. (with contempt) Without equivocation, sir, you are a villain!

Guests *rush between them.*

ACT IV

Marguerite's *sleeping chamber, meanly furnished. Window on* L, *with curtains half drawn; door* R. *Fireplace,* R, *with poker, tongs and fender; sofa in front of the fireplace. Table with toilette glass and tea things; chairs round. Bed at back; near it a small table with medicines, letter and night-light.*

Marguerite *discovered in bed asleep;* Gaston Rieux *stretched out on the sofa; no light except the night-light.*

Gaston. (raising his head and listening) I must have dozed off for a
    moment. I hope she has not wanted anything. No; still asleep.
    I wonder what the time is. Seven o'clock! No daylight yet, and the
    fire has gone out. I must get it going again.   *(He pokes the fire)*
Marguerite. (waking up) Nanine, give me something to drink.
Gaston. Here you are.
Marguerite. (lifting her head slightly) Who is that?
Gaston. (preparing a cup of tea) It's only me, Gaston.
Marguerite. What are you doing in my room?
Gaston. (giving her the cup) Drink this first, and then I will tell you. Is it
    sweet enough?
Marguerite. Yes.
Gaston. I was born to be a nurse.
Marguerite. But where is Nanine?
Gaston. Fast asleep. When I came at eleven last night to learn how
    you were, the poor girl was ready to drop with fatigue while I,
    as usual, was wide awake. You had already fallen asleep, so I
    bundled Nanine off to bed, settled myself on the sofa there near the
    fire, and have passed a beautiful night. You slept so quietly that it
    did me more good than if I had had the finest snooze in the world.
    And now, how are you this morning?
Marguerite. Very well, my good Gaston; but why should you wear
    yourself out like this——
Gaston. Rubbish! I spend enough nights on the town; it would do me
    much more good to pass some of them watching by a sick-bed!
    Besides, I have something to say to you.
Marguerite. To me?
Gaston. Yes. You are in need.
Marguerite. In need of what?
Gaston. Money. When I arrived here yesterday there was a bailiff
    in the drawing-room; I paid him off and turned him out of doors.
    But that's not all. You need some ready money here, and I happen
    to have some—not much, for I have lost a fair amount at cards and

bought a pile of useless presents for New Year's Day. —May you be well and happy all the year! (*He embraces her*) — But, to be brief, look here, here are twenty-five louis anyway; I am going to put them in that table drawer over there, and when they are gone there will be more.

Marguerite. (*moved*) Gaston, you are very kind. And to think it should be you who takes such care of me! You, whom all suppose a scatter-brain, you who have never been more than my friend——

Gaston. Why, it is always so. Now, do you know what we are going to do?

Marguerite. Tell me.

Gaston. 'Twill be a splendid day! You have slept for eight good hours and must sleep a little more. From one to three the sun will be quite warm; I will come for you; wrap yourself up well; we will go for a drive in a carriage; and who will sleep well tomorrow night? Marguerite. Till then, I must go and see my mother. Heaven knows how she will receive me; it's more than a fortnight since I saw her last! I shall lunch with her and be here at one. How will that suit you?

Marguerite. I shall try to find the strength——

Gaston. You shall find it, never fear!

Enter Nanine.

Come in, come in, Nanine. Marguerite is awake.

Marguerite. Were you very tired, my poor Nanine?

Nanine. A little, madame.

Marguerite. Open the window, I need a little air. I want to get up.

Nanine. (*opening the window and looking into the street*) Madame, the doctor is here.

Marguerite. He is a good man. His first visit is always here. Gaston, open the door to him as you are leaving. Nanine, help me to get up.

Nanine. But madame——

Marguerite. No objections now!

Gaston. Goodbye for the present!

Marguerite. For the present.   (*Exit* Gaston)

Marguerite *rises, but sinks back again exhausted. At length, supported by* Nanine, *she walks to the sofa; the* Doctor *enters in time to help her sit.*

Good morning, doctor. How kind you are to think of me the first thing in the morning! Nanine, see if there are any letters.

(*Exit* Nanine)

Doctor. Give me your hand. (*He feels her pulse*) How do you feel today?

Marguerite. Better and worse; better in spirit but worse in body. Last evening, I felt myself so near to death I called a priest. I was wretched, afraid of death and driven to despair. He came, talked with me for an hour, and took away with him all my remorse and terror and despair. And then I fell asleep and woke just now.

Doctor. All goes well, madame, and I promise you a total cure by the first days of spring.

Marguerite. Thank you, doctor; but I know it is your duty to speak thus. When God said it was a sin to lie, he made an exception for all doctors.

Re-enter Nanine.

(*To* Nanine) What have you there?

Nanine. Some presents for you, madame.

Marguerite. Ah, yes, 'tis New Year's Day. How much has happened this last year! At this hour a year ago, we were at table, singing, greeting the New Year with the self-same smile we had just given to the old. When shall we laugh again, I wonder? (*Opening the packages*) A ring, from Saint-Gaudens. Bless him! A bracelet, from the Count de Giray in London. What would he say if he could see me now? And then some bonbons. Well, the world has a better memory than I expected.

Nanine. And here is a letter, madame.

Marguerite. Let me see. (*Taking the letter and opening it*) 'Dear Marguerite, I have called to see you twenty times but could never be admitted. However, I must share my happiness with you. Gustave and I are to be married on the first of January in the Magdalen Chapel at St Theresa's Church. It is a New Year's present which Gustave has been keeping for me. Do, my love, try to be present: nine o'clock in the morning is the hour. Believe me, your happy and devoted friend, Nichette.' There is, then, happiness for all the world but me; yet, no, I am ungrateful! Doctor, pray close that window, I am cold, and give me pen and paper.

Marguerite *buries her head in her hands. The* Doctor *places writing materials on a table near her, and retires.*

Nanine. (*to the* Doctor, *in an undertone*) Well, doctor?

Doctor. (*shaking his head*) She is very, very ill.

Marguerite. (*aside*) They think I cannot hear them. (*Aloud*) Doctor, as you pass by, would you be kind enough to leave this letter at the church where Nichette is to be married, and beg them not to give it her until after the ceremony. (*She writes the letter, folds and seals it*) There—and thank you. (*She presses his hand*) Don't forget, and come back soon if you are able! (*Exit* Doctor) Now to tidy up this room a little. (*Bell rings*) Some one rings; go to the door, Nanine. (*Exit* Nanine)

Nanine *re-enters*.

Nanine. It is Madame Duvernoy, who wishes to see madame.
Marguerite. Show her in. (*Exit* Nanine)

Nanine *re-enters with* Prudence.

Prudence. Well, my dear Marguerite, and how are you this morning?
Marguerite. Better, thank you, my dear Prudence.
Prudence. Send Nanine away for a moment; I have something to say to you alone.
Marguerite. Nanine, tidy the next room, will you? I will call when I need you. (*Exit* Nanine)
Prudence. My dear Marguerite, I have a great favour to ask you.
Marguerite. What is it?
Prudence. Have you any money?
Marguerite. As you know, I have been in difficulties for some time. But, anyway, go on.
Prudence. It's New Year's Day, and I have presents to give. Could you lend me two hundred francs until the end of the month?
Marguerite. (*casting up her eyes*) The end of the month!
Prudence. If it inconveniences you——
Marguerite. I have but little money, of which indeed I am in urgent want.
Prudence. Then we will say no more about it.
Marguerite. But no matter. Open that drawer.
Prudence. Which one? (*She opens several*) Ah, the middle one.
Marguerite. How much is there?
Prudence. Five hundred francs.
Marguerite. Well, take the two hundred that you need.
Prudence. And the rest will be enough for you?
Marguerite. Never mind me; I have all that I shall want.
Prudence. (*taking the money*) You do me a great kindness.
Marguerite. So much the better, dear Prudence!
Prudence. Now I must go, but I shall see you again soon. You are looking much better.
Marguerite. Oh yes, much better.
Prudence. The fine weather will come soon, and the country air will complete your recovery.
Marguerite. No doubt.
Prudence. (*going*) Thank you again!
Marguerite. Send Nanine to me.
Prudence. Of course. (*Exit* Prudence)

Nanine *re-enters*.

Nanine. Did she come to ask you for money again?
Marguerite. Yes.

Nanine. And you gave it her?

Marguerite. It was so small a sum, and she needed it so greatly, she
said. But so do we, Nanine; there are New Year's gifts to give.
So take this bracelet I was given to the jeweller's, and sell it. Come
back quickly.

Nanine. But in the mean time——

Marguerite. I can remain alone—shall want for nothing. Besides, you
will not be long, you know the way; that jeweller has bought
enough from me these last three months. *(Exit* Nanine; Marguerite
takes a letter from her bosom and reads) 'Madame, I have learned
of the duel between Armand and Monsieur de Varville, not from
my son for—you will scarcely believe it—he fled without bidding
me farewell. De Varville is now out of danger, thank heaven, and I
know all. You have kept your oath at hazard of your life. I have
today written to Armand, explaining all. He is far distant, but will
return to ask your pardon for us both; for I have been forced
to do you harm, and wish to make amends. Take especial care
of yourself, my child, and hope; your courage and your self-
denial merit a bright future, and I promise you it shall be yours.
Believe me your friend, Georges Duval. 15th November.' 'Tis six
weeks since I received this letter. How many times have I re-read it,
to gain a little courage! If only I could hear one word from Armand!
If only I could live until the spring! *(She rises and looks in the glass)*
Oh, how changed I am! And yet the doctor promised me I should
recover. I will have patience. Yet, just now, with Nanine, he gave
me up. I heard him; he said that I was very ill. Very ill! Yet there
is hope; I have some months yet to live, and if Armand returns
within that time, I shall be saved. New Year's Day! Ah, 'tis the
time for hope! And I am right to do so; if I were in real danger,
Gaston would not have the courage to laugh at my bedside as he did
but now; the doctor would not have left me. *(At the window)* How
happy the children are! Oh, how that pretty infant laughs and
gambols with his toys! I should like to kiss him.

Nanine *enters. She puts the money she has brought upon the mantelpiece,
and comes to* Marguerite.

Nanine. Madame——

Marguerite. What is it, Nanine?

Nanine. You feel better today, do you not?

Marguerite. Yes—why?

Nanine. Promise me you will be calm.

Marguerite. What has happened?

Nanine. I wanted to forewarn you . . . too sudden joy is difficult to bear!

Marguerite. Joy, you say?

Nanine. Yes, madame.

Marguerite. Armand! You have seen Armand? Armand is coming to see
me! (Nanine *nods assent.* Marguerite *runs to the door*) Armand!

Armand *enters, looking pale.* Marguerite *flings her arms round his neck
and holds him tight.* Nanine *withdraws.*

Oh, is it really you? It is impossible that God should be so kind!
Armand. Yes, Marguerite, it is I—so penitent, so troubled, and so
guilty that I did not dare to cross your threshold. Had I not
met Nanine, I should be still weeping and praying underneath
your window. Do not curse me, Marguerite! My father wrote to me,
explaining everything. I was very far from you; I knew not where
to go to flee my love and my remorse. I left at once, travelled like a
madman, night and day, without repose or respite, without sleep,
pursued by ominous foreboding, seeing from afar your house
draped with mourning black. Oh, had I not found you living, I
should have killed myself, knowing that I had killed you. I have
not yet seen my father; Marguerite, tell me that you will forgive
us both. Oh, how miraculous it is to see you once again!
Marguerite. Forgive you, my beloved? But I, alone, was guilty!
Yet could I have acted otherwise? I sought your happiness, even
at the cost of mine. But now your father will not separate us,
is it not so? 'Tis not the Marguerite of former days you meet
with here; but I am still young, and will grow beautiful again
because I now am happy. You will forget the past. 'Tis only from
today we will begin to live.
Armand. Oh yes, we shall no more be separated. Listen, Marguerite.
We will leave this house this very minute, and never see Paris
again. My father knows your true worth; he will love you
as his son's good genius. My sister is married—the future is ours.
Marguerite. Oh, speak on, speak on! I feel my soul, my health,
reviving with your words. I said this morning but a single thing
could save me; I no longer hoped for it—and here you are! We
have no time to lose; come, and since life is passing from me, I
must arrest its passage. Oh, you do not know—Nichette and Gustave
are married now, this very morning. We shall see them. It will do
us good to go into a church, give thanks to God, and share in the
happiness of others. What a surprise did heaven keep for me for
New Year's Day! But, Armand, tell me once again you love me!
Armand. Yes, Marguerite, I love you; all my life is yours.
Marguerite. (*calling*) Nanine—my shawl; I am going out.

Re-enter Nanine.

Armand. Dear Nanine! You have taken such good care of her. Thank
you.
Marguerite. Every day we talked of you, the pair of us; for no one

else dared speak your name. It was she who consoled me, who said
that we should meet again. And she was not mistaken.   (*She totters*)

Armand. Marguerite, what is it? How pale you are!

Marguerite. (*with an effort*) Nothing, my beloved, nothing! When
happiness thus floods a heart so long left desolate, it takes away
the breath—that's all.   (*She sits down, her head falling back*)

Armand. Marguerite, speak to me, I implore you—Marguerite!

Marguerite. (*coming to herself*) Fear nothing, my beloved. I have, you
know, been always subject to these fainting fits; but they quickly
pass. Look, I am smiling, I am strong! Come. 'Tis the joy of
knowing I shall live which stifles me.

Armand. (*taking her hand*) You are shaking.

Marguerite. It is nothing! Come, Nanine, give me my shawl, my hat——

Armand. (*terrified*) My God! My God!

Marguerite. (*pulling off the shawl angrily, after trying to walk*) Oh, I cannot!
              (*She falls upon the sofa*)

Armand. Nanine, run and find the doctor!

Marguerite. Yes, yes; tell him that Armand has returned, that I want
to live, that I must live. (Nanine *goes out*) But if your return cannot
save me, nothing will. I have lived for love; now I am dying for it.

Armand. Hush now, Marguerite; you will live—you must!

Marguerite. Sit near me, Armand, as close as you can; and listen to me
well. I am sorry that a moment since I was angry at death's approach;
'tis inevitable, and I welcome it, since it has awaited your return to
strike me down. If my death had not been certain, your father
would not have told you to return——

Armand. Marguerite, speak no more thus, or you will drive me mad.
Do not tell me you are dying; tell me that you do not believe it,
that it may not—must not—will not be.

Marguerite. But since God wills it, I must yield, whether I will or
no. If my life were innocent and chaste, perhaps I would weep
to leave a world where you remain, because the future would be
full of promises and all my past life would give me rightful claim to
them. When I die, all your memories of me will be pure; if I lived,
there would always be some stain upon our love. Believe me, that
which heaven does, is ever well done.

Armand. (*rising*) Ah, I am choking——

Marguerite. (*detaining him*) What, am I forced to give you courage?
Come then, obey me. Open that drawer, and take the locket that
you find there. It is my portrait, drawn at a time when I was pretty.
I had it done for you; keep it, it will help you to remember me.
But if, one day, a beautiful young girl should fall in love with you
and you should marry her—as well may be, as I sincerely hope—and
she should find this portrait, tell her it is that of a friend who, if
God permits her an obscure place in heaven, prays every day

216

for her, and for thee. If she is jealous of the past, as we women often are, if she begs of you to sacrifice that portrait, then grant it her without fear, without remorse. It would be justice, and I forgive you in advance. When a woman loves, she suffers too much if she does not feel beloved. Are you listening, Armand; have you well understood me?

Nanine *enters with* Nichette, Gustave, *and* Gaston. Nichette *enters with some fear, and becomes bolder as she sees* Marguerite *smile at her and* Armand *at her feet.*

Nichette. My dear Marguerite, you wrote to me that you were dying, and I find you up and smiling.
Armand. (in an undertone) Oh, Gustave, I am utterly wretched!
Marguerite. I am dying, but I am happy too, and my happiness takes the sting from death. There you are now, married! You will be yet happier than before! You will think of me sometimes, will you not? Armand, give me your hand. I promise you, it is not difficult to die. And here is Gaston come to look for me. I am glad to see you once again, dear Gaston. In happiness we are ungrateful, and I had forgotten you. *(To* Armand) He has been very, very good to me. Ah, how strange! *(She rises)*
Armand. What is it?
Marguerite. There is no more pain. Life seems to be returning to me. I feel better than ever before. Yes, yes, I shall live! Ah, how well I am! *(She sits and seems to fall asleep)*
Gaston. She sleeps.
Armand. (at first uneasily, then with terror) Marguerite! Marguerite! Marguerite! *(A great cry. He has difficulty in withdrawing his hand from that of* Marguerite) Ah! *(He steps back, appalled)* Dead! *(Running to* (Gustave) My God! My God! What will become of me?
Gustave. (to Armand) She loved you well, poor girl!
Nichette. (who has fallen on her knees) Sleep in peace, Marguerite! Much will be forgiven you, because you greatly loved!

London by Night

A DRAMA IN TWO ACTS sometimes attributed to CHARLES SELBY

CHARACTERS

HENRY MARCHMONT, a naval officer
FRANK MARCHMONT, his profligate brother
JONATHAN HAWKHURST *alias* BERNARD JACKSON, a
   character not unknown to the police
SHADRACK SHABNER, a bill discounter of the Hebrew
   persuasion
MR FAIRLEIGH, a wealthy merchant banker, living in Kent
ROBERT WILLIS, also known as the drunkard DOGNOSE,
   a dram-drinker
ANKLE JACK, a shoeblack
NED DAWKINS, a crossing-sweeper and member of the cadging
   fraternity.
MR NOBLEY COLE, a popular entertainer
CHAIRMAN at 'The Apollo' public house

LOUISA WILLIS, deserted and betrayed

Policemen, cadgers, vagrants, shoeblacks, newspaper boys, vendors of
fruit and cigar-lights, railway servants, waiters and members of the
public.

The action takes place in London and its suburbs.

Period: 1868

LONDON BY NIGHT

This is a hybrid melodrama, stolen from several sources and written up
by several authors over a period of years. The basic plot derives from
Eugène Sue, the railway scene from Daly, and the title from another play
which may be by Charles Selby. These elements were first combined by
Dion Boucicault in 1868, and probably achieved their present form a
few months later that same year.

The lurid tales of urban vice which Sue collected in *Les Mystères de
Paris* (1842–3) gave many melodramas to the Boulevard du Crime.
One of them, by Sue and Dinaux, was promptly pirated by Dennery
and Grangé as *Les Bohémiens de Paris* (1843). Their adaptation
crossed the Channel as *The Rogues of Paris*, *The Bohemians* and
Moncrieff's *The Scamps of London*, which first gave the characters and
settings English names. This, clearly, is the version upon which
London by Night is based. In both plays a pair of crooks persuade a
profligate to impersonate his elder brother so that he can marry a rich
heiress. In both, the girl he ruined leaps into the Thames but is fished
up by an old dram-drinking vagabond who turns out to be her father.
In both, the villains trick him into an attempt to kill her, but he
discovers her identity in time and is reunited with her in a scene of
rapturous forgiveness. And in both the hero is a gallant naval officer
who is ambushed by the villains and survives to bowl them out and
claim his wealthy bride. Many of the settings are identical, for both
plays open at a London railway station, move to a bridge over the
Thames, take in a fashionable café and a low dive full of cadgers,
and then choose moonlit brickfields for the murder threat and family
reunion. And although the names of characters occasionally vary,
it is not difficult to see Louisa Willis in Louisa Johnson, or Henry and
Frank Marchmont in Frank and Herbert Danvers, or Hawkhurst and
Shadrack Shabner in Hawksworth Shabner and his leader Devereux.

The Scamps of London opened at Sadler's Wells on 13 November 1843.
It was another twenty years before a railway engine made its début on
the stage. The play was Bolton's *The Engineer* at the Old Vic (23 March
1863), and in the thunderous finale young George Stephenson mounts
the footplate, shunts the heroine to safety in a ballast truck, and crushes
her prostrate seducer beneath his cardboard wheels. The sensation was
repeated in *The London Arab* (29 March 1866), migrated to the Porte St

Martin Theatre in Paris, and then turned up at the New York Theatre
as the climax of *Under the Gaslight* by Augustin Daly (13 August 1867). In
this play, Laura is locked inside a station hut and faithful Snorkey
roped to the railroad track. The down express is due at any moment.

> *Laura.* (*in agony*) Oh, I must get out! (*Shakes window bars*) What
> shall I do?
> *Snorkey.* Can't you burst the door?
> *Laura.* It is locked fast.
> *Snorkey.* Is there nothing in there? no hammer? no crowbar?
> *Laura.* Nothing. (*Faint steam whistle heard in the distance*) Oh, heavens!
> The train! (*Paralysed for an instant*) The axe!!!
> *Snorkey.* Cut the woodwork! Don't mind the lock, cut round it. How
> my neck tingles! (*A blow at door is heard*) Courage! (*Another*)
> Courage! (*The steam whistle heard again—nearer, and rumble of train on
> track—another blow*) That's a true woman. Courage! (*Noise of
> locomotive heard, with whistle. A last blow—the door swings open,
> mutilated, the lock hanging—and* Laura *appears, axe in hand*)
> *Snorkey.* Here—quick! (*She runs and unfastens him. The locomotive lights
> glare on scene*) Victory! Saved! Hooray! (*Laura leans exhausted against
> switch*) And these are the women who ain't to have a vote! (*As*
> Laura *takes his head from the track, the train of cars rushes past with roar
> and whistle*)

Compare this with the railway scene of *London by Night.* Louisa is
locked inside a lone house by the track and her father Dognose left
senseless on the railway line. The down express is again due at any
moment.

> *Louisa.* (*in agony*) Oh, I must get out.   (*Shakes gate again*)
> *Dognose.* Can't you force out a bar? I am too weak to move.
> *Louisa.* Lock and bars alike defy me.
> *Dognose.* Is there nothing there? No hammer—no crowbar?
> *Louisa.* Nothing. (*She searches the apartment. Faint steam whistle in the
> distance*) Great God! The train! (*Paralysed a moment, then resumes her
> search; shrieks as she discovers an axe*) Heaven has not deserted me.
> Courage! (*Strikes gate*) Courage! (*The steam whistle is heard again
> nearer, and rumble of train on the track*) It must give!
>
> *Noise of train increases. A last blow. Gate flies open and* Louisa *rushes to*
> Dognose. *Just as his head is removed from the track, the train passes
> with a roar and a whistle.*

Clearly, *London by Night* is no more than the sum of Moncrieff's plot
and Daly's railway rescue. The man who brought the two together in a
single play was Dion Boucicault.

During the winter of 1867, Boucicault prepared an adaptation of
Les Bohémiens de Paris for production at the Princess's Theatre, London.
There were the usual scenes at Victoria Station and Waterloo Bridge,
but when his hero was drugged at the Elysium Music Hall Boucicault
took a leaf from Daly's book and left him senseless on the track of the
Metropolitan Underground Railway, whence he is rescued—only just in
time—by the vagabond whom we know as Dognose. To prevent some
wretched hack from stealing his new play, Boucicault registered its title
at Stationers' Hall. It was called *London by Night*. Meanwhile, a wretched
hack named William Travers was just finishing an exciting play about a
wicked French madame who inveigles unsuspecting virgins to her
private bawdy house. On 11 May 1868, Sarah Lane staged it at the
Britannia Theatre, Hoxton. It was called *London by Night*. Boucicault at
once sent her a copy of his Stationers' certificate, and next day the
theatre advertised 'Mr Travers' last new original play' as *The Dark Side
of the Great Metropolis*. For several days letters of defence and protest
swelled the columns of *The Daily Telegraph*, as Boucicault cried 'Thief!'
and Travers claimed that he had drawn the title from a cartoon in *The
Tomahawk* (which indeed had published an engraving labelled 'London
by night' on 18 January 1868). Boucicault soon found himself on the
defensive. To avoid confusion with Travers' play, he renamed *London
by Night* as *After Dark*. When it appeared at the Princess's on 15 August,
everyone knew where the railway scene had come from, for Daly's play,
complete with train, had opened at the Whitechapel Pavilion some four
weeks earlier (18 July). Worse still, the September issue of *The Mask*
drew attention to the amazing similarities between *After Dark* and *The
Scamps of London*, commented adversely on Boucicault's departures from
his source, and invited other dramatists to follow his example and bring
out their own new versions of Moncrieff's old play with the railway
rescue added as a novelty sensation.

This, of course, is exactly what the minor theatres did. The next
few months saw *The Scamps of London* staged at Sadler's Wells (19
September), the Whitechapel Pavilion (17 October) and the Grecian
Saloon in Hoxton (26 October). All three used Frederick Marchant's
adaptation, which follows Moncrieff closely for the first two acts, but
tacks onto Louisa's reunion with her father a final scene in which he
saves her from the wheels of the express. Before the end of 1868,
other scamp shows were produced at Highbury, Greenock, Brighton,
Dublin, Hull and Leeds.

The present text, no doubt written for performance at a minor or
provincial theatre about this time, was published in Dicks' Standard
Plays in 1886. In order to avoid a charge of copyright infringement,
Dicks' editor gave the play another name and a wholly false stage
history. The title-page impudently borrows Boucicault's old title of
London by Night, but then identifies the author as Charles Selby, locates

the first performance at the Strand Theatre on 11 January 1844, and
assigns the leading roles to Webster, Hall, Lee, Roberts, Searle, Cockrill,
Broadfoot and Miss Walcott. Like all good lies, this is a plausible
conflation of acknowledged fact and undefined deception. Many
of the minor theatres did indeed perform *The Scamps of London* during
the winter months of 1843–4, but the Strand was not among them.
On 11 January 1844 it was still busy with the holiday attraction,
Rodwell's *The Roué Brother*, but a play called *London by Night* was
eventually produced there on 19 May 1845, and it had John Webster,
Henry Lee and Harriet Walcott in the cast. Of the other actors in
Dicks' list, Roberts, Searle and Cockrill were in *The Roué Brother*, Hall
was the Strand stage manager and Broadfoot manager at Sadler's
Wells. The play itself, about a country lad's adventures in the great
metropolis, has several scenes indebted to Moncrieff's more sensational
attractions. One shows a busy crowd at the Elephant and Castle, with
potato sellers and news vendors crying their wares, and omnibuses
setting down and taking up their passengers. Another visits the
Illuminated Gardens at Vauxhall, filled with masked revellers calling out
for strawberries, iced champagne and devilled kidneys. And of course
there is the usual view of Blackfriars Bridge by moonlight, with
the usual throng of riff-raff and the usual female suicide who is, as
usual, saved. And although no author is acknowledged on the playbills
or in the manuscript submitted for the Lord Chamberlain's approval,
the piece may very well be Selby's, who wrote several plays for this
theatre in 1844–5. All in all, Dicks' editor cooked up a very clever
fraud, and one totally in keeping with the tangled history of this most
fascinating play.

ACT I

Scene 1. A London railway terminus, exterior. The stage filled with passengers, newspaper boys calling out the names of their papers, shoeblacks following their occupation, vendors of fruit and cigar-lights, porters with luggage. Railway and engine heard without; the scene, in fact, to realise the arrival of a train.

Ankle Jack discovered. Henry Marchmont *appears among the crowd directing a* Porter, *who carries his luggage on a truck.*

Henry. Convey my kit to the Europa Hotel and return to me here, for I shall require further assistance with the cargo I've left in the store-room.

Porter. Ay, ay, sir. I'll be there and back in a jiffy. (*Exit*)

Jack. (*coming up to* Henry *and touching his hat*) Clean your boots, your honour? Only a penny! Put on an extra polish——

Henry. Eh, what? I can't be mistaken! Your face should be known to me. Why, you're Jack——

Jack. Yes! And you're Henry Marchmont, my old school-fellow, who used to pitch into all the big boys that pitched into me. Tip us your fist. I see you are not too proud to shake hands with an old pal who has seen better days. (*They shake hands*)

Henry. No; a true seaman never turns his back when the wind of adversity blows in his teeth.

Jack. Ah! I heard you'd gone for a sailor.

Henry. Yes; I've only just arrived from a long voyage. Since last I saw you I've travelled far and wide. My father dying in China, I have returned to England, from which love had driven me.

Jack. Love! You don't say so.

Henry. Yes, love for a young, innocent, beautiful girl. I could not declare to her my passion because I felt myself unworthy. I quitted London, bearing the sweet remembrance of Louisa in my heart. Her name whispered hope and comfort to my soul in the dreary watch, the howling storm, the raging battle! When the shots fell like rain, and death stared me in the face at every turn, the thought of her enabled me to overcome any obstacle, surmount every danger. and secure a fortune which I might lay at her feet.

Jack. I see how it is. You are now steering for the haven of happiness, and having passed the barrier will drop anchor in the smooth waters of contentment?

Henry. No. The broad arrow is branded on her name, and my anticipation is but a dream. On reaching my native shore, I learn that a more favoured rival has taken advantage of her weak, credulous, and unsuspecting disposition. Louisa is betrayed to ruin, shame, and dishonour. She who would have shared my name and wealth is not the wife, but the mistress of another man!

Jack. Do you mean to follow up the guilty pair?

Henry. Not I! Let the frail one follow her own bent; I am too old a salt to allow myself to drift on the quicksand of woman's perfidy. I have returned to London to seek an only brother that I have not seen for many years, and who by this time must be a wealthy and prosperous man.

Jack. I knew and still know him well, but regret to say with regard to his circumstances you are quite in the dark.

Henry. What do you mean?

Jack. My meaning will soon be made plain enough. When your brother came to London, he lived like a lord. He kept a carriage, gave dinner parties, and acted like a real gentleman—as he was. But he who goes beyond his means is sure to find a balance on the wrong side of the account, and poor Frank learnt this truth by experience. He is now without a penny, and the associate of some of the worst characters in the metropolis.

Henry. If you know his haunts, you shall conduct me to them—for in spite of his faults, his crimes, I feel it is my duty not to abandon him in extremity. Meet me after dusk at my hotel, and we will talk this matter over more fully.

Re-enter Porter.

Ah, the porter returns for the remainder of my luggage. I must accompany him, for I have some valuables among it.

(Henry Marchmont *follows* Porter *off*)

Enter Hawkhurst *and* Shadrack Shabner. Ankle Jack *meets them.*

Jack. Clean your boots, gents! Clean your boots!

Shadrack. I always clean my own.

Jack. Clean your boots! Clean your boots!

Hawkhurst. Hang the fellow! His noise goes far to crack the drum of my ear. Ah, Ankle Jack!

Jack. (*aside*) Hawkhurst! I'd better mizzle![1] I wonder what he's up to?

(*Sneaks out*)

---

[1] *mizzle* disappear suddenly

Shadrack. Now, Mr Hawkhurst, as I'm a man of business, let me know
　yours at once. You wrote to me, and——

Hawkhurst. I am about to confide an important secret to your keeping.

Shadrack. Is it safe to do so?

Hawkhurst. Yes; for if I saw the slightest sign of your betraying it, I
　should peach [1]—and Shadrack Shabner might chance to pay a visit
　to one of the penal settlements.

Shadrack. There, there, Mr Hawkhurst, that'll do! I never in my life
　injured anybody, unless——

Hawkhurst. It suited your purpose. But that is neither here nor there,
　so I'll proceed with my communication. I wrote to you from Canter-
　bury to lend me some money upon my word alone.

Shadrack. You did; but I was afraid the security wasn't very good.

Hawkhurst. On receiving a refusal, I was at a non-plus. I wandered to
　the outskirts of the city without a shilling in my pocket. Suddenly a
　house presented itself to my view. Dark thoughts prompted me,
　and I cleared the garden wall at a bound!

Shadrack. You had your tools with you?

Hawkhurst. I never travel without them. I was not disappointed with
　the squeeze,[2] for entering the first room I discovered an open cabinet
　with a bowl of silver coin.

Shadrack. Providence is bountiful!

Hawkhurst. I was disturbed as I took the money, and was compelled to
　leap through the window to prevent my detection. On returning to
　my lodgings, I unrolled my booty, which I had enveloped in the
　first piece of paper I felt under my hand. This turned out to be a
　letter addressed by one bearing the name of Marchmont.

Shadrack. Marchmont! How singular! Had you the curiosity to read
　this same letter?

Hawkhurst. Yes. It was dated China, and the contents gave me to learn
　that Henry Marchmont was destined to become the husband of the
　only daughter of the wealthy Kentish banker, Fairleigh.

Shadrack. Fairleigh—um—yes, he stands well in the City.

Hawkhurst. Old Marchmont had sanctioned, by writing, the union on
　his death-bed. The singularity of the name caused me to think of
　Frank Marchmont, whom we both know so well. He was the younger
　of two brothers, and I was informed further by the letter that the
　intended father-in-law was acquainted with neither the one or the
　other.

Shadrack. Well, what then?

Hawkhurst. A glorious scheme then developed itself to my teeming
　brain. Though in semblance I had stolen a few shillings, I had in
　reality purloined more than a million. Disguised, I sought the

[1] *peach* turn informer

[2] *squeeze* loot, 'the dibs'

banker Fairleigh, and represented myself as the friend of Henry Marchmont returned from China, and whom, I added, was detained in London by pressing business. My story, plausibly told, took the old gentleman off his guard; in fact, so much so, that he will come to London to conclude his daughter's marriage.

Shadrack. But suppose the bird shouldn't come, Mr Hawkhurst?

Hawkhurst. He is come, and by this time is comfortably seated with his daughter in the Europa Hotel. Our next business must be to find out Frank Marchmont, and bestow on him a rich bride and a handsome dowry—the dowry we share together.

Shadrack. Of course. People can't be expected to take all this trouble for nothing.

Hawkhurst. By the by, Shadrack, you must shell out at once for contingencies.

Shadrack. So I expected. Well, well—here's a couple of fivers.

Hawkhurst. I must have a hundred pounds at least.

Shadrack. One hundred pounds, Mr Hawkhurst! I never heard of such a sum.

Hawkhurst. You hear of it now. To carry out our plan successfully, I must provide our dupe with dress, cash, and all the requirements of a gentleman—so dub up! [1]

Shadrack. How much did you say?

Hawkhurst. One hundred pounds.

Shadrack. Don't you think fifty would do?

Hawkhurst. I must have a hundred.

Shadrack. The game is hazardous, and I——

Hawkhurst. There is no risk. For every shilling you advance, you will receive a thousand back. But time is on the wing. Fetch the sum I have asked for, while I seek the man who shall make our fortune.

Music. Hawkhurst *and* Shadrack *go off. The bustle of another arrival of a train. The stage is cleared to*

Scene 2. *The banks of the Thames and Adelphi Arches by moonlight. Craft moored in the river. Waterloo Bridge in the distance.*

Ned Dawkins *and numerous vagrants discovered. Some are sleeping, some playing at dominoes, some smoking. Cadgers' chorus as scene opens. Whistle heard off.*

Ned. Ah, that's Ankle Jack. I can tell his whistle from a hundred. (*Calling off*) Come along, my pippin! Here's prog and gatter [2] in galore for an old pal.

[1] *dub up* pay up
[2] *prog and gatter* food and liquor, usually beer

Enter Ankle Jack *down the archway.*

Ha, Jack, how goes it tonight?

Jack. Plummy and slam! [1] How do you feel?

Ned. Not quite up to the knocker——[2]

Jack. Why, what's in the wind, my rum cull? [3]

Ned. If things goes on this way, I shall soon find myself in the Bankruptcy Court, or——

Jack. Or some other court. How did this misfortune happen?

Ned. I gave too much credit.

Jack. That's a good 'un—a crossing-sweeper giving credit!

Ned. Yes, it's the ruin of business! The reg'lar customers with clean boots pays well, but when it comes to *premiscous* customers, it's quite t'other way. 'Remember the sweeper' says I. 'Never forget you' say they. 'Got a copper for the sweeper?' continues I. 'Got no change —pay when I comes back!' Catch 'em coming back! I've got more nor a hundred pound bad debts owing me that way!

Enter Frank Marchmont *at back.*

Jack. Ah! Who goes there?

Frank. A friend and comrade, if a residence in these dark and wretched haunts can entitle you to call me so.

Jack. We are poor, unfortunate, and——

Frank. I, too, am unfortunate—or say rather guilty, for my errors have brought me misery, penury, and shame. Till I fell in with you I had not tasted food for two days; and but for you I might have perished with want in the streets of this opulent city!

Ned. 'Never say die' is the cadger's motto. You shall regale, now. We are going to sit down to supper, and as far as an ingun, pannum, [4] and cheese, and a drop of heavy [5] goes, you are perfectly welcome.

Frank. My abject necessities compel me to accept and thank you for such generosity.

Jack. Our fare is homely, but you possess in hunger a sauce that an alderman's table might envy. We're rough spun, but always go upon the same tack: that is, if we can't bring our means to our wishes, we can keep our wishes down to our means, and that comes to the same point—namely, content.

Music. All seat themselves and eat. Ankle Jack *beckons on* Henry Marchmont, *disguised and poorly clad.*

Jack. (aside to Henry) All right, I've dropped upon him!

[1] *plummy and slam* fine and dandy
[2] *up to the knocker* in first-class condition
[3] *rum cull* odd fellow
[4] *ingun, pannum* faggot (?), bread
[5] *heavy* i.e. *heavy wet* malt liquor

Henry. And is it among the forlorn creatures that I see around that I am to find my unhappy brother?

Jack. Yes. He's at present busily engaged, but will make his appearance shortly. For eight days he has associated with this rude fraternity.

Henry. I cannot brook delay! Let me at once see Frank, that I may take him from this haunt of wretchedness!

Jack. No; in doing so you will defeat the object I have in view.

Henry. What object?

Jack. I have by mere accident found out that we are not the only persons who are seeking him.

Henry. What do you mean?

Jack. That there are two others on the same errand as ourselves.

Henry. Who are they?

Jack. Jonathan Hawkhurst and Shadrack Shabner.

Henry. I do not know these individuals.

Jack. But I do—and for two of the greatest scoundrels in London!

Hawkhurst *and* Shadrack Shabner *appear at back.*

Hush! Talk of the devil, they say, and his imps appear; for the very men of whom we have been speaking are coming down the archway. Let us stand back and watch their movements; there's mischief brewing, as sure as there are fish in the sea.

Henry *and* Jack *retire. The cadgers rise simultaneously.*

Ned. Hark, footsteps! The police! No—two strangers.

Enter Hawkhurst *and* Shadrack Shabner.

Shadrack. Don't disturb yourselves, my dear boys; we're on the square, not on the cross,[1] and——

Ned. No gammon?[2]

Shadrack. No gammon, upon my honour.

Ned. Oh, let me touch my castor![3] (*Aside*) His honour! I wonder the word didn't stick in his throat and choke him. (*Aloud*) Then what's your little game, Smouchy?

Shadrack. That's impolite. My business is told in a few words: I and this gentleman are in search of a scapegrace.

Ned. Scapegrace? There ain't no such person here; we're all respectable people.

Hawkhurst. Tell me, my good fellow, have you not among you a young man of good figure and good looks?

Ned. To be sure we have.

Hawkhurst. Where is he?

[1] *on the square . . . cross* engaged in honest dealing, not in fraud.
[2] *gammon* humbug
[3] *castor* hat

Ned. Here. I'm the covey [1] indicated.

Hawkhurst. No, no. I allude to an associate who answers to the name of Frank Marchmont.

Frank. (coming forward) I am Frank Marchmont. What do you want with me? Ah, Hawkhurst—Shabner!

Henry. (aside) 'Tis indeed my brother.

Frank. Your presence here, I fear, bodes me no good.

Shadrack. How we are deceived by appearances! We come to do you an important service.

Hawkhurst. Can we speak with you alone?

Frank. I know not whether I dare trust you.

Hawkhurst. If you doubt us, we can depart; but you will remain without the information that leads to the high road of fortune.

Frank. Sincerity prompts such words. Friends, leave us. (*The cadgers retire*) Now you can speak with freedom. What brings you here?

Hawkhurst. A friendly purpose. We would exchange your rags for better clothing, in order that tomorrow you may enjoy the luxurious life you have quitted but lately.

Frank. You are mocking me.

Hawkhurst. I do not jest, I assure you. Shabner, for once in his life, is about to be generous. You will have the command of his purse-strings.

Shadrack. Yes, yes; I shall not object to a few hundreds. You must appear with an equipage, of course.

Hawkhurst. You will live *en prince*. You will have——

Shadrack. Apartments in the best hotel.

Hawkhurst. A box at the opera.

Shadrack. A seat in Parliament, and——

Hawkhurst. Wealth unlimited.

Frank. Stop—stop! I know you too well to suppose you will confer all these favours without your interest being concerned. Tell me then, without prevarication, what hellish deed you expect me to perform for these obligations.

Hawkhurst. You may accomplish all we shall ask without crime, dishonour, or bloodshed. Come with us, and you shall judge for yourself. We shall leave it for you to ratify or destroy the compact.

(*Music. Exeunt* Frank, Hawkhurst, *and* Shabner)

Henry. (comes forward) 'Tis evident they meditate some infamous scheme. We will apprise the authorities, and——

Jack. Perhaps spoil all. Leave the matter for the present in my hands, and who knows but these sons of Lucifer may find a match in Ankle Jack. (*Runs off*)

During the above, Louisa *has appeared on bridge at back.*

[1] *covey* i.e. *cove* fellow, customer

231

Louisa. My sufferings have made me desperate, and I must no longer hesitate. Abandoned, without hope, let these flowing waters become my grave! Heaven pardon this dreadful crime, and forgive the hapless woman who wishes to die!

(Louisa *throws herself into the water.* Henry, *paralysed, witnesses the act*)

Henry. Help, help, for mercy's sake! There is a woman drowning! Is there no one to aid her?

Dognose *appears on bridge.*

Dognose. Yes, here is one—the drunkard Dognose!

Dognose *leaps into water. The cadgers group. Lights on the stage.* Henry *puts off in a boat;* Dognose, *bearing* Louisa, *swims towards it. Tableau as scene closes.*

Scene 3.   *A dilapidated garret.*

Enter Dognose, *still bearing* Louisa *insensible in his arms, and* Henry Marchmont. Louisa *recovers. They place her on a chair.*

Louisa. What place is this? Where—where am I?

Henry. With friends. Do you not recognise me? I am Henry Marchmont.

Louisa. Yes, I remember all now—you have saved my life. But I cannot thank you, for I wished to die.

Henry. Suicide is a terrible crime.

Louisa. Alas, you know not my sorrow, my suffering! Destitute of relations and friends, I consented to place my love and honour in the hands of one who became my only consolation in the hours of tribulation. The act was guilty, and heaven meted out its punishment.

Henry. You loved this man?

Louisa. Yes; his language, sweet and gentle, won my heart. I, a friendless orphan, believed his vows, and under a promise that I should become his wife consented to accompany him to London. Here, in the whirl of gaiety, I learnt that he had become a confirmed gambler, and that his passion for play was so overwhelming and irresistible as to subvert every good resolution.

Henry. He, then, upon whose plighted word you had implicitly relied, was ensnared by toils from which a woman's affection failed to deliver him.

Louisa. Our resources diminished at last; gaunt poverty stared us in the face, and my needle procured us bread. I laboured night and day for a scanty pittance, but I worked cheerfully, for I worked for Frank alone.

Henry. To abandon you after such devotion was the act of a coward and a scoundrel.

Louisa. For eight days he was absent. I became restless and unsettled; I sought my bed each night to think, but not to sleep. I thought he would return, but I pondered to meet only disappointment. In a paroxysm of despair, hopeless and blighted, I saw relief only in self-destruction.

Henry. All hope is not yet annihilated. I feel that the good genius of Frank Marchmont has not deserted him, and that he has yet force enough to shake off his thraldom. Calm your fears. You shall again behold my erring brother, and shall become his wife.

Louisa. Bless you for those words! (*Turning to* Dognose) And you who saved me——

Dognose. Saved you? Yes; you were too young to die. You resembled her, too. Ha, ha, ha!

Louisa. Why does he laugh so terribly? He appears to——

Henry. Hush! He is deeply to be pitied; his reason is impaired by drink and affliction. In that vacant stare lurks grief and remembrance of the past.

Dognose. (*musing*) Yes, there she lies, the pride of my heart, cut off in the morning of life, in her bloom and beauty, destroyed by him, the villain who—oh, madness is in the thought! I must have drink to quench this fire of the brain, to dissipate anguish. (*Laughs wildly.* Henry *puts money in his hand*) Money! Good. It will buy brandy. I love brandy—I love brandy! (*Exit*)

Ankle Jack *appears.*

Jack. I thought I should find you here, and you see I'm not mistaken. I've good news—I may say, rare news!

Henry. Speak, and quickly.

Jack. I've discovered the rascals, their project, and their victim, who is no other than your friend Mr Fairleigh.

Henry. Can this be true?

Jack. Oh, I had it on the very best authority. Leave Ankle Jack alone for nosing out a secret. Hawkhurst and the infernal jew intended to make a good thing of it, but I fancy we shall spoil their pretty little game.

Henry. Acquaint me at once with the particulars of the plot you have spoken of.

Jack. Well, as Mr Fairleigh is what the world calls 'warm', his newly-found friends are about to appropriate a portion of his capital to their own use; and as to Frank——

Henry. My brother.

Jack. Yes; he's going to marry the banker's daughter.

Louisa. Frank marry another! Can he be so base?

Henry. Be calm; this marriage will not take place. Acquainted with the whereabouts of these desperate men, I possess the means of foiling

their plot even at the moment of its consummation. Louisa, you must remain here till you hear from me further. Ankle Jack—quick, follow me!
(*Exeunt opposite sides*)

Scene 4. *The handsomely furnished saloon of a café restaurant in the neighbourhood of Leicester Square.*

Enter Hawkhurst, Shadrack Shabner, *and* Frank *elegantly dressed.*

Frank. Before I proceed further in this matter, you must explain everything, as you promised. Tell me, why do I find myself in the midst of this luxury and pleasure?

Hawkhurst. Frank, my dear fellow, you really are doing your old friends an injustice to distrust them. Have we not hitherto kept faith with you? You possess an equipage that puts Rotten Row to blush. You have money, clothes, and will soon be heir to eighty thousand pounds. If these are inadequate to your desires, I must confess you are a man more difficult to please than myself.

Frank. I am quite satisfied with my good fortune, Jonathan Hawkhurst, but simply wish to know at what price I purchase it.

Hawkhurst. Your name.

Frank. My name? I do not understand you.

Hawkhurst. You must put your signature to a marriage contract.

Shadrack. Yes; the bride is a lovely creature, and but for conscientious scruples I should have made her my wife.

Frank. What you demand is impossible. Louisa yet lives.

Hawkhurst. Psha! Louisa can still remain your mistress.

Frank. Withered be the tongue that profanes her name! She is an angel of goodness and loves me still, only as a heart like hers can love. Well do I remember, when first I pressed her to my bosom and asked if she would be content to follow the star of my destiny, her gentle murmur of 'I will'. Oh, why did guilt, with face averted, impress on mine the brand of infamy?

Hawkhurst. Are we then to understand that from a false sense of delicacy you refuse the dowry we offer to you? Remember that with eighty thousand pounds you render yourself, Louisa, and your two friends here, happy.

Shadrack. Yes, take your friends into consideration, by all means.

Frank. I cannot consent.

Shadrack. Don't say that, there's a dear boy; or you will drive me to the cruel necessity of suing you for damages and goods ordered.

Hawkhurst. Reflect. Would you return to the misery from which we have taken you? Poverty, and disease, a bed of straw, and a wretched death? Come; dispel the darkness which hangs over you. Act with determination while Fortune smiles. The father of the bride is within.

Shadrack. Yes, the good Mr Fairleigh—a very worthy man, just like myself.

Frank. What! Wed with Mr Fairleigh's daughter? Do you not know she was the intended of my brother, Henry?

Hawkhurst. You are over-scrupulous. Your brother is in China, where he has—so I am told—acquired wealth through the agency of a lady who will shortly become his wife. Knowing this, why should you hesitate?

Shadrack. You may depend upon it, your brother will be much obliged to us all for taking Miss Fairleigh off his hands. So, as we may consider the matter now settled, we will, if you please, proceed to complete our final arrangements.

Frank. What arrangements?

Shadrack. Merely a bond to——

Frank. (*snatching the bond which* Shadrack *has produced, and reading it*) What! A bond for forty thousand pounds!

Shadrack. Don't be alarmed, my good young man. We shan't expect a penny till you touch the money.

Frank. The sum is exorbitant.

Hawkhurst. You must remember that it is by our means alone you are enabled to mount this ladder of fortune.

Shadrack. Yes, my dear creature, you see how we have your interest at heart.

Frank. But suppose circumstances arise by which the marriage may be prevented?

Hawkhurst. That is improbable—I may say, impossible. Decide at once: is it to be wealth or poverty?

Frank. (*after a pause*) Wealth.

Hawkhurst. Then sign the bond.

Shadrack. Yes, sign; that's most essential (*aside*)—for a court of law!

Frank. Give it to me.

Music till the end of the scene. Frank *reads and signs the paper.*

Hawkhurst. (*aside*) Caught in the toils! The bird is ours.

Frank. I have given my name in full. To whom am I to deliver the document?

Henry *appears suddenly.*

Henry. To your brother, Henry Marchmont!

Henry *snatches the bond before* Hawkhurst *can take it. Picture as the scene closes.*

Scene 5. *Exterior of the café.*

Enter Hawkhurst *and* Shadrack Shabner, *hurriedly.*

Hawkhurst. Confusion! They have escaped us!

Shadrack. There's the other door. Suppose we——

Hawkhurst. No; that only leads to a blind alley. There's no outlet that way.

Shadrack. Why not call a cab, and follow up the pursuit?

Hawkhurst. It would be useless. We cannot tell the direction they have taken.

Shadrack. The return of his brother from China at such a moment is most unfortunate. I'm afraid the game's up. (*Aside*) Oh, Shadrack, Shadrack Shabner, why do you let the milk of human kindness flow so freely in your tender bosom? I oughtn't to have advanced so much money without proper security.

Hawkhurst. Hell's curses! To think that after all my precautions I should be thus entrapped! (*Turning fiercely on* Shadrack, *and shaking him*) It's all your fault, you shaking coward! You should have closed with the one as I attacked the other. I've a great mind to shake the life out of you! (*Throws off* Shadrack)

Shadrack. Confound his headstrong temper! How he has rumpled the clean shirt I put on only an hour ago! Really, Mr Hawkhurst, I cannot imagine why I am treated in this manner. I hope that in future you will guard against——

Hawkhurst. Keep quiet, fool! My head's at work.

Shadrack. Fool? Mr Hawkhurst, you know me better.

Hawkhurst. I beg your pardon; I should have said rogue. (*Muses*) Yes, I must resort to artifice, then violence. I have the means, and will employ them. Shabner, all is not yet lost. There remains but two obstacles to our success.

Shadrack. Two obstacles?

Hawkhurst. Yes—the girl Louisa, and Henry Marchmont. Both shall be removed. A desperate man resolves and acts.

Shadrack. Jonathan Hawkhurst, you're a clever fellow; and were I not so extremely sensitive, I should admire your courage and cunning.

Hawkhurst. Quick! Follow me. We must not trifle with time in this affair. (*Exeunt*)

Enter Fairleigh.

Fairleigh. So the paper and contract are all regular, says the lawyer. Good! Then tomorrow the affair will be terminated, I hope, to the satisfaction of all parties concerned. My daughter will make a charming bride, Henry Marchmont a handsome bridegroom, and I——.

(*Clock strikes*) Five o'clock! Bless me! so near the hour I appointed to dine with Mr What's-his-name. I shall never get dressed in time. Ah, the thought of this marriage has well-nigh driven every other out of my head. (*Re-enters café*)

Scene 6.   *A back room in a public house in the Borough. A group of low persons discovered seated, drinking, smoking, and gambling, as the scene opens. Waiters in attendance.*

Chairman. Gentlemen, give your orders. The waiters are in the room. (*Orders are given for rum hot, two pickwicks,*[1] *ale, stout, &c.*) Chair, gentlemen, chair! Mr Nobley Cole will give a song! (*Uses his hammer*)

All. Bravo—bravo! He's a stunner, he is!

Enter Ned Dawkins.

Ned. (*entering*) Yes, Nobley's fust-rate. He beats Ward into fits and Herring into convulsions. His doing a hornpipe on his nut upside-down is the most wonderful effort of genius I ever witnessed.

Chairman. Order and harmony, if you please, gentlemen!
(*He plies his hammer more vigorously than ever*)

Song by Mr Nobley Cole.

At its conclusion, enter Hawkhurst *and* Shadrack Shabner.

Shadrack. I'm afraid, Mr Hawkhurst, your plan is attended with con-siderable danger.

Hawkhurst. May be so, but it will rest with me alone. Should I need your assistance, you must not fail to give it; but I shall not trouble you unless it is absolutely necessary. If I only make sure of Henry Marchmont, we shall yet pocket the eighty thousand pounds.

Shadrack. Will he come to your appointment, think you?

Hawkhurst. I have sent Ankle Jack with a message that compels him to keep it.

Shadrack. But why have you chosen such a strange meeting place as this?

Hawkhurst. Because in this place he will be without a defence, sur-rounded by those who are devoted to my cause. Besides, I have other motives.

Shadrack. Other motives?

Hawkhurst. Yes; which it is as well not to divulge under the present circumstances.

Enter Ankle Jack.

Jack. What a rum place for an appointment! But I suppose they know

[1] *pickwicks* cheap cigars

237

their business best. I don't think much of the company I see hanging
about; they may be very respectable, though they have more or less
the appearance of pickpockets.

Hawkhurst. (*meeting* Jack) Will he come?

Jack. Yes; he'll be here in a minute. I've made it all right with Mr
Marchmont.

Hawkhurst. (*to* Shabner) Get rid of this idiot.

Shadrack. How am I to do it?

Hawkhurst. Let me see. Ah, I have it! Entice him into yonder bar, then
make him drunk.

Shadrack. (*to* Jack) Here, young man, if you've no objection, we'll
have a glass of brandy-and-water. Follow me!

(Shadrack *and* Jack *go off*)

Enter Henry.

Hawkhurst. Mr Marchmont, I am glad to find you are punctual.

Henry. This is a strange place to appoint a meeting.

Hawkhurst. Not so strange as it may appear, as you will find before we
leave.

Henry. Let us at once to business, if you please. You say the honour
of my brother is yet in your hands. I would prove the truth of that
assertion.

Hawkhurst. You are looking suspiciously around. You need be under
no apprehension.

Henry. Fear is the word omitted in a seaman's vocabulary. Therefore,
let me hear what you have to say.

Hawkhurst. I will be brief. In the first place, you have interfered with
an arrangement between myself and your brother, Frank Marchmont.

Henry. It was a compact sealed by shame, disgrace, and infamy, which
I refused to sanction.

Hawkhurst. I have yet to learn that your sanction was required.

Henry. I might have expected sarcasm from one who has acted most
unjustly towards his dupe.

Hawkhurst. I am at a loss to arrive at your meaning.

Henry. Then I will speak more freely. You have encouraged the weakness and folly of my poor brother for your own ends. You have
placed temptation in his path, and would have completed his ruin
by surrounding him with vicious associates.

Hawkhurst. You have painted my portrait; whether it is true or not I
leave others to judge. But we are wasting time. I must beg of you to
deliver up the document you snatched from my hand a few hours
since.

Henry. Say, rather, you exact it.

Hawkhurst. Precisely so. (Henry *is about to go*) Stop! You must not leave
me thus. (*Detains* Henry)

Henry. This is madness! Would you use violence in a place of public resort? (*Approaches door, against which* Ned Dawkins *is leaning smoking*) Ah, you have your myrmidons here! But surely some one will aid me? Gentlemen, will you permit this ruffianism in your presence? (*Struggles to escape, and pauses*) They heed me not. Accomplices, one and all! Into what a snare have I fallen!

Hawkhurst. Again I demand the paper. Return it to me, or you are a dead man before you are five minutes older.

Henry. Never will I leave you free to consummate my brother's ruin; and rather than yield it, shall my heart's blood flow like water from a running spring.

Hawkhurst. For the last time I ask——

Henry. Villain! You are at present all-powerful, I defenceless. But heaven, who watches over all its creatures, will never in the end suffer so cowardly, heartless, and infamous a man as yourself to triumph.

Hawkhurst. Indeed! (*To* Ned Dawkins) Quick! Open the trap, and descend with him to the cellars.

At a sign from Hawkhurst, *several men rush upon* Henry. *A desperate struggle.* Henry *calls aloud for help. They gag his mouth. The trap-door is forced open, and* Henry *driven to the brink of the cellar beneath.*

Ned. Hush! His cries have aroused the police.

Henry. (*tearing off gag*) The police! They come to my rescue. Help, help!

They are forcing Henry *down trap and forming a picture of consternation as act drop falls.*

ACT II

Scene 1. *A public tea gardens in the suburbs of London. As the drop ascends, numerous parties are discovered seated in the alcoves, taking refreshments. Waiters continually pass to and fro.*

Enter Ankle Jack, *extravagantly dressed.*

Jack. Well, I fancy I shall do. My togs being in keeping with this nobby [1] place, I can pass for a regular swell and nobody will twig the swindle. Mr Fairleigh sups here tonight, I understand, so I must keep a sharp look-out and not let him leave the gardens till I have made my communication. Bless me, who's this coming along? Some

[1] *nobby* belonging to 'the nobs'; hence, extremely smart

great man, I suppose, for the gardens don't appear large enough to hold him.

Enter Ned Dawkins, *attired in the extreme of modern fashion.*

Eh? Why, no—yes, but it is! What, Ned! Is that really you?

Ned. Go away, my *good* man! Apply to the parish. I can't think of relieving beggars——

Jack. Good man? What do you mean? (*Showing fight*) Perhaps I am a better man than you.

Ned. Fellow, when next you address a gentleman, eschew onions. You're positively obnoxious! (*Takes out smelling-bottle*)

Jack. Stand up! (*Squaring up to him*) I ain't going to be insulted in this manner.

Ned. Eh—what? It's Ankle Jack! A thousand pardons! I really didn't know you.

Jack. Well, I oughtn't to be surprised, then, for I hardly know myself in this toggery.

Ned. I see an improvement in the financial position. Lucky, like myself.

Jack. (*aside*) Lots of mopusses,[1] no doubt. I'm devilish faint. I hope he'll ask me to take something. (*Aloud*) Have you tea'd?

Ned. Not yet—I dined late. (*Aside*) I had a baked tater. (*Aloud*) Well, suppose we tea together?

Jack. With pleasure, my dear boy. Ho, waiter! (Waiter *enters*) Tea for three.

Ned. There are only two of us.

Jack. I require a double quantity. Tea for three, and bread and butter for thirty-three.

Ned. Let's take a seat.

They seat themselves. Waiter *brings tea. The* Waiter *presents bill.* Jack *glances at bill.*

Jack. Three shillings. Very moderate.

Ned. (*looking at it*) I wonder how they can do it for the money.

Jack. (*casting it*) Quite correct.

Ned. (*ditto*) Right to a fraction.

Jack. Who's to pay?

Ned. Whichever you please.

Jack. Oh, in that case you may as well settle it.

Ned. Not for Joseph! You asked me to tea. I appeal to the waiter; you ordered everything. In fact, I can't pay; I've no change.

Jack. And I haven't a rap.

Waiter. Oh, this is a bilk![2] Here—police, police!

A scuffle. The Police *enter and secure* Jack. Ned *escapes.*

[1] *mopusses* money
[2] *bilk* cheat

Jack. Really, gentlemen, this is all a mistake. I was not aware of the circumstance that I had forgot my purse.

Waiter. Forgot his purse! Ha, ha, ha!

Jack. No, I didn't forget my purse—here it is. I only forgot to put any money in it.

Waiter. Let him tell that tale to the magistrate. He's an old offender. Take him off!

As the Police *are dragging off* Jack, *they encounter* Hawkhurst.

Jack. Ah, here's a gentleman that will answer for my respectability. Won't you?

Hawkhurst. Absurd! I don't know you, fellow.

Jack. Well then, I know *you.*

Hawkhurst. I never saw the man before in all my life.

Jack. Oh, yes, you have.

Hawkhurst. Indeed! Where?

Jack. At 'The Apollo' public-house in the Borough.

Hawkhurst. (*aside*) Ah! Can he have witnessed the murder? I must ascertain the truth. (*Aloud*) Waiter!

Waiter. Yes, sir.

Hawkhurst. How much is this rascal's bill?

Waiter. Three shillings, without remembering the waiter.

Hawkhurst. Let the bill be mine. (Waiter *hesitates*) You hesitate—you doubt? Doubt no longer. Here is your money, and a shilling for yourself.

Waiter. (*altering his manner*) Oh, sir, a thousand pardons for my apparent rudeness. I saw you were a gentleman at the fust glance. You could have paid at your convenience.

Hawkhurst. Vamoose—scarper—fly!

Waiter *bows himself off. The rest disperse.*

Hawkhurst. So you were going to betray me.

Jack. No! I never splits upon a pal.

Hawkhurst. Depend upon it, if you do my vengeance will reach you even to the extremity of the earth.

Jack. (*aside*) What a stretch of imagination. (*Going*)

Hawkhurst. Stay! I cannot suffer you to depart till I am certain that I have nothing to fear from your tongue. You must give me some further account of yourself. (*Glances off*) But I see Dognose approaching; I must speak with him. Till my leisure permits, you must stay in yonder pavilion.

Jack. I hope you won't keep me long, for I've an assassination with my young woman.

The moment Jack *goes into pavilion,* Hawkhurst *fastens door.*

241

Hawkhurst. Safe bind, safe find. (*Calling*) Waiter, a bottle of cognac!

It is brought. Then Dognose *enters.*

Ah, old fellow, I want to speak to you. Sit down; take a drop of brandy. (Dognose *seats himself and eyes bottle vacantly*) Drink, man. Tell me how you like it. (*Fills a glass*)

Dognose. (*drinks*) Good—very good. Nothing like brandy. It is light—comfort—life to me.

Hawkhurst. Take another glass. You may need it, for I'm about to speak of Amy Willis.

Dognose. Oh, name her not! The recollection of my wrongs rushes upon my brain and drives me mad. Remind me not of the past, if you have mercy. Alas, darkness is upon my days, and the shadow of desolation is flung over my soul.

Hawkhurst. I speak not in sport of poor Amy, but that I knew her.

Dognose. You knew her? Ha, ha! Was she not beautiful, spotless, good?

Hawkhurst. She came from Jersey, did she not?

Dognose. Yes, yes; you say you knew her?

Hawkhurst. It was a sad day when her husband was arrested.

Dognose. He was no felon! The accusation was false, and I was condemned unjustly.

Hawkhurst. (*aside*) My suspicions, then, are confirmed! (*Aloud*) You are, then, no other than my old fellow-workman, Robert Willis?

Dognose. Yes; Amy called me so. But others call me Dognose—dog and drunkard!

Hawkhurst. But had you no friends to interest themselves in your behalf? An innocent man had surely some claim!

Dognose. I was believed guilty, and guilt meets not with commiseration. For twenty-one years I was a convict, forced to herd with criminals of the worst class; but the misery I then endured was followed by a greater trial. On my return to England I found my wife dead, my child dishonoured!

Hawkhurst. Such affliction cannot be endured.

Dognose. No; 'tis that which makes me drink and support life, that I may one day be avenged on the destroyer of my happiness!

Hawkhurst. That day has arrived. I will impart to you a secret. (*Sees his empty glass*) You don't drink. (*Fills.* Dognose *drinks*) I knew the murderer of your wife. It was not, as you suppose, a man—but a woman!

Dognose. A woman!

Hawkhurst. She was envious of her charms, and poisoned her!

Dognose. Another glass of brandy. (*Drinks*) Can you show me this woman? I will be calm; I will speak to her, and then——

Hawkhurst. This very evening you may see her.

Dognose. Where?

Hawkhurst. Across the river, some miles from this spot, there is a brick-field, and on the left a lone house. At the hour of twelve the woman you would meet will be there.

Dognose. How shall I know her? There may be others passing.

Hawkhurst. She will pronounce these words: 'I saw Amy Willis die'. (Dognose *rises*) Where are you going?

Dognose. To avenge her whose name you have uttered!

Hawkhurst. Take the brandy with you.

Dognose. No; I want no drink now. I only want this!

(*Takes out knife and hurries off*)

Hawkhurst. The birds fall into the fowler's net. Louisa will not fail to keep the appointment, for the name of Frank Marchmont would draw her to the Antipodes. But I must not forget my last victim. Ankle Jack, I suspect, knows more than he will tell; prudence and caution may worm out the secret.

Hawkhurst *enters the pavilion in which* Ankle Jack *has been confined. A rustic quadrille is commenced by the characters on the stage with great spirit, as the scene closes.*

Scene 2. *An apartment in The Cedars, at Wandsworth, the residence of Mr Fairleigh the banker.*

Enter Hawkhurst *and* Frank Marchmont.

Hawkhurst. Yes, this is the house. Welcome, Frank Marchmont, to The Cedars, at Wandsworth. Charming prospect, no end of meadow and pasture land, sylvan scenery, the Thames at your feet, and——

Frank. I do not come to admire the beauties of this suburban villa, but simply to see my brother.

Hawkhurst. Your brother—yes—um—. What would you say if I tell you I do not know where he is?

Frank. Assuredly, I should say you have brought me here on a false pretence. But I am too generous to suppose you would play me such a trick. Whose house is this?

Hawkhurst. It is at present occupied by a gentleman named Fairleigh.

Frank. That name at once discloses to me your project—a project that can only be accomplished by fraud! I have told you already that I will have nothing to do with the affair.

Hawkhurst. Very well, then; I must find some other friend to assist me. I wish you good morning; my carriage will convey you back to town.

Frank. Am I then not to see Henry?

Hawkhurst. His whereabouts will remain a secret, unless——

Frank. Unless what?

Hawkhurst. You sign the marriage contract, and take to wife the banker's daughter.

Frank. Hawkhurst, you are a clever rascal—but you have over-reached yourself. A word from my lips will bring you to the felon's dock!

Hawkhurst. That word you will never utter!

Frank. And why so?

Hawkhurst. Because your brother's life depends entirely on your silence! He is now alone, imprisoned by me, and without succour. My will can enforce life or death! Knowing this, let me know if you still refuse to wed Miss Fairleigh.

Frank. (*aside*) If what he asserts be true, I must make the sacrifice for Henry's sake. I can only choose between my dishonour and a brother's death!

Hawkhurst. Well, have you reconsidered my proposal?

Frank. Yes, as well as my distraught senses will permit me. I find I must agree to your wishes.

Hawkhurst. You have decided wisely. The contract is within.

Enter Fairleigh, *abruptly.*

Fairleigh. Yes, the contract is within; but I don't think that the person you are conducting will be allowed to sign it.

Hawkhurst. Absurd! Who shall prevent it?

Fairleigh. I shall. You stare; but I have just received information that you are a pair of scoundrels. The one, I hear, is the seducer of an unsuspecting girl; the other I must look upon only in the light of an assassin.

Hawkhurst. (*aside*) Dognose in his drunken cups has betrayed me! But I will be even with him yet. (*Aloud*) Before I refute so false a charge, Mr Fairleigh, I must acquaint you that my accuser is more than partially insane, the affliction being aggravated by the use of ardent spirits. This is not the first time the madman and drunkard has made a charge of this kind.

Fairleigh. (*aside*) Villain! But I will remain calm, that I may confound and frustrate him. (*Aloud*) Matters are taking a very serious turn. My informant appears neither drunk nor mad. The more I think, the more I am perplexed, Mr Hawkhurst. It is for you to speak, and——

Hawkhurst. Really, Mr Fairleigh, I am surprised that you should so readily believe a charge made against a friend by an entire stranger to you. In the first place, I know some of the antecedents of my accuser. He is a returned convict!

Fairleigh. A returned convict?

Hawkhurst. Yes; and allowing his statement to be true, there is no evidence of my guilt.

Enter Henry Marchmont.

244

Henry. Villain! There is evidence, and I can produce it.

Hawkhurst. (staggered) Henry Marchmont!

Frank. My brother!

Henry. Yes, 'tis Henry Marchmont—and living! The man you doomed
to death by a miracle escaped it. For two days, without food or
drink, I remained in the cellar in which you and your base accomplices had imprisoned me, when one came to my assistance.

Hawkhurst. I'd give a good round sum to know the name of the
treacherous rascal.

Enter Ankle Jack.

Jack. Then hand over the dibs, for I did the trick. You locked me in
the pavilion but forgot to secure the window. I knew all about the
cellar business at 'The Apollo', and thought I'd take advantage of
my knowledge.

Hawkhurst. You may yet suffer for this meddling.

Jack. Sixty-sixth and last round! (*Pointing to* Hawkhurst) The big 'un's
floored, and Ankle Jack's as fresh as a daisy.

Henry. Yes, to you I owe a life; and while that life remains I shall not
forget the obligation.

Hawkhurst. There must be some mistake here. Frank Marchmont can
answer for me.

Jack. Ain't he a cool 'un? If ever I set up an ice-cream shop, I'll have
him for head freezer.

Henry. Frank, if you still retain a particle of honour, you will leave that
man. Your past errors are forgiven. Let us hope that your future
conduct will cause them to be forgotten. As an earnest of affection,
I resign to you Louisa, whom I so well loved.

Frank. Henry, I do not deserve this. (*Takes* Henry's *hand*) You are too
generous.

Hawkhurst. An affecting scene, truly; highly agreeable to the parties
concerned, and anything but pleasurable to those who have no
interest in the family affairs. (*Aside*) Shall I bolt, or remain and face
it out? I will remain. Assurance elbows ability out of the apartments
of common sense.

Henry. (*goes up to* Hawkhurst. *They regard each other*) Inhuman villain!
The hour has now arrived when you and I must settle scores.

Jack. Yes, and I opine which will come off second best by long chalks.

Hawkhurst. I am quite content. You will find I shall not hesitate to
give you ample satisfaction. Name your friend, your time, and place.

Henry. Insolent! Do you suppose I would appeal to weapons? No law
of honour compels a gentleman to exchange shots with a ruffian.
When last we met, I registered a vow that I would denounce you.
I kept my word, and the police are now in the house.

Hawkhurst. I am fully aware of it. But I am not to be terrified, and it

will be to your advantage not to molest me. In the first place, I
never venture forth without being armed. In the second, I am provided against all contingencies by having your brother's bride in
the custody of my confederates. Should I not return by a certain
time, she may suffer more than if she remained under my protection.

Henry. You are in my power, and your threats shall not save you from
my resentment. (*Calling to* Police, *who enter*) Officers! Do your duty!
Secure that man!

Hawkhurst *wounds several of the* Police *with a revolver, which he draws
from the breast pocket of his coat. After a desperate struggle, he escapes.
The others follow in pursuit.*

Scene 3. *The brick-fields at Battersea. Lone house, L. The river in the
distance. Night, and moonlight. A railroad track runs at back from L to R.*

Enter Dognose.

Dognose. 'Tis near the hour; she will soon be here. I must not contem-
plate the scene. It is one of horror and darkness, such as to freeze
the current of my blood. For myself, I might spare her; but Amy's
soul denies pity. Hark! Footsteps in the distance! They are those of a
woman. Let me retire. My limbs, as if palsied, seem to refuse performance of their functions. (*He retires*)

Enter Louisa.

Louisa. What could induce Frank to choose so lonely a place as this for
the rendezvous? Doubtless he is compelled to do so, to evade the
snares and treachery that surround him. Oh, why did he not confide
in me? Had he acted honourably in the first instance, what misery
might have been spared him! (Dognose *comes down*) Ah! A stranger!

Dognose. Start not, but answer. Are you the woman I am here to kill?

Louisa. Kill? Mercy! Why do you utter such a terrible word?

Dognose. What do you want in this deserted spot?

Louisa. I am seeking some one, but it cannot be you. He desired me to
be near the lone house, and this should be——

Dognose. I ask again what you want, and why you approach yonder
crazy tenement.

Louisa. I expected to meet a person here.

Dognose. Your token?

Louisa. I was bid to pronounce a sentence.

Dognose. Then speak the words!

Louisa. 'I saw Amy Willis die!' (Dognose *raises his knife*) Ah, wretched
man, what would you do? You surely would not take the life of one
who never injured you?

Dognose. Never injured! Ha, ha, ha! But I came not to bandy words. My object is revenge—dire and fearful! You think I am acting under the impulses of insanity, but my reason is as lucid as your own.

Louisa. Stay, miserable man, your murd'rous hand awhile! There is some terrible mistake! You cannot believe that a poor, lone girl can possibly be your enemy?

Dognose. (*regards her*) Had it been any other than yourself, you would have been a dead woman ere this. But there is mildness in your eyes, innocence in your speech. I hesitate—I tremble—I freeze beneath your glance. Repeat your words.

Louisa. 'I saw Amy Willis die!'

Dognose. It is, then, true?

Louisa. Yes; for Amy Willis died in these arms—she was my mother. (Dognose *lets the knife fall, and stands transfixed*) Oh, why do you gaze on me thus wildly? A shadow is thrown over my heart, and a blight over my young and ardent spirit! (Dognose *caresses her*) Oh, why do you press me to your bosom, and grasp my hand so earnestly? You, who would but in the past moment have been my murderer?

Dognose. My tongue cleaves to my mouth. I can hardly speak! Emotion —happiness—joy—stifle me! Learn, girl, that your mother was my wife!

Louisa. Great God! Then you are——

Dognose. Thy father!   (Louisa *rushes into his arms*)

Louisa. My father—my father!

Dognose. 'Tis the first time that thou hast ever addressed me by that endearing word, for thy infant lips had not learnt to lisp it when I was cruelly torn from my home. (*Embraces her*) This happy hour repays the years of misery and suffering I have endured!

Louisa. From this time, dear father, we will never part.

Dognose. Never—never! I cannot afford to give up my newly-found treasure! (*Embraces her again*) We will often speak of thy mother, who rests in heaven.

Louisa. Yes; for she was kind and good. She often bade me cherish my father, and with her dying breath blessed him.

Dognose. Poor Amy! She knew that I was innocent.

Louisa. Yes; and for that reason a monster sought her life. He murdered her because she held proofs of his own guilt.

Dognose. Proofs, say you?

Louisa. Yes. She by a fortuitous circumstance discovered the culprit and his real name.

Dognose. What was it?

Louisa. Bernard Jackson. After poor mother's death he made away with the evidence against him, and the stigma of the robbery of which you were unjustly accused still attaches itself to your name.

Dognose. The villain! But the day of retribution is at hand. I have now the means of vengeance, and will use them. Come, girl; you've seen a father's downfall. Be now the witness of his exaltation. Conceal yourself in yonder habitation while I circumvent our deadly enemy.

Music. Louisa *enters the lone house, the interior of which is visible to the audience.* Dognose *locks the door, holds up the key, and then places it in his pocket. Enter* Hawkhurst *and* Shadrack Shabner.

Hawkhurst. Well, Dognose, have you been successful?

Dognose. (*abstractedly*) I will do it—so good an opportunity may never occur again.

Hawkhurst. You do not answer me.

Shadrack. He seems in one of his moody fits. He has been drinking, no doubt. Let me question him. (*To* Dognose) Mr Hawkhurst wishes to know whether you have been as good as your word with respect to the girl Louisa.

Hawkhurst. Is your work complete?

Dognose. No—for you yet live, villain!

Rushes upon Hawkhurst. Hawkhurst *with the assistance of* Shabner *is enabled to wound* Dognose. *He falls senseless, and is left on the iron track of the railway by the assassins.*

Hawkhurst. I think I've settled him. If not, the coming engine will complete the work. Now then, to secure the girl. She can't be far off. (*Exit, followed by* Shadrack Shabner)

Louisa. (*in the house*) All seems quiet, and yet just now fancy pictured to my mind a struggle of contending men. I hope my father will soon return. I was very wrong to suffer him to depart alone. (*Goes to iron grating which forms the door*) From this spot I can witness his approach. Ah, what is that? My eyes surely cannot deceive—there is some object lying across the iron road before me. It can never be a human being in such a dangerous position! I must warn them. Ah, the gate is locked! How unfortunate! The train will be down in ten minutes. If the poor creature is not sleeping, my voice may be heard. (*Shouts loudly*)

Dognose. (*feebly*) Who's that?

Louisa. Heavens! 'Tis my father!

Dognose. Listen to me and restrain your grief, for I have only five minutes to live.

Louisa. (*shaking gate*) Oh, and I cannot aid him!

Dognose. Never mind, you can avenge me. Hawkhurst is a——

Louisa. (*in agony*) Oh, I must get out. (*Shakes gate again*)

Dognose. Can't you force out a bar? I am too weak to move.

Louisa. Lock and bars alike defy me.

Dognose. Is there nothing in there? No hammer—no crowbar?

Louisa. Nothing. (*She searches the apartment. Faint steam whistle in the distance*) Great God! The train! (*Paralysed a moment, then resumes her search; shrieks as she discovers an axe*) Heaven has not deserted me. Courage! (*Strikes gate*) Courage! (*The steam whistle is heard again nearer, and rumble of train on the track*) It must give!

Noise of train increases. A last blow. Gate flies open and Louisa *rushes to* Dognose. *Just as his head is removed from the track, the train passes with a roar and a whistle. Enter* Henry *and the whole of the characters, except* Hawkhurst.

Henry. Providence be praised! You are saved and restored to happiness. Frank, accept from my hand your wife—Louisa!

Dognose. The villain Hawkhurst—where is he?

Henry. He is now a prisoner of the law. As Bernard Jackson, your old enemy, let the law punish him. Your existence hitherto has been a long night, but there is a morning. Let us hope that it will bring sunlight, genial gales, and comfort to your future days, while it banishes the remembrance of those scenes which have been enacted in London at Night.

Curtain.

FURTHER READING

Plays

Most of the plays collected in this book were first published in crudely printed acting texts now rarely found outside the great national libraries. Among the principal collections are Cumberland's Minor Theatre (1828–43), Dicks' Standard Plays (1875 ff.), Duncombe's British Theatre (1828–52) and Lacy's Acting Edition (1849–55), which has continued to the present day as French's Standard Drama and French's American Plays. Thousands of unprinted melodramas are preserved in the Library of Congress and the Bibliothèque de l'Arsenal in Paris; the Lord Chamberlain's vast manuscript collection of nineteenth-century plays is now divided between the Huntingdon Library at San Marino, California, and the British Library, London.

Happily, some of the most important plays have recently been edited in scholarly anthologies. George Rowell's *Nineteenth Century Plays* (1953 revised 1972) includes *Black-ey'd Susan, Lady Audley's Secret, The Colleen Bawn, The Ticket-of-Leave Man* and *The Bells*. In *Hiss the Villain* (1964), Michael Booth has edited *The Miller and his Men, My Poll and my Partner Joe, Ten Nights in a Bar-Room, Lost in London, Under the Gaslight* and *The Bells*. The first volume of his *English Plays of the Nineteenth Century* (1969) includes *Black-ey'd Susan, The Miller and his Men* and *The Factory Lad*; volume two (1969) adds *The Ticket-of-Leave Man, The Corsican Brothers* and *The Shaughraun*. *Black-ey'd Susan, The Lady of Lyons* and T. A. Palmer's version of *East Lynne* are in Leonard R. N. Ashley's *Nineteenth-Century British Drama* (1967), while the melodrama section of J. O. Bailey's *British Plays of the Nineteenth Century* (1966) has *A Tale of Mystery, The Rent Day, Luke the Labourer, After Dark, Our American Cousin*, an American version of *East Lynne* and *The Silver King*. *Uncle Tom's Cabin* may be read in *Representative Plays by American Dramatists*, ed. Montrose J. Moses (1918–25), and Fechter's version of Dumas' *Monte Cristo* in Robert Saffron's *Great Melodramas* (1966), which also includes Gillette's *Secret Service* and some more recent plays. Many melodramas are included in the twenty volumes of *America's Lost Plays* (1940–9), under the general editorship of Barrett H. Clark. A list of modern burlesque melodramas is available from French's Theatre Bookshop, 26 Southampton Street, London WC2.

Further Reading

Reviews

Much valuable information about Victorian melodrama on the stage can be gleaned from the reviews published in contemporary newspapers and magazines, the best of which were sometimes rescued from oblivion by later publication in book form. Hazlitt reprinted many of his notices in *A View of the English Stage* (1818), and Leigh Hunt's *Dramatic Criticism: 1808–1831* is now readily available in a scholarly edition by L. H. and C. W. Houtchens (1950). Henry Morley's *Journal of a London Playgoer from 1851 to 1866* was published in 1866. George Henry Lewes' essays for the *Pall Mall Gazette* in 1875 were collected the same year as *On Actors and the Art of Acting*. Edward Dutton Cook compiled several volumes of his criticism: *A Book of the Play* (1876), *Hours with the Players* (1881), *Nights at the Play* (1883) and *On the Stage* (1883). Also valuable are John Westland Marston's *Our Recent Actors* (1888), A. B. Walkley's *Playhouse Impressions* (1892) and Joseph Knight's *Theatrical Notes* (1893). Irving's first nights at the Lyceum are chronicled in Clement Scott's *From 'The Bells' to 'King Arthur'* (1896). Shaw's notices for the *Saturday Review* were edited by James Huneker as *Dramatic Opinions and Essays* (1916); selections from the work of Max Beerbohm, his successor, were published as *Around Theatres* (1924), *More Theatres* (1969) and *Last Theatres* (1970). Allan Wade has edited the dramatic papers of Henry James under the title of *The Scenic Art* (1948). George Rowell's *Victorian Dramatic Criticism* (1971) creams off the best notices from many of these volumes.

Literary Criticism

The introduction to this book draws freely on the present author's *Melodrama* (1973). Other recent studies are Michael Booth's *English Melodrama* (1965) and David Grimsted's *Melodrama Unveiled: American Theater and Culture 1800–1850* (1968). Frank Rahill's *The World of Melodrama* (1967) deals thoroughly with English, French and American melodrama and supplies a valuable bibliography of contemporary and modern criticism. More general studies which include some discussion of the form are E. B. Watson's *Sheridan to Robertson* (1926), Ernest Reynolds' *Early Victorian Drama: 1830–1870* (1936), and George Rowell's *The Victorian Theatre* (1956). A. H. Saxon has a chapter on *Mazeppa* in *Enter Foot and Horse* (1968), and *The Factory Lad* is treated by Robin Estill's article for *Theatre Quarterly* I (December 1971). The nineteenth-century volumes of Allardyce Nicoll's *History of English Drama: 1660–1900* (1946 revised 1959, 1930 revised 1955) are an invaluable reference tool.